Quetzalcoatl
and the Irony of Empire

Quetzalcoatl
and the Irony of Empire

Myths and Prophecies
in the Aztec Tradition

Davíd Carrasco

The University of Chicago Press

Chicago & London

DAVÍD CARRASCO is associate professor of religious studies at the University of
Colorado, Boulder.

THE UNIVERSITY OF CHICAGO PRESS, CHICAGO 60637
THE UNIVERSITY OF CHICAGO PRESS, LTD., LONDON

© 1982 by The University of Chicago
All rights reserved. Published 1982
Printed in the United States of America

5 4 3 2 1   82 83 84 85 86 87 88

Library of Congress Cataloging in Publication Data

Carrasco, Davíd.
    Quetzalcoatl and the irony of empire.

    Bibliography: p.
    Includes index.
    1. Aztecs—Religion and mythology.   2. Aztecs—
Urban residence.   3. Quetzalcoatl.   4. Indians of
Mexico—Religion and mythology.   5. Indians of Mexico—
Urban residence.   I. Title.
F1219.76.R45C37   1982   299'.73   82-13356
ISBN 0-226-09487-1

To my mythic figures Ira G. Zepp,
who first taught me about
shadows and symbols, and
Milena Soforo, my aunt,
who first took me to
the castle and the museum

Contents

Illustrations

Acknowledgments

Teachers, friends, and colleagues have assisted me at every stage of this book's creation. The brilliant and inspiring writings of Mircea Eliade on the nature and meaning of archetypes and symbols provided the foundation for my study. Jonathan Z. Smith's illuminating work on symbols and social change enlarged my perspective and helped me utilize the primary sources more efficiently. Charles H. Long's excellent teaching and wonderful support helped me focus my work on the intriguing relationships between cities and symbols in Mesoamerican history. My greatest intellectual debt is to Paul Wheatley, whose probing questions about Mesoamerican society and symbols combined with his extensive knowledge of urban geography helped me make my way through the final stages of the analysis. Wheatley's work on spatial organization in traditional cities constitutes a very significant advance in our understanding of the history of religions. Professor Friedrich Katz stimulated me to think hard about the problems of historical reconstruction in Mesoamerican culture and helped me understand the distinct character of Aztec social organization. Another Americanist, Pedro Armillas, who was teaching at the University of Illinois, was especially helpful in the conception and organization of chapter 3. Pedro was kind enough to sponsor my research at archaeological zones in Mexico by introducing me to Eduardo Matos Moctezuma, general coordinator of the Templo Mayor Project in Mexico City. Eduardo's generous response to my interest in the Aztec temple tradition made my work more enjoyable and vital.

Other colleagues in Mexico who made critical comments include Johanna Broda, Doris Heyden, and

Alfredo López Austin. Dr. Broda made insightful suggestions about all aspects of the book and her own scholarship assisted me in the construction of chapters 1 and 4. Doris Heyden's ideas about sacred space in Mesoamerica contributed to my understanding of the Toltec heritage. Alfredo López Austin challenged and confirmed a number of my ideas about Quetzalcoatl's political significance.

Throughout the project, I depended on Henry B. Nicholson's precise textual analysis of the primary sources concerning the Toltec tradition. This distinguished Mesoamericanist's doctoral thesis remains the foundation for our understanding of the historical significance of the Toltec heritage.

I extend a special word of gratitude to my friend and colleague William B. Taylor, a Latin America historian at the University of Colorado. He read the first draft carefully and provided a number of very helpful and challenging suggestions on how to improve the manuscript and organize the discussion. Bill's encouragement and the quality of his mind provided a gentle inspiration for the book.

Others at the University of Colorado who assisted me were John Hoag, whose comments on Aztec sculpture proved illuminating, Jack Kelso, who taught me the value of a sense of humor while trying to get published, Betty Theoatokatos, Fine Arts librarian, Ellsworth Mason and Sonia Jacobs, of the Rare Books Room, and Robert Lester, chairman of Religious Studies.

I also wish to thank my typists, Maxine Kluck, Jean Pfleiderer, and Gail Maxwell for their excellent care with the manuscript and for helpful editorial suggestions. Also, thanks to John S. Meyer, who helped in the proofreading. Special gratitude goes to Larry Desmond for his excellent illustrations and to Jane Swanberg for her invaluable assistance with the final editing.

Research for the book was supported by generous grants from the National Chicano Council on Higher Education and the Council on Research and Creative Writing at the University of Colorado.

Thanks to Richard Glass, Jacob Jacobson, and Calvern Narcisi for their insightful reflections on the growing pains involved in expressing my own point of view.

My wife Cresson provided many helpful thoughts on the project and I am grateful for her patience and good spirits.

David Carrasco

Introduction: Mosaics and Centers

The Aztec Empire was a mosaic of cities.

—Jacques Soustelle
Daily Life of the Aztecs

 The story of ancient Mexico is the story of places and symbols of places. The little footprints crossing and looping the ancient maps suggest that archaic Mexicans visited such places as Teotihuacán, "Abode of the Gods," Tollan, "Place of Reeds," Xochicalco, "Place of the House of Flowers," Colhuacán, "Place of the Ancestors," and Teocolhuacán, "Place of the Divine Ancestors." In a sense, ancient Mexican history is the story of people and their symbols moving from place to place.

This volume is concerned with a network of places in pre-Hispanic Mexico that conform dramatically to that social order known as the traditional city[1] and with the role one complex symbolic form, Quetzalcoatl, "Plumed Serpent," played in the organization, legitimation, and subversion of a large segment of the urban tradition. It seeks to present a new understanding of Quetzalcoatl's significance by emphasizing the urban setting of the ancient culture and the ways in which ancient Mexicans regarded their society as a cosmo-magical construct. It strives to do this by focusing on the meaning of Quetzalcoatl's relationship to the great Toltec capital of Tollan, which appears in the primary sources as both a historical capital and a fabulous symbol of a mythical city.

Contemporary scholars are aware of the urban character of ancient Mexico, but an old and stubborn Europocentric approach to the New World has deflected scholarship away from a sustained awareness

1

that the ancient Mexican city-state was the center of life and that this has great significance for the meaning of religious symbols, including the plumed serpent. Working from a comparative analysis of pristine urbanism, Paul Wheatley, an urban geographer, has summarized the significance cities have for an understanding of the ancient world: "It is the city which has been, and to a large extent still is, the style center in the traditional world, disseminating social, political, technical, religious and aesthetic values and functioning as an organizing principle, conditioning the manner and quality of life in the countryside."[2]

One outstanding characteristic in the history of pre-Columbian cities is the eccentric periodicity of settlement and stability. The urban tradition had an erratic pattern, "marked by political fragmentation, discontinuity in occupation and decline in the crafts between the successive periods of intensified integrations."[3] This pattern of discontinuity was accompanied by the persistence of several religious symbols, among them the feathered serpent, which appeared in a number of regional capitals over a long period of time. It is impressive that Quetzalcoatl, acting in the written sources as a creator god, the morning star, the wind god, a culture hero, the emblem of the priesthood, is inlaid not only within the mosaic of cities constituting the Aztec empire, but also within the obscurer mosaic of cities dominating the long history that led up to the empire. The present study attempts to elucidate the manner in which the symbol of Quetzalcoatl contributed to the organization of six capitals—Teotihuacán, Cholollan, Tula, Xochicalco, Chichén Itzá, and Tenochtitlán—by symbolizing the legitimation of power and authority in a trembling world. The overall significance of this pattern is that Quetzalcoatl can be understood, along with his myriad other meanings, as the patron of capital cities in a significant part of Mesoamerica. Quetzalcoatl was a symbol of authority, not only in terms of his expression in specific circumstances, but in terms of the origin and sanctification of authority in capital cities.

Quetzalcoatl and the city of Tollan present one of the most complex puzzles for the historian of religions to work with. For years scholars have spoken of the Quetzalcoatl "problem" or the Toltec "problem." Some years ago, Henry B. Nicholson, one of the leading experts in Mesoamerican religions, wrote a work entitled "Topiltzin Quetzalcoatl of Tollan: A Problem in Mesoamerican Ethnohistory." There and elsewhere Nicholson has shown that the "tangle and complexity" of the deity Quetzalcoatl is heightened by "his inextricable interdigitation with the life and personality of a figure whose fundamental historicity seems likely but who can be discerned only through a dense screen of mythical, legendary, and folkloristic accretions: Topiltzin Quetzalcoatl."[4] In my view, we can untangle some of the complex and frustrating lines of meaning by seeing Quetzalcoatl, Topiltzin Quetzalcoatl, and Tollan as combined to form one of the major competing traditions in the sanctification of supreme authority which resided in major ceremonial centers and capital cities in Mesoamerica. While it is clear that Quetzalcoatl was not the only symbol of sanctified authority in central Mesoamerica, he was a distinctly valued, resilient, and indispensable paradigm of authority. Although the meaning of the Quetzalcoatl tradition changed in content over time—it received marvelous and startling elaborations in different cities—it maintained its importance as a symbol of sanctified authority from Teotihuacán's empire (A.D. 250) to the very end of the Aztec empire (A.D. 1521). This book attempts to interpret the history of this religious tradition.

This is a hermeneutical task. It is an attempt to understand the meanings of a variety of texts (painted, sculptured, written) that carried apparent and hidden messages concerning the nature and character of authority in Mesoamerican cities. My approach depends on the use of the discipline and categories of the history of religions, especially the renewed concern for relating the religious texts of a people to the social and historical contexts in which they were read, danced, applied, and reinterpreted. In attempting to comprehend the enigmatic figure of Quetzalcoatl and his importance as a dynastic paradigm, I will draw upon the inspirational and insightful writings of Mircea Eliade, Charles Long, and Jonathan Z. Smith, whose contributions toward a method of deciphering the meaning of myth, symbol, and religion in traditional cultures have set the stage for a deeper and more comprehensive understanding of Mesoamerican religion. Special use will be made of the categories of sacred space and the sacred human because they enable us to understand the currents of thought and action that organized and animated life in the pre-Columbian city. Advantage will be gained by bringing the "Great Tradition" of the Toltecs and their capital city, Tollan, into dynamic interplay with the notions of the symbolism of the center, sacred genealogies, cosmogonic models, and hierocosmic symbols. "Great Tradition" refers to the canonical traditions about the Toltec civilization that contained paradigms for spatial order, kingship, sanctity, priesthood, and major institutions of the city. The longer I read Mesoamerican texts, the more I am convinced that a significant advance in understanding can be accomplished through the sensitive and sustained use of history of religions' categories and methods.

This hermeneutical effort will also benefit from a recent reinterpretation of the theory of the central place by the urban geographer Paul Wheatley, which is articulated in *The Pivot of the Four Quarters*. There and elsewhere, Wheatley has combined the methods of urban studies with the insights from the history of religions and tested them against a multitude of sources from seven areas of primary urban generation to show that ceremonial centers were the "primary instruments for the creation of political, social, economic and sacred space," that constituted traditional cities and their spheres of influence.[5] Developing the insights articulated by Fustel de Coulanges a hundred years before ("We have seen how the religion of the city is mixed up with everything"),[6] Wheatley has demonstrated some of the complex ways in which religious symbols and meanings contributed to the origin and development of cities. In Mesoamerica, it is becoming clear that the symbol of Quetzalcoatl integrated and was used to integrate the multitude of social processes that constituted the urban tradition. Though it is obvious that the cities under Quetzalcoatl's patronage were complex worlds of economic trade, hydraulic systems, and military expansion, it has been less obvious how the symbolic structures managed and interpreted by elites in the ceremonial centers directed these processes.

Quetzalcoatl and Tollan were religious symbols in the sense that they revealed and were utilized to demonstrate sacred modes of being in pre-Columbian society. Their sacrality derived from their capacity to participate in powers that transcended the pragmatic realms of textures, spaces, and beings, or what Mircea Eliade calls celestial archetypes.[7] Put simply, Tollan was a symbol of sacred space and Quetzalcoatl was a symbol of sacred authority. These symbols were models for two types of orientation in Mesoamerican culture; orientation in space and orientation in the social hierarchy. Tollan expressed and gave sacred prestige to the effective organization of space associated with ceremonial cities while Quetzalcoatl was the standard for the vital relationship between kingship and divinity. Religious symbols, however, are never simple expressions, but always multivalent and complex. They have the capacity to express simultaneously a number of meanings that have hidden but vital correspondences. Within the history of Mesoamerican urbanism, the symbol of Quetzalcoatl imbued kings, merchants, artists, and priests with sacrality and celestial power. Also, there were many Tollans—cities that symbolized in different ways the interaction between terrestrial space and celestial design. These two symbols revealed a vision of the cosmos that depended on the intimacy of city, kingship, and the gods, a vision that helped a number of cultures and capitals achieve stability and legitimacy in a changing world.

But there is also an irony in this vision which derives in part from the nature of religious symbols and in part from the Mesoamerican conception of authority, for, as Eliade notes, religious symbols can express contradictory aspects of ultimate reality, combining them in a coincidence of opposites. The tradition of Quetzalcoatl in Tollan reveals that at critical moments in the urban process, when kingship and city had achieved a marvelous stability, there appeared a contradiction of this stability from within the tradition itself. Mesoamerican empires, which are founded on an obsession for order, place, stability, and continuity, were based on a paradigm that had an "other" dimension and destiny. The symbols of Quetzalcoatl and Tollan contained the promise of disjunction, collapse, and abdication of order and authority. This study of the Mesoamerican urban tradition will attempt to show both the imperial security of Quetzalcoatl's symbol and the ironic subversion embedded in the myths and prophecies about Quetzalcoatl. When the Aztec elites utilized the prophecy of Quetzalcoatl's return to interpret the arrival of Spaniards in their kingdom, the Aztecs contributed to the reversal of their efforts to control their destiny. It is the combination of the Aztec dependence on the Toltec tradition for legitimacy and their application of the myth of Quetzalcoatl's return which constitutes the irony of empire.

This relationship between sacred symbol and social process is reflected in the fact that at least six important Mesoamerican cities, Teotihuacán, Tula, Xochicalco, Cholollan, Chichén Itzá, and Tenochtitlán, were organized around shrines that carried the image of Quetzalcoatl and integrated the social complexities of regional kingdoms, city-states, or empires. These centers were places where the sacred, as it was conceived in Mesoamerica, had manifested itself in elementary hierophanies (through caves, springs, mountains, rocks, animals) or in more evolved hierophanies (manifestations of specific deities to priestly elites) and so were considered the quintessential meeting places of the supernatural and natural realms. The temples and pyramid temples marking these "world axes" received their sanctity and authority, in part, from the traditions of meanings associated with Quetzalcoatl.

This study does not seek merely to confirm the efficacy of history of religions' categories in the study of Mesoamerican religions. Its aim is to sketch out the lines of force that related the central shrines associated with Quetzalcoatl to the social and historical processes that animated the cities in question. From studying the history of Mesoamerican urbanism and the complex changes that influenced the long tradition of legitimacy and authority, I have become convinced that some categories, for example, the symbolism of the center, need to be enlarged upon in order to reach a fuller understanding of Quetzalcoatl and the city in Mesoamerica. More attention must be given to the centrifugal functions and influences of sacred centers and sacred cities. Great centers like Tenochtitlán, Chichén Itzá, and Tula did not just integrate, attract, and consolidate peoples and process; they also extended, pushed, and broke the boundaries of their cosmos. Capital cities with their ceremonial centers were involved in rebellions, subversive movements, competing traditions, conquests, and military defeats. The centrifugal tendencies of Tenochtitlán, for instance, weakened the power we usually attribute to the symbolism of the center. The recent excavations at the Templo Mayor in Mexico City suggest that the Aztec "Center of the World" not only integrated the periphery, but also was manipulated by peripheral kingdoms to magnify its ideological and ritual system to the point of near self-destruction. In short, more focus needs to be placed on the periphery and the role of the periphery in the expression of Mesoamerican religion. In this study I attempt to expand the notion of a creative hermeneutic by utilizing the shape and character of ancient Mexican history to expand concepts like symbolism of the center and the *axis mundi* by noting the interplay between centers and peripheries and their social and symbolic consequences.

One major difficulty facing the historian of religions interpreting this pattern is the difficulty of "establishing the text." This arises from the fragmentary nature of the mute and written primary sources, the colonial nature of most of the written works, and the amazing variety of feathered serpents found in these texts. Recently, scholars such as Jacques Soustelle and Robert McC. Adams have argued that the primary sources are adequate, yielding in their archaeological sequence a detailed picture of Aztec life just prior to the conquest. But this optimistic view minimizes and obscures the rupture in transmission of indigenous traditions caused not only by pre-Columbian upheavals, but also by the conquest of Mexico and the colonial pressures of the sixteenth century. It is common for scholars working in this area to skim over the significant hermeneutical adjustments made by Spanish and Indian writers influenced by colonial politics, personal needs, mendicant theology and goals, and language differences. Alfredo López Austin refers to our predicament when he notes, "the indigenous sources . . . appear to have been elaborated with malevolent delight in the prospect of confusing future historians."[8] In a number of cases (Sahagún's celebrated *Florentine Codex* is one), what we call primary sources are elaborate Spanish glosses of original sources now lost. This hazardous situation invites an exegesis not only of the content concerning Quetzalcoatl but of the sources themselves.

The scholar or layman who enters upon these archives is not in the same position as one who studies the texts of most other religious traditions, like Christian, Judaic, Buddhist, or Hindu, or even one who does field work among contemporary native peoples. Between us and the pre-Columbian city and its symbols stand not just time and wear, distance and cultural diversity, and renewal within a tradition of wisdom, but also the conquest of Mexico and the invention of the American Indian. Before building my own interpretation of Quetzalcoatl and the ancient city, I will begin to define the "text" by discussing the transformation in primary texts that will serve as the basis for my interpretation. I call this transformation "from storybook to encyclopedia." It is outlined in chapter 1, where I identify the history, nature, and reliability of those sources carrying significant versions of the Quetzalcoatl tradition. I also review the ways in which scholars encountering this fragmented situation and the enigmatic Quetzalcoatl have attempted to design and redesign the symbol's significance according to their theories of culture, religion, civilization, and Indians.

The unusual nature of the evidence demands a skillful interweaving of material from both archaeological and written sources. In some instances it is not simply a matter of weaving, but also of tentative reconstruction, projection, and just plain guessing. For example, two of the six capitals we are examining are known almost exclusively through archaeological work. This presents the historian of religions seeking to understand social and symbolic changes with serious methodological problems. One distinguished scholar has described the limits of archaeological evidence:

> Emphasis is given to objects and institutions evoking consensual patterns of behavior, art styles, cult objects, rituals, rather than to those which might suggest incipient patterns of differentiation and stratification. . . . Art tends to deal mainly with traditionalized symbolic themes which probably always were most resistant to change.[9]

The static messages of ruins, monuments, and inscriptions demand a delicate caution in deciphering the meaning, enrichments, and alterations in a symbolic complex over time. But if we look at the evidence through a different lens, the limits of the evidence can work to our advantage. While it is apparent that archaeological data does not yield pictures of changes "taking place," it does provide statements about continuities and discontinuities in traditions that have "taken place." The possibilities of such a view are enhanced by the exciting advances made in recent decades, up to the present, by scientists working in the archaeological zones that dot Mexico's landscape. This is especially true regarding the discoveries at the Templo Mayor in Mexico City. As a recent conference of Mesoamerican specialists has shown, a new reconstruction of Tenochtitlán's history is possible through the examination of chronicles and archaeological evidence concerning the Templo Mayor.[10]

A second problem presented by working with archaeological sources is locating a fruitful starting place. The historian of religions must wade into the pools of evidence at the safest starting point. In terms of the Mesoamerican iconography of the city and the feathered serpent, the safest entry point is the Post-Classic iconographic tradition, which is accompanied by abundant if hazardous documentation. We must work backward from the known Aztec and Toltec periods to the unknown or partially known Classic and pre-Classic periods with sensitivity and skill. I am not, however, suggesting a thoughtless use of analogy and comparison to drive the understood messages of one time period back into the obscurer puzzles of another. I am saying that, after analyzing the sacred temple tradition in Mesoamerica's many Tollans, it is possible to trace the modes of symbolic, stylistic, and architectural connections between relevant data and, with the "eyes of critical restraint and disciplined imagination,"[11] to identify authentic continuities and changes in the iconographic tradition back to Teotihuacán and its contemporaries.

My approach is based on the observation of the coincidence of two images in Mesoamerican urbanism, the original image of Tollan in the written sources and the sculptured, painted, and written images of Quetzalcoatl. In his fullest and most enigmatic manifestations, the plumed serpent appears within, at the center of, or related to the image of Tollan and its urban replications. While the two images have been discussed in relation to one another before, more advantage can be gained by focusing on the significance of Tollan as a city symbolizing the magnificent achievement of an elaborate level of social integration, creativity, and influence, and by utilizing this significance as a context in which to interpret Quetzalcoatl as patron of the urban structure as a living and vital form in ancient Mexico. The point is not merely that Quetzalcoatl was the symbol of authority in a number of cities in Central Mexico, but that Quetzalcoatl was the symbol of the authority of the urban form and structure itself. Chapter 2 contains a discussion of the paradigmatic meaning of this conjunction of Quetzalcoatl and Tollan utilizing evidence associated with the ceremonial city of Tula Xicocotitlan. This chapter also includes a discussion and interpretation of Quetzalcoatl's role in Mesoamerican cosmology. Chapter 3 demonstrates how the symbol of Quetzalcoatl functioned in "other Tollans," a series of regional capitals that renewed the Toltec tradition by serving as the social and cultural pivots on which the culture of the time stood and from which came the social and symbolic powers that dominated the society. A series of short histories is presented to show the variety of Quetzalcoatls manifest in the urban traditions and the ways in which the general orientation of Quetzalcoatl and city persisted and was altered by social changes, and yet continued to sanction and justify those changes.

This study will also reveal how Quetzalcoatl finally became an ironic symbol of urban authority. For not only did he function to guide, inspire, and stabilize the Aztec elites of fifteenth- and sixteenth-century Mexico, but with the detail of the prophesied return of the ancient priest-king, he worked to undermine the structure of sovereignty in Aztec Mexico. Chapter 4 shows how the ideal image of Quetzalcoatl in Tollan functioned as a subversive genealogy, a critique against the royal line that ordered the capital of an empire, in the face of the sixteenth-century crisis that threatened Tenochtitlán. Our discussion utilizes the notions of center and periphery as interpretive devices to help us understand the meaning of the evidence uncovered at the Templo Mayor, the great Aztec shrine of this last Tollan of pre-Columbian history. Through our focus on the mythic drama of the return of Quetzalcoatl and his identification with Cortes, we will see how the Toltec paradigms related to and overpowered the other deities and ancestral heroes in the last days of the Aztec kingdom. Quetzalcoatl and Tollan maintained their prestige as the preeminent symbols of place and the authority of place. In this way, we can come to understand how the myths and prophecies of Quetzalcoatl reflected the irony of the last Mesoamerican empire.

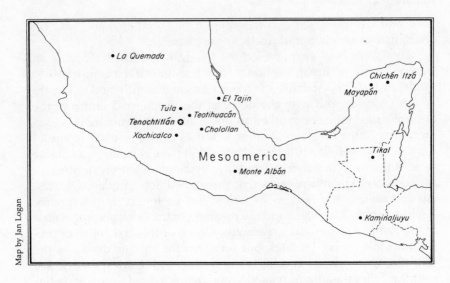

Selected Mesoamerican Ceremonial Centers

Periods of Regional Dominance

Chichén Itzá	650 A.D.–1200 A.D.
Cholollán	1000 B.C.–Conquest
Kaminaljuyú	700 B.C.–800 A.D.
La Quemada	850 A.D.–1050 A.D.
Mayapán	1200 A.D.–1450 A.D.
Monte Alban	350 B.C.–1200 A.D.
Tenochtitlán	1425 A.D.–Conquest
Teotihuacán	100 A.D.–750 A.D.
Tula	900 A.D.–1200 A.D.
El Tajín	600 A.D.–900 A.D.
Tikal	100 B.C.–900 A.D.
Xochicalco	600 A.D.–1200 A.D.

One

The Sources: From Storybook to Encyclopedia

Quetzalcoatl in the Primary Sources
Text and Context

These religious documents are at the same time historical documents; they are an integral part of different cultural contexts.

Mircea Eliade

 The historian of religions working with primary sources representing Mesoamerican religions is faced with a distinctly complex relationship between the texts and their contexts. Not only is he faced with the problem of understanding the usual idiosyncratic influences of indigenous cultural and historical realities upon the origin, contents, and purposes of these sources, but also with the problem of understanding the influences of a foreign, conquering culture upon the bulk of the primary evidence. The documents that record events under the dynasties of the Aztecs, their neighbors, and precursors reflect not only the world views, beliefs, and artistic styles of ancient Mexican society, but also the world views, beliefs, and millennial dreams of the dynamic conquest culture of New Spain. To use Mircea Eliade's phrase in a way he did not intend, the religious documents from Mesoamerica are a part of at least two different cultural contexts, the pre-Columbian and the colonial world of New Spain.[1]

It is not that authentic pre-Columbian material is unavailable to the scholar because of the oppressive strategies of conquering Spaniards. But the student of pre-Columbian cultures needs to practice a special form of the "hermeneutics of suspicion" when addressing and using those documents classified as primary sources. "Hermeneutics of suspicion" means

that before we display a "willingness to listen" and try to make
something meaningful out of the material available, we must ask
penetrating questions about the nature, reliability, and intentions of
the material itself.[2] Reading the evidence shows that the impact of
Spanish colonial processes generated a heated, pressurized, danger-
ous social atmosphere which penetrated the sixteenth-century transmission of indigenous historical and religious traditions to the extent
that almost all of the available documents contain alterations in the
picture of pre-Columbian life. This does not eliminate the possibility
of interpreting creatively, if cautiously, the evidence about Quetzalcoatl and the pre-Columbian city, but it does require that we postpone
interpretation until we have examined the historical and hermeneutical circumstances that affected the transmission of information about
pre-Columbian life. We find ourselves faced with a perplexing situation. On the one hand, it is clear that a thick Spanish, colonial,
Christian gloss has been brushed across the ideas, beliefs, symbols,
and dramas of ancient Mexican culture. At times, the evidence seems
distorted, confused, and inconsistent. Our attempt to understand and
interpret pre-Hispanic religion is thwarted by what one scholar calls
"an acute consciousness of what may have been lost."[3] On the other
hand, it appears that significant segments of authentic pre-Hispanic
culture can be discerned and understood in an illuminating fashion.
Through the gloss, indigenous images and patterns show themselves
in an engaging manner.

A close look at the primary sources reveals that during the sixteenth century there were important changes in the types of documents that carried the evidence about ancient Mexico. The scholar is
faced with a broad spectrum of sources; at one end we have the pre-
Columbian storybook, which consists of elaborately painted scenes
depicting Indian genealogies, calendars, wars, rituals, and creation
myths. At the other end we have the same material presented in
European style prose histories (in one instance in encyclopedic form),
often with Christian polemics and interpretations inserted. These
changes reflect, to some degree, the social dynamics of the colonial
culture. Social, religious, and political developments in New Spain
altered the style and content of those documents that are today classified as primary sources. This dynamic literary situation demands
our attention and caution so that we can realistically assess the degree
of European manipulation and the persistence of authentic pre-Columbian beliefs. In the short section that follows, I briefly summarize
the influences the conquest had on the transmission and destruction
of the pre-Columbian world view in the sixteenth century. Then we
shall look at the specific documents that carry important evidence
about the Toltec tradition and Quetzalcoatl. Thus, our account of the

textual meanings of Quetzalcoatl and city begins by using what Robert McC. Adams calls a contextual approach, which formulates "a series of structured summaries or syntheses, rather than confining analyses to fragmentary, isolated cultural components."[4] As will be clear, Quetzalcoatl's role in the history of Mesoamerican cities can best be discovered through combining a synthetic outlook with "a tolerance for ambiguity" found in all the primary sources. It is through the combination of suspicion, synthesis, and tolerance that one is free to practice a creative hermeneutics in Mesoamerican studies.

Conquerors and Apostles

In 1535 the apostolic inquisitor of Mexico, Juan de Zumárraga, ordered the collection and destruction of the pictorial libraries belonging to the Nahuatl cultural capital Tezcoco. Tradition tells us that the abundance of existing manuscripts, when gathered together, formed a mountain-heap in the local marketplace. In a Christian ceremony marked by a religious fervor aimed at wiping out Indian idolatry, the brilliant intellectual and artistic treasures of ancient Mexico were committed to the flames and became ashes. Although this particular story may be apocryphal,[5] it is a fact, bitter to the minds of scholars, that of the scores of pictorial manuscripts extant in Mexico in 1519 showing the histories, genealogies, cosmologies, and cartographies of the ancient culture, only sixteen remain today.[6]

The destruction and defacing of ancient Mexican symbols and images was by no means restricted to the picture books. The earliest conquerors, priests and soldiers alike, saw the destruction of the symbols of the indigenous religion as one of their purposes. Hernán Cortes's march from Villa Rica de la Vera Cruz to Tenochtitlán was punctuated with the removal, destruction, and whitewashing of religious monuments, idols, and images. Temples were whitewashed, idols were broken and crosses were set up in their place. This process was often characterized by symbolic and structural superimposition of Spanish Christian forms. Consider Bernal Díaz del Castillo's report of an amusing event that took place in the Aztec capital soon after the arrival of the Spanish troops. Moctezuma had invited Cortes and his inner circle of officers and priests to visit the major ceremonial pyramid located in the center of the city. The scene supposedly took place on the summit of the "great Cue" in Tlatelolco. Díaz del Castillo writes:

> Let us leave this and return to our captain who said to Fray Bartolome de Olmedo, who happened to be nearby him, "It seems to me, Señor Padre, that it would be a good thing to throw out a feeler to Montezuma as to whether he would allow

us to build our church here," and the Padre replied that it would be a good thing if it were successful, but it seemed to him that it was not quite a suitable time to speak about it, for Montezuma did not appear to be inclined to do such a thing.[7]

In the end Moctezuma's inclinations worked to enhance the Spanish conquest and the superimposition of Spanish Catholic forms became a common practice in many cities and towns that contained important ceremonial centers. The material and spiritual conquest of the Mexican kingdom was partially accomplished by the destruction of indigenous monuments, books, images, and symbols.

The Spanish effort to eliminate Indian symbols and images was successful enough that scholars debate whether we should lament the extinction of pre-Columbian cultural forms or study their fragmented survivals. Aztec society was so seriously wrecked that colonial historians were faced with reconstructing parts of a dead civilization. A careful examination of the art motifs in sixteenth-century Mexican art and architecture has led the distinguished art historian George Kubler to lament, "nearly all symbolic expressions of native origin were suppressed by the colonial authorities as well as by native leaders whose position depended upon conforming obedience." There were a number of distinctive dimensions to the conquest of Mexico. One was speed. Kubler summarized the situation: "One generation after the conquest of Mexico, by 1550, a great colonial state stood upon the ruins of Indian civilization. The rapid creation of this ordered polity was beset by factional disputes, contradictory methods, and the familiar struggle for power."[8] Seldom, if ever, has a developing civilization, with its economic, political, and spiritual processes intact and alive, ended with such sweeping finality. Although important vestiges of pre-Columbian life continued into the sixteenth century, indeed some survive today, the complex processes that constituted the native literary tradition, its manuscript art, and the political, religious, and economic systems of Aztec society were used for Spanish gain or destroyed altogether. As Kubler has noted, the confrontation of Spaniard and American Indian "produced a reaction violent enough to strip apart the symbolic system from the practical behavior of an entire continent." But it is important to be aware that the many fires and purification rituals of the conquerors were ignited as part of a much larger plan of cultural alteration, a plan to gain control of the content and transmission of the ancient world view in order to transform it. One does not have to read far into the documents to see that the Spaniards had more in mind than the destruction of dead men's thoughts lingering in the screenfolds. The fires of Zumárraga destroyed the brilliant colors and signs of the Nahuatl picture books—

they became black ashes. But the event symbolized a more profound, if less dramatic, change—a kind of literary conquest that was central to the transformation of world views. We refer to the intense and intricate changes in the documentary evidence that took place during the last three-quarters of the sixteenth century. These changes, as we shall see, were directed by religious and cultural preferences that resulted not merely in the evolution of one kind of document into another, but in the transmutation of one general form and style into a radically different form and style. And the content was changed as well on more than a few occasions.

In the decades immediately following the fall of Tenochtitlán, another strategy concerning the indigenous historical and religious traditions operated in the minds of the colonizers. Along with the campaign to eliminate idolatrous documents, to "put an end to everything indigenous, especially in the realm of ideas, even so far as to leave no sign of them,"[9] there developed a movement to collect, reproduce, and interpret selected parts of the native pictorial and oral tradition so that they could be used (a) to inform European society, especially the Spanish court and literate public, about the natives of New Spain, (b) to organize the developing colonial society, and (c) to enhance the missionary work of New World Mendicants and insure the effective conversion of the natives who had so abruptly become a part of Spanish colonial society. In each instance, the native pictorial and oral tradition was revived and the results are immensely valuable for our understanding of pre-Columbian life and religion.

The conquest of Mexico was one aggressive part of the Iberian project to expand its hegemony beyond the known world. One result of this amazing adventure was, surprisingly, a reorientation in world view that, in cartographic terms, saw the growing outline of America replace Jerusalem as the symbolic center of the world.[10] The enchanting places and inhabitants of the Indies were the focus of tremendous curiosity and confusion in Spain. This led to a flurry of published accounts and histories of the explorations, discoveries, and conquests, as well as descriptions of the societies that had been subdued. In this context, there was an effort to produce documents "more satisfying to the Europeans and make them more readable to one not versed in the native traditions."[11] This resulted in the limited but enthusiastic encouragement of Indian painters still conversant with the preconquest picture-writing tradition to reproduce picture books that would attract and please European eyes. The best example of this can be seen in the work sponsored by the greatest patron of the native artists, the viceroy of Mexico, Don Antonio de Mendoza, an enthusiastic collector of native "curios." Called by one scholar a "Renaissance Maecenas," Mendoza noted that the ravages of the conquest had destroyed countless native artifacts and had effaced the craft traditions that generated them.[12] He responded in the 1540s by hiring native artists and establishing them in workshops where they could fabricate "curios" for his own collection and for King Charles I of Spain. One of the most beautiful and revealing pictorial documents composed under his patronage was the *Codex Mendoza*, which consisted of seventy-one folios bound at the spine in the manner of European books, but painted largely in the native style. Picture pages alternate with Spanish translations of the pictographs and ideographs. Although the pre-Columbian mode of pictorial representation had been altered somewhat in this document, authentic Aztec patterns of symbolic thought, tribute collection, and daily life were presented, making this codex extremely valuable for interpreting Mesoamerican urbanism. In this manner, the ancient tradition was revived and Spanish understanding of Aztec life increased.

In New Spain the task of building a new system forced both the colonizers and the colonized to utilize the indigenous maps, tribute records, land claims, and genealogies in order for Spanish political and administrative order to be imposed and maintained in such a rapidly changing society. In order to gain a comprehensive understanding of the new colonial communities, a research effort was ordered by Philip II of Spain. He had a series of questionnaires sent to the colony, compelling the local administrators of each town and region to compile organized descriptions of native society. A large number of *Relaciones Geográficas* and *Descripciones* were compiled, each requiring a map or *pintura* of the local community's geography.[13] These maps carried vestiges of the native pictorial tradition and served to reanimate the art in local situations. These administrative documents are invaluable for understanding the geography, political organization, and social character of parts of pre-Hispanic Mexico. In several instances, they provide illuminating views of religious traditions including beliefs about Quetzalcoatl and the Toltecs.

The great stimulation for the transmission of native beliefs and pictorial and oral traditions into the colonial period came from the friars who were committed to transforming Indian consciousness.[14] It is from the documents generated through contact with Mendicant institutions that we draw a great deal of information about pre-Columbian religion and the city. Within the charged political atmosphere of the developing colony, the Mendicant orders had immense influence on all parts of life. The most influential religious order was the Franciscan. Along with the Dominicans and Augustinians, they became the guardians, teachers, and spokesmen for Indian peoples. They planned the new towns, built the churches, and controlled the formation of the new social order. These Christian missionaries were driven by an especially intense spiritual vision. They wanted to establish a new world and new church in America that would imitate the primitive church of the Apostles of Christ. This apostolic mission was symbolically initiated in 1524, when twelve Franciscans were ceremoniously welcomed by Cortes in Mexico City to begin the evangelization of the New World. This illustrious moment was memorialized in a mural at the convent of Huejotzingo, where the Apostolic Twelve kneel in prayer before a cross set up in Mexico. These original New World apostles and their brothers spread out rapidly to set up missionary centers in the major Indian towns. An intense millennial attitude inspired some of these friars to work speedily with the Indians so that the gospel would finally be spread to all members of the human race and the Kingdom of God could be realized on earth.[15] However, following the initial claims of large-scale instant conversion of the Indians to Christianity, it became clear that Indian religious attitudes continued to influence all aspects of Indian life. Within a decade after the military conquest, a number of priests realized that the spiritual conquest would be a long-term process, and they took the approach of learning about Indian religion and life so that it could be effectively transformed. This approach of learning about pagans in order to transform them resulted in the discovery of a wealth of pre-Columbian beliefs and practices.

This apostolic strategy and the research that accompanied it were legitimated by a patronage system, the *Patronato Real*, which gave Catholic priests the power to exercise total control and authority over the Indians, holding them in "protective custody until the time when their spiritual and temporal maturity should have arrived."[16] This mission was officially authorized by the pope who dispensed power to the Spanish Crown to assign the task of evangelization to its chosen missionary groups. One expression of this patronage system was the establishment of a college, El Colegio de la Santa Cruz, in Tlatelolco, that attempted to train Indian students in the doctrines of the Christian religion and in the classical educational system of the Spanish Renaissance. Here, as elsewhere, the priests not only trained Indian youth, but also used them and their contacts to gain deeper views into the pagan religion. The priests became the patrons of Indian education and of recording the guarded expressions of the pre-Columbian world view. Interaction with the native priests who survived the conquest and the native students who transcribed their statements greatly stimulated a number of Mendicants like Toribio de Motolinía, Bernardino de Sahagún, and Andrés de Olmos, all of whom produced books with rich and detailed information about pre-Columbian society. Still, these works must be approached cautiously because most of the informants were from urban centers and had already undergone some acculturation to Spanish Christianity. Also, in some cases the scribes who recorded the statements and memories of Aztec life were trained by the Spaniards. Complicating the accuracy of the documents further, different local traditions were often lumped together in the final versions. Yet, a remarkable amount of valuable information about pre-Columbian life can be mined from these sources.

One important result of these approaches was the extensive and often intricate change in the documentary evidence generated during the sixteenth century. One embryonic expression of colonial alterations is reflected in the *Codex Kingsborough*, where we are presented with two maps drawn in colonial terms, representing the same general landscape, but in two radically different ways. One map, the unfinished pre-Columbian style map (folio 208r), was the model for the other (folio 209r). The earlier map consists of roads and place signs done in the native pictorial style, whereas the second map, showing the same space, has been radically transformed into a landscape painting with natural images of forests, mountains, and hills, a practice not seen in pre-Columbian pictures of space. In the native style map we have, according to Donald Robertson, "signs of nature," while in the colonial map we have a Renaissance "image of nature."[17] This development suggests two different orientations to space and its qualities. The more native style map, like other storybooks, with their place signs, fantastic animals, empty spaces, human and divine figures in communication, was used as a text for oral stories about events that took place at special locations imbued with power and significance. In the second map, done for the European eye, the same space was transformed into a lush landscape, a garden of the New World, where man and nature had no discernible pattern of interaction. Much more than a style of painting was lost in this transformation: a way of perceiving the powers of space and the telling of stories about these powerful spaces was replaced by comforting images of a fresh, attractive world of nature.

This kind of change was intensified when the "images of nature" were further translated into prose descriptions of nature, gods, history, rites, and politics—indeed all aspects of pre-Columbian life. Often, it is the end product of this process of transformation that we must trust for interpreting Mesoamerican religion. Indeed, in a recent highly respected bibliography of Mesoamerican religions, it is stated that "the best single source for the study of ancient Mexican religions is Sahagún's *General History*,"[18] which is a prose Spanish and Nahuatl account of pictorial and oral traditions originally done in the native style. Cartoonlike Renaissance versions of the native pictures accompany parts of the text. A literary conquest has brought about the evolution of one kind of document into another and the transmutation of the general form and style into another. Donald Robertson has divided this process into three steps. First, there were picture books done in the native style without prose commentary. Second, the conquest produced documents with pictorial events glossed in Spanish, Nahuatl, or French. Third, prose works appeared that occasionally included Europeanized pictorials.

The result of this process is a hazardous field of evidence characterized by a pervasive dichotomy.[19] The division in its most general sense consists of pre-Columbian archaeology and storybooks on the one hand, and post-Columbian storybooks and prose works painted and written by Indians or Spaniards on the other. Within this dichotomy is a series of types of documents that reflect both Spanish influence and pre-Columbian attitudes, practices, and beliefs. More specifically, the present study will rely on seven types of documents, which include (a) pre-Columbian storybooks that escaped destruction, (b) post-Columbian storybooks generated through Spanish patronage and independently by Indians with Spanish glosses, (c) early prose works in Nahuatl and Spanish, largely anonymous, (d) prose writings of descendants of Indian elites, (e) letters and histories by Spanish witnesses of the conquest and its aftermath, (f) priestly writings best represented by Sahagún's works, and (g) archaeological evidence. All of these types of "texts" contain native pictorial or historical traditions, or both, though the degree of European influence varies significantly. In what follows I will discuss briefly the types and character of pre-Columbian storybooks since, strictly speaking, they constitute "the primary source." The bulk of this chapter will trace the transformation from storybook to encyclopedia by focusing on those works that contain important information about Quetzalcoatl as god and god-man. In this manner, our suspicions will be both confirmed and illuminated and our awareness of Quetzalcoatl's meaning will begin to expand.

The Storybooks

Form of Writing. If we attempt to identify the primary sources for the study of Quetzalcoatl and the ancient city, it becomes apparent that we are dealing, in part, with literary echoes. But, instead of just facing the problems of identifying a shout that grows fainter, we must face the phenomenon of other voices picking up the shouted word and re-shouting it, adding on and leaving off tones and timbres according to their particular capacity, education, and purpose. Johanna Broda's study of ethnohistorical sources concerning ancient Mexico reveals emphatically that a few of the earliest colonial sources, which depended on storybooks, were copied by later writers who changed the context of the earlier material.[20] More original material—already a combination of both clear and vague allusions, mythical acts, and historical events—was seriously changed in its context and significance according to the interests of later authors. Her study makes it clear that it is more accurate to speak of primary source material within works rather than to label them primary sources.

Behind these distortions in the colonial sources is the original pre-Columbian form of transmission, the pictorial sign and the oral interpreter. These two elements constitute, in pure form, the primary source, or what Jill Leslie Furst calls "the final authority." She notes that when the chronicler diverges from the pictorial material, "the pictorial version must take precedence—the manuscript as the presumably faithful rendition of the oral tradition, must be the final authority."[21] It is this combination of painted images explained by the oral specialists that leads to the use of the term "storybook" here. The pre-Columbian pictorials were not used by merely looking at the pictures, but also by explaining them verbally and telling the stories they depicted. In her fine analysis of picture writing from ancient southern Mexico, Mary E. Smith claims that the Mixtec codices "may be considered as possible prototypes of the lost pre-Columbian manuscripts of the Valley of Mexico,"[22] and she notes that in some of these documents we witness dynastic histories focusing on the genealogies and achievements of Mixtec rulers from major towns and cities. It appears that pre-Columbian storybooks were part of the art of the ruling classes and contained stories painted and understood by very few individuals, usually the priestly sons of noble families who memorized the stories and pictorial conventions of their culture.

While Jill Furst's claim about the "final authority" is ideally accurate, it is not always relevant because the majority of the documents have no related pictorial tradition. Prose works usually exist independent of pictorial images. Yet, in spite of the rupture of the conquest, it is apparent that certain symbols, metaphors, and traditions from the indigenous system of storytelling and writing have persisted through time and conflict. It is clear that the majority of sixteenth-century scholarship done under Spanish patronage depended heavily, though with a variety of methods and intentions, on extant painted manuscripts and their *nahuatlato* interpreters. While this heartens us with its suggestion of authentic nearness to the primary source, the problem of echoes comes into play when we realize that most of the painted manuscripts were destroyed or lost after the "translation." The problem intensifies when we remember that the Mesoamerican writing system, symbolic forms, and types of history were different from those of the documents in which we place the burden of our interpretation. Still, the recent systematic analysis of ethnohistorical sources in the *Handbook of Middle American Indians* has settled on the

FIG. 1. This image, from the Codex Fejérváry-Mayer, presents a typical Meso-american view of the cosmos as divided into five major sections corresponding to the four quarters and the center. Each quarter contains a cosmic tree and bird flanked by the deities of that direction. The fire god occupies the center.

judgment that in spite of all the disruption of the pre-Columbian literary tradition, "probably a gross compatibility" exists between the surviving texts and the types and quantities of original documentation.[23]

This writing system, studied seriously since 1849, has been named the Mixteca-Puebla tradition, referring to stylistic and iconographic forms that appeared in parts of Mesoamerica around the tenth century and most clearly articulated in the storybooks from the Puebla and Mixtec regions. This pictoral system is found in two types of sources: (a) a series of storybooks of both preconquest and postconquest composition, and (b) low relief sculpture carved in such famous structures as the Aztec calendar stones, the Tizoc stone, the Teocalli de la Guerra

Sagrada, as well as sparse examples of wood or bone fragments and smaller stone objects. The system is partially understood because it was flourishing at the time of the conquest and continued to be used in numerous ways throughout the sixteenth century. Some of the surviving examples are glossed in Spanish or in indigenous languages, principally Nahuatl.

I. J. Gelb's lucid *Study of Writing* is helpful to our understanding of these primary sources in two ways, first, through its classification of writing systems and, second, through the comments on the evolution of writing. Gelb defines writing and its relationship to forms of speech through a descriptive and comparative method. His analysis of writing systems from different parts of the world and different eras in history, including ancient America, led him to recognize that though writing can be defined as a "system of human intercommunication by means of conventional visible marks," there exist radical differences in the forms of writing. On one end of the spectrum is the semasiographic writing system in which "pictures convey the general meaning intended by the writer . . . who can express meaning directly without an intervening linguistic form," and on the other end is the phonographic writing system, which exists when phoneticism and syllables of speech are central.[24] Roughly speaking, these two forms are equivalent to the dichotomy of pre-Columbian storybook and post-Columbian encyclopedia.

Gelb's second relevant point is that there is no smooth emergence of one form of writing from the other. There is a great difference between the stage of writing where notions are communicated by signs having a loose connection with speech and the "phonographic stage (expressing speech)." In the former system, a loose relationship between writing and speech fosters the independence of picture writing from phonetic forms, an independence which is lost in the developed systems of writing where phonetics reduces signs and pictures to written substitutions for its spoken counterparts. It seems that, in spite of the confusing labels for Mesoamerican writing systems (ikological, elliptical, symbolic, descriptive, representational), we are dealing with a semasiographic system consisting principally of two types of messages. First, we have pictographs where the images of the objects referred to are used individually or in a series to tell something in general terms.

> Animals, plants, birds, mountains, streams and trees are recognizable as such; the scenes depicted are comparable to photographs of dances, processions, self-castigation, sacrifice or battles. Gods, goddesses or priests and common people are rec-

ognizable by their actions, their postures, their clothing, painting and headdress.[25]

In other words, we have images of the things themselves.

Second, we have ideographs in that images of objects stand for ideas associated with the images. For instance, the picture of a flower could represent a flower as a pictograph, while as an ideograph it could mean sacrificial blood. The image of a bundle of reeds would likely signify a bundle of reeds as a pictograph; but a tied bundle of reeds appearing as an ideograph can refer to the end of a great fifty-two-year calendrical period. Usually ideographs and pictographs occur on the same page.[26] In all cases, these signs form narrative drawings, that is, drawings whose meanings are communicated through the oral telling of the picture sequences. The already noted independence of picture writing from speech forms resulted in a creative leeway in interpretation for specialists. It is clear from the available sources that these specialists had a "penchant for varying place names and name signs, employing different graphemes and grapheme combinations to produce the same result."[27] One good illustration of the ambiguity and richness of this system is given in Jill Leslie Furst's discussion of Mixtec star symbolism. She notes that the image of stars in the *Codex Vienna* is a representation of human eyes, reflecting a pun on the Mixtec word for star.[28] This ideographic pun is further complicated by the fact that Mixtec languages are tonal and more precise meanings depend in part on pitch. Through careful comparison of interior evidence of *Codex Vienna* star symbols, she demonstrates how one single image could have been used, by a skillful teller of stories, to mean "the chief or head (e.g., the most important) eye of the heavens, an object that moves and returns to its proper place— and that in doing so, marks the passage of time." Complex metaphorical meanings are embedded in these apparently simple signs. This complexity and ambiguity is perhaps behind the report of the translator (from picture to Nahuatl to Spanish) of the *Codex Mendoza*, that the Indian interpreters of the pictures in the document argued so intensely over a number of images that he had only ten days to prepare his manuscript before it was to be sent from Mexico to the court of Charles V.

It is apparent that a phonetic subsystem was developing within the narrative drawing system, specifically in personal and place names. Although the extent of phoneticism is contested, it seems likely that an indigenous phonetic system was developing during late Aztec times, a system which, along with its more stable picture-writing system, was abruptly stifled and transformed by the conquest. Concerning the rupture caused by this development, Robert Ricard notes, "In whatever way it was done, the introduction of the Latin alphabet for the transcription of native tongues was a revolution in the intellectual history of Mexico, the importance of which cannot be exaggerated."

The Documents. Picture writing in the native style is found in codices that, in Mesoamerican studies, include complete documents or isolated pages, cloth paintings or European style manuscripts containing indigenous material and symbolic conventions, in an indigenous style. These codices are sometimes referred to as *mapas* or *pinturas.* The basic format is called the *tira,* which consists of long, narrow strips of native paper or animal hides, glued together, with drawings and paintings on them. The most typical form is the screenfold, a large accordion-pleated *tira* with a series of paintings that can be read in a number of directions, sometimes indicated by guiding lines. Third, we have the roll, a *tira* that has been rolled rather than folded. This type is rare, though there is at least one, the *Selden Roll,* which has important information about Quetzalcoatl on it. Finally, there are *lienzos,* which consist of large sheets of picture writing on cotton or maguey cloth sewn together. Although no preconquest *lienzos* still exist, there is no doubt that they were abundant in pre-Hispanic Mexico.

There are sixteen pre-Columbian documents still in existence. While the exact provenance of these surviving gems is often in doubt, the following summary can be made. Five ritual calendrical manuscripts which form the celebrated *Borgia* group are known to have originated somewhere in the Puebla-Tlaxcala region. They survived, perhaps, because they were sent to Europe during or soon after the conquest, before zealous priests and officials could get possession of them. Six historical-genealogical manuscripts survive from the western Oaxaca region and are known generally as the *Nuttal* group screenfolds. From the extremely brilliant lowland Maya culture, we have only three surviving ritual-calendrical screenfolds known as *Codex Dresden, Codex Paris,* and *Codex Madrid.* From the central Mexican region, where the destruction of manuscripts was most intense, we have two disputed pre-Columbian ritual calendrical works, the *Codex Borbonicus* and the *Tonalamatl Aubin.* The history of all these documents is as obscure as some of their meanings. We know that twelve reached Europe in the first half of the sixteenth century; two of these were sent by Cortes before the conquest ended. Two others probably remained in Mexican libraries, passing from collection to collection until they emerged in the Boturini collection in 1743. Two others were kept hidden in Indian communities until the end of the nineteenth century.

For a sampling of the dispersal of these primary sources, let us note
when and where a few emerged into public awareness: '

Codex Borgia, Cardinal Stephano Borgia, Rome, 1792–97
Codex Fejérváry-Mayer, Gabriel Fejérváry, Pest, Hungary, 1829
Codex Laud, William Laud, Oxford, England, 1636
Codex Vienna, King Emmanuel I of Portugal, Portugal, 1521
Codex Paris, Bibliothèque imperiale, Paris, 1829–37
Codex Colombino, Local Cacique, Tututepec, Oaxaca, 1717[29]

The Obsession with Time. One of the problems facing the historian
of religions results from the fact that the various forms and content
of the "original vehicles" did not die out after the conquest. In fact,
much of what we know about the original vehicles comes from colonial documents that carry pre-Columbian materials. H. B. Nicholson
points out that picture manuscripts produced under Spanish patronage, "despite their post-conquest date, . . . are often of the greatest
value to the student of late Pre-Hispanic culture."[30] This has caused
confusion and controversy about the principles of composition of
preconquest narrative drawings. Nevertheless, one of the distinctive
characteristics of storybook composition was the interest in, indeed,
the obsession with time, its shape, and meaning. This obsession with
time is also evident on the calendar stones, sculpture, and architecture
of the various ceremonial centers of ancient Mexico. Together, these
texts reflect the intense involvement in marking, measuring, and deciphering the patterns of celestial and social events. Consider the
"Introductory Letter" by Motolinía:

> the Indians observed close order in reckoning time—days,
> weeks, months and years—and also feasts, as will appear later.
> Similarly, they related in figures the achievement of victory and
> the conduct of wars; the succession of chief lords, weather con-
> ditions and noteworthy signs in the heavens; and general epi-
> demics; at what time and under which lord these things
> occurred; and all the lords who took a leading part in subjugat-
> ing New Spain up to the time that the Spaniards arrived.[31]

This observation by one of the more alert Spanish priests reflects
several important characteristics about the Aztec preoccupation with
time. Time was closely observed and measured in varying units. These
units were used to depict stories of human and natural phenomena.
There was a special concern for sequences of events that revealed the
nature of destiny. Although it is not true that all the storybooks were
dominated by this obsession, it is accurate that the two dominant
types of picture writing, the ritual-divinatory and the historical-genealogical, reflect a peculiar form of what Alexander Marshack calls
"time-factored thinking."[32] We will see in the books discussed here

stories about the vital processes and relationships that animate and renew society and the gods.

The ritual-calendrical manuscripts, which include the *Borgia Codex*, the *Tonalamatl Aubin*, *Codex Borbonicus*, and the three Mayan screenfolds, reflect the ingenious attempt to measure, worship, and control time—a special characteristic of Mesoamerican religions. Paul Wheatley notes in his comments on the development of the sciences in urban cultures that "It was in the realms of Nuclear America . . . that the most complex and accurate of all calendrical systems was devised."[33] The manuscripts of this category were "primarily devoted to religion and the calendar, and such related topics as divination and

FIG. 2. The Aztec Piedra del Sol reflects the five-part cosmology applied to the conception of the ages of the universe. Each of the four cosmic eras surrounds the central or fifth (Aztec) age, known as 4 *nahui ollin*, represented here with the god in the center; his tongue is a sacrificial knife. Courtesy of Lawrence G. Desmond.

religious ceremonies, and the systematic depiction of gods of the native pantheon."[34] Within this category we find three types of documents, each with a different ordering of cosmic and human time: First was the *tonalpohualli*, a 260-day cycle with 20 named days and 13 signs, known in book form as the *tonalamatl*. This type of book was the favorite target of the missionary priests. It served as the basis for prophecy, determined the favorable and unfavorable days, and was the source for names given to children. Second was the eighteen-month festival calendar, which organized "fixed" ceremonies with an eighteen-month, twenty-day count to form the solar year. Third was the calendar wheel, found only in colonial sources that contain both the divinatory and solar cycles. These manuscripts also carried related mythological and cosmological information not restricted to calendar ritual.

The historical-genealogical manuscripts have three orientations: time, place, and event. Running throughout all three is the presence of time-factored thought. Robertson notes that sources both before and after contact are ordered as year-to-year accounts of families, dynasties, and towns. The narratives are presented in linear composition in *tira* or screenfold with pictured events attached to dates or clustered dates by extended lines. Even when a map composition dominates the *tira*, the narrative consists of the history of a family that occupied that space. Time-factoring, though less prominent, is still fundamental. And when we come across event-oriented manuscripts, we are dealing with genealogical narratives covering many generations. In each case, the emphasis on sequence is present. Although it is undoubtedly true that other types of primary sources, such as economic and ethnographic records, existed in ancient America, the evidence suggests the same influence of time-factored thinking. Economic records include the historical notations of tribute relationship and the ethnographic documents have Indian life cycles woven throughout.

In my view, one of the important relations expressed in these books is the relation between ancient or mythic events and future or prophetic events. Whether in the cosmogonic myths, which tell of the universe's origins, or in the sacred history of the Toltec tradition, we see the focus on sequences of events, loaded with sacred meanings, which were set in motion in a remembered past, are enacted in the present, and will lead toward an expected repetition in the future. There is a special connection between the myths and the prophecies. This time-factored attitude permeates all the documents to various degrees, and, as the testimony of the storybooks will show, it influences the Aztec perception of Quetzalcoatl's meaning, especially the

Aztec interpretation of the events related to the coming of the Spaniards to Tenochtitlán.

The Testimony of the Storybooks

Not surprisingly, the surviving storybooks provide little evidence of Quetzalcoatl's significance in pre-Columbian society. Since the great majority of pre-Columbian storybooks are from the Mixtec region, the Toltec and Aztec traditions are barely represented in the pictorials.[35] There is, however, apparent reference to the Quetzalcoatl tradition in two pictorials containing Mixtec genealogies. In these pre-Columbian sources, figures that seem to have a clear relationship to Quetzalcoatl as god and god-man demand our attention.

It is probable that there was some contact between Toltec culture and Mixtec, and this apparently resulted in the exchange of mythical and historical traditions between the two culture areas.[36] Two related Mixtec prose sources, the *Descripción Geográfica* of 1674 and the *Origen de los Indios del Nuevo Mundo*[37] of 1606, contain stories about the deities El Corazon del Pueblo and 9 Ehécatl (9 Wind, a flying serpent), whose careers are reminiscent of the Toltec god and high priest Quetzalcoatl. These similarities are explicit in a cosmogony portrayed in the *Codex Vienna*, repeated in the *Codex Nuttal*,[38] and appearing in the postconquest *Selden Roll*.[39] The most complete version is in *Codex Vienna*, folios 49a–38c. This section of the codex, apparently a sacred genealogy, depicts in magnificent detail, the birth of a culture hero, his ascension to heaven, investiture by the Creative Pair, descent to earth, and raising of the heavens. Apparently the figure 9 Ehécatl (called by at least one commentator 9 Ehécatl Quetzalcoatl)[40] is the figure from whom Mixtec rulers claim their descent. The hero 9 Ehécatl is born from a stone knife and is followed by the birth of sixteen males representing his different guises and powers as a shamanic healer, painter, singer, recorder of history, ritual expert, and warrior, among others. He ascends to heaven, where he confers with the Creative Pair, who instruct him in his mission and show him the elaborate paraphernalia of his future career. Then, elaborately dressed in his sacred costume, which includes a truncated cap, red buccal mask, a shell pectoral, feather bundle, and flowered weapons, he is given four decorated temples and descends to earth on a rope. He is accompanied by two companions, Fire Serpent and Descending Eagle, diving head first to earth. A bird sacrifice is performed in his honor. He confers again with the Creative Pair and then performs the amazing act of lifting the heavens, revealing the earth as a hilly, fertile place with rivers and turbulent water and nine place signs, six of which have divinatory dates. Under the instruction of the high gods, he has created cosmic and ceremonial space.[41] A similar scene depicting another figure, 12 Ehécatl, in his flight and descent in *Codex Nuttal* has led Jill Furst to suggest that the creation scenario of the *Codex Vienna* is a prototype for the events in the *Nuttal*. I am inclined to favor an interpretation along the lines suggested by H. B. Nicholson, that we are presented with a story depicting one widespread indigenous pattern of the creation of a culture hero and his divinely ordained creative power. The story and its painted elements are strikingly similar to the careers of Quetzalcoatl-Ehécatl and Topiltzin Quetzalcoatl from the central plateau. The details of this pattern of world creation, including a) the miraculous birth of the hero, b) his ascent and conference with the Divine Pair, c) the costumes worn, d) the raising of the sky to reveal the earth and create an age, and e) the presence of four special buildings along with the cosmic dive of related deities, are all duplicated in fragmentary form in a large number of other pictorial and prose sources concerning the Toltec god and godman. Cautiously, we can suggest that we have a pre-Columbian example of a widespread cosmogonic tradition depicting the creation of terrestrial space, the original ceremonial center, and legitimate authority—all symbolized in the career of Quetzalcoatl or one of his doubles.

The second category of primary documents is the post-Columbian storybook done in the native style which conveys pre-Columbian historical and cosmological traditions. Some of these documents were commissioned by Spaniards in the manner already described and some were generated independently by Indians, as, for instance, the prototype for the *Codex Telleriano-Remensis*[42] and the *Codex Vaticanus A*.[43] A third document that shares this native character is the *Historia Tolteca-Chichimeca*.[44] Though several dozen similar documents exist, these three contain significant material on Quetzalcoatl and will be discussed briefly.

The history of two of the documents—the *Vaticanus A* and the *Telleriano-Remensis*, which are storybooks with written annotations—demonstrates in an astonishing way the complex relationship between text and context summarized here. Consider the following steps in the pictorial and prose composition of these two important pieces, which were copies of a pre- or post-Columbian pictorial document that was subsequently lost. Apparently, a copy of the original was made in Mexico around 1563 and later taken to Europe, where it was eventually named the *Telleriano-Remensis*. The copy consists of three parts, and it was compiled using several other documents as well as the prototype. The annotations explaining the pictorial material were done in three different hands. The prototype of the Telleriano-Remensis copy was sent to the Vatican library and copied again; this copy became known as *Vaticanus A*. This important source contains two sections missing entirely from the *Telleriano-Remensis*. The *Vaticanus A* was copied after 1569. The prototype for both codex copies was lost! The annotations on the *Vaticanus A* were done by at least two scribes who copied an earlier Italian translation of a Spanish text. To complicate the situation, the final annotations were done by a Spaniard who had an imperfect knowledge of Italian. It appears that we have two copies of an early post-Columbian storybook, probably itself a copy of a pre-Columbian storybook, which was never, as far as we know, seen by European eyes. As Henry Nicholson has demonstrated in his invaluable discussion of these sources,[45] the paintings that serve as the basis for the written narrative, along with the more acculturated pictures in the *Florentine Codex*, are the only coherent group of native style illustrations of the Toltec priest-king still available. In spite of heavy Christian additions to the text, these works constitute, along with some of the stone carvings at Tula, the closest thing we have to the "final authority" about Quetzalcoatl.

Taking these two documents together,[46] the Quetzalcoatl material reveals the intimate relationship that existed between the Toltec hero Topiltzin Quetzalcoatl and the deity Quetzalcoatl, sometimes called Quetzalcoatl-Ehécatl. Following an account of the creation of the world and its organization, Topiltzin Quetzalcoatl (it is stated in the commentary that he was named after "the other Quetzalcoatl," meaning the god) is divinely conceived and born to the virgin Chimalman. The engenderer was the creator sky god Citlallatonac-Tonacatechuhtli. As an adult, Topiltzin Quetzalcoatl sees that Tollan is suffering from a famine and degradation, and he initiates new ritual practices to end the famine and gain divine pardon for his people who have committed errors. The famine ends and he is appreciated for his ritual bloodlettings, which are imitated by the people. He constructs four temples that become famous: the House of Nobles, the House of the Common Man, the House of the Serpent, and the Temple of Shame. He also invents round temples. One of his fervent disciples, Totec, carries out several penitential adventures following his frightening dream experiences. Then, the two lead a group of devotees from Tollan, boring a tunnel through a mountain in which some of his followers are turned to stone. Topiltzin Quetzalcoatl arrives in Tlapallan and disappears over the water, telling his people not to mourn too much because he will return and that a bearded people will eventually rule in the land. It is noted that this belief, heightened by the coincidence of his birth on the day 1 Reed and the arrival of the Spaniards in Mexico in the year 1 Reed, encouraged the Indians to think Quetzalcoatl had returned. When the hero died, he ascended to heaven and became the Morning Star and was identified as Tlahuizcalpantecuhtli. In other parts of the two documents it is noted that Topiltzin

Quetzalcoatl was also the god who created human life and the world and was the wind god who was worshiped in the city of Cholula. (Throughout this book, the pre-Columbian city of Cholollan will be referred to both as Cholollan and as Cholula, its modern name.) The connection with Cholula, as Eloise Quiñones Keber has shown, was elaborately referred to in the glosses for the fourth, fifth, and ninth trecena periods.[47] In one case, Topiltzin Quetzalcoatl was celebrated at a great feast in this city on the special days 7 Reed and 1 Reed once every fifty-two years. Elsewhere we find that a Topiltzin–Morning Star cult was celebrated in Cholula, suggesting that a fusion of the culture hero and deity Ehécatl and Morning Star developed. From her analysis of these documents, Keber shows that the commentators were making active interpretations of the storybooks and not merely copying what was already before them. She writes, "from its first written expression, the tale of Topiltzin Quetzalcoatl can be seen in a continuous state of flux, meshing legendary, historical and myth-ological elements from both the native and Christian European tra-ditions."[48]

Remembering the story line in the *Codex Vienna*, we can see some striking similarities and additions to our scenario. As in the *Codex Vienna*, this culture hero is miraculously born, this time by the union of a deity with a Toltec virgin. He is a ritual expert whose sacrifices become models for the populace and, as in the *Vienna*, he is associated with four important temples which organize his ceremonial center and activities. A clearly unique episode occurs when he leaves Tollan and dies in Tlapallan, after announcing that he will one day return—this is related to the Spanish conquest. His identification with deities, including Quetzalcoatl, Ehécatl and Tlahuizcalpantecuhtli, is impor-tant and will be repeated elsewhere.

A third colonial pictorial source, also with accompanying com-ments, this time in Nahuatl, is the *Historia Tolteca-Chichimeca*. Probably copied from a pre-Hispanic storybook before 1546, it contains three short but important references to Quetzalcoatl and expands our view of his significance in space and time. We first hear of the Toltec deity Quetzalcoatl during an account of a mighty conflict which brings about the fall of Tollan.[49] One of the warring groups within Tollan, the Nonoalco-Chichimeca, prepares to abandon their city, but on the night before their flight they hide all the treasures of Quetzalcoatl and guard them carefully. A second reference appears during the flight of the other faction, the Tolteca-Chichimeca, fifteen years later. Their high priest Coenan is sent to the city of Cholollan[50] to plead with the deity Ipalnemouani, "Through Whom All Live," to allow his people to relocate there. He performs special rituals before the great shrine and, surprisingly, Quetzalcoatl answers, telling him that his people are welcome. The identity of this deity changes, however, when Coenan returns to Tollan to report his success and informs his followers that it was Topiltzin Quetzalcoatl who promised them a new home. Inspired by the oracle's welcome, the Tolteca-Chichimeca leave Tollan and eventually arrive in Cholollan.

Again, we have an explicit identification of Topiltzin Quetzalcoatl with the deity Quetzalcoatl and a clear statement that both were significant sacred figures in Cholollan. This Cholollan location is expanded in the third reference to Quetzalcoatl, where it is stated that his shrine in that city made it a truce center for warring factions who periodically made peace and visited the ceremonial center to attend religious festivals. Truces were not always successful, however, for it is stated that one of the enemies of the Tolteca "shot the face of Quetzalcoatl" and initiated a new war in Cholollan.[51]

A number of other post-Columbian storybooks, although they do not carry the Quetzalcoatl tradition, contribute to our understanding of Mesoamerican cities and the pre-Columbian conception of legitimate authority. These include the splendid *Codex Mendoza* and the pictorial histories *Codex Xólotl* and *Codex Azcatitlan*.

If all we had to work with were the storybooks from pre- and postconquest times, we could make the following profile. Quetzalcoatl the deity, in his manifestations as Morning Star, Creator God, and Wind God, is clearly related to the culture hero Topiltzin Quetzalcoatl. The latter was divinely born and became a sacred figure in Tollan and Cholollan as a result of ritual actions, establishment of four temples, his flight from Tollan, and his death. His promise to return led to his identification with the Spaniards during the conquest. When we hazard the identification of this figure with the career of 9 Ehécatl in the *Codex Vienna*, we see striking similarities. Basically, Quetzalcoatl is the divinely ordained creator of life, ceremony, ceremonial structures, and social authority. Let us move into the prose sources to see if these connections and meanings can be illuminated.

Transitional Prose Sources
During the early decades of the colonial period, at least five documents were produced which contained significant information concerning Quetzalcoatl. We call these documents transitional prose documents; that is, early postconquest accounts, written in prose Nahuatl, Spanish, or French, which were based to a large extent directly on pre-Columbian and post-Columbian storybooks. One important fact that distinguishes these from the former documents is the almost total absence of pictorial images, although it is clear that in several cases the prose translator had pictures before him. The five relevant works are the *Anales de Cuauhtitlán*, the *Leyenda de los Soles*,

FIG. 3. The frontispiece of the *Codex Mendoza*, depicting the founding of Ten-ochtitlán, reflects the application of the Aztec cosmology to the spatial order of the capital. In the center of the four sections of the city is the image of the Aztec god perched on the cactus growing from a rock in the lake of Mexico. The human action below the central section represents Aztec conquests of nearby towns.

the *Historia de los Mexicanos por sus pinturas*, the *Juan Cano Relaciónes*, and the *Histoyre du Mechique*.

An extremely valuable document, the *Códice Chimalpopoca*, contains two rare and beautiful sources, the *Anales de Cuauhtitlán* and the *Leyenda de los Soles*, which are based on different preconquest storybooks and are written by anonymous hands. The *Anales*, completed by 1570, consists of a number of interwoven local histories from major towns and cities in the Valley of Mexico and the basin of Puebla, including Tezcoco, Tenochtitlán, Chalco, Tula, Tlaxcala, and Azcapotzalco. Robert Barlow's intense analysis of this Nahuatl document[52] shows that it is based on ancient songs, storybook images, memories of old men in Cuauhtitlán, two written sources from Tezcoco and Chalco, and other unknown sources. It emphasizes the tradition of Cuauhtitlán, a city founded after the fall of Teotihuacán in the tenth century, and includes an account of the rise and fall of Tula.

A full, lyrical, and confused version of the Quetzalcoatl tradition confronts the reader in the *Anales*. Quetzalcoatl, under the sign 7 Ehécatl, creates human beings from ashes in an early sequence. "He had them made and raised them." This scenario is greatly expanded in the *Leyenda* version. Later in the source, a full-blown account of Ce Acatl Topiltzin Quetzalcoatl's career is offered, providing us with an invaluable look at the indigenous appreciation for the Toltec king. This account includes such important events as his miraculous birth when Chimalman swallowed a precious stone, his search for and reburial of his father's bones, his installation as king in Tollan, and the construction of his four temples.[53] Then, in a new scenario, he prepared for an ecstatic flight through intense ritual action and communicates, as in the *Codex Vienna* scene, with the Creative Pair above the ninefold heavens. His kingdom is portrayed as an ideal natural and social landscape, and he is described as the discoverer of valuable stones, feathers, cotton, and birds. Also, he is a marvelous craftsman. He begins to build a great temple with feathered serpent columns, but cannot complete it. This paradise crumbles through the tricks of his rival Tezcatlipoca who, angry that the king will not sacrifice humans, leads him to drunkenness and an apparent incestuous episode with his sister Quetzalpetlatl. Stricken with grief, Quetzalcoatl departs from Tollan and arrives at Tlapallan-Tlatlayan, where he sacrifices himself by fire and is transformed into the Morning Star. The story ends with the summary: "Such was the life, in its entirety, of him who was called Quetzalcoatl. He was born in 1 Reed. And also he died in 1 Reed and so it is reckoned he lived for fifty-two years. And so it is finished, in the time, in the year 1 Reed."[54] This account, adding marvelous details of his sacred career, stresses that a conflict about human sacrifice was one of the major causes for his downfall. It is also important to note here that the historical survey which runs throughout the work positions the rise and the zenith of Aztec power purposely in line with Quetzalcoatl's Tollan, suggesting this figure's importance in Mesoamerican traditions of legitimate rule.

The companion document, the *Leyenda de los Soles*, presents a fuller account of the god Quetzalcoatl's creative acts and offers a short version of the hero Ce Acatl's career. (Ce Acatl, Topiltzin Quetzalcoatl, and Quetzalcoatl, when referring to a human being, all refer in my view to a single historical individual or mythical hero.) This Nahuatl document, written by a Spanish-educated Indian, was completed by 1558. It contains a sacred history of the Aztec world from the point of view of Tenochtitlán's surviving elites and was constructed free of priestly direction. It is apparently a concise commentary on several pictorial codices in the possession of the writer. One page includes a rough diagram of Topiltzin seated on a ruler's throne surrounded by the four temples of his ceremonial center, apparently copied from the original storybook. The document is especially important because it consists of poetic fragments which were most likely recited and sung in the *calmecacs* of Aztec society and its precursors.

During the cosmogonic sequences, Quetzalcoatl is chosen by a group of deities to travel to the land of the dead and recreate human life. His cosmic dive results in a dramatic confrontation with the Lords of the Underworld and he is miraculously successful in his quest.[55] Later on, he participates in the creation of man's most important food, corn.

Referred to later as Ce Acatl, the culture hero follows some of the lines of his career in the *Anales* version, with an account of his unusual birth and the recovery of his murdered father's bones, but it differs in its emphasis on the vicious revenge sacrifice of his uncles. And Ce Acatl is pictured as a ruler of Tollan who becomes a military conqueror, eventually reaching Tlapallan, where he falls sick, dies, and is burned on a funeral pyre. This simpler account is followed by a description of the Aztec royal dynasty and their conquests.

The most appealing and picturesque transitional prose document is the *Historia de los Mexicanos por sus pinturas*, written before 1536. There is circumstantial evidence that the famous Franciscan priest and linguist, Andrés de Olmos, translated it from a surviving storybook which was originally attached to the prose commentary. It may well be the earliest account we have of an official Aztec history of the world. Myths of creation swing into dramatic motion, a motion which seems unique in its shape. Quetzalcoatl, one son of the Creative Pair, shares in the creation of the universe, the destruction of different ages, and the arrangement of the earth. He is one of the two deities who lift the sky to reveal the earth. He bleeds himself in penitence, gets kicked out of heaven, and in one sequence casts his own divine child into the sacrificial fire in order to create the sun.[56] He is a cosmic tumbler in a circus of eccentric divinities.

Following this cosmogony, there is an account of Ce Acatl of Tula who as a youth distinguished himself as a great warrior and religious hermit. He emerges from seclusion to construct a wonderful temple where he performs rituals and worships until he is cast out of Tula. He travels to Cholula and finally to Tlapallan, where he dies. In the last sections of this document there is a clear effort made to link the Aztecs with the Toltec remnant residing in the city-state of Culhuacán, suggesting again the Aztec perception that Tollan's priestly ruler was the founder of legitimate rule in Mexico.

An unusual work, *Libro de oro y tesoro indico* contains thirteen documents, two of which, the *Origen de los Mexicanos* and the *Relación de la genealogía y linaje de los señores que han senoreado esta tierra de la Nueva España*, provide important early evidence of Quetzalcoatl's significance for dynastic succession in central Mexico. Called the *Juan Cano Relaciones* by Nicholson because a *primero conquistador*, Juan Cano, commissioned a Franciscan friar to trace the pedigree of his Indian wife Doña Isabel, daughter of Moctezuma II, back to the creation of the world, these two documents contain important variants of Quetzalcoatl's career, copied from a common prototype.[57] Both documents demonstrate that the ruling dynasty of Tenochtitlán traced its heritage through the rulers of Culhuacán to Ce Acatl Topiltzin of Tollan. Compiled in 1532, the *Relación* is one of the earliest accounts we have of preconquest history, going back to the eighth century, and the prototype was obviously based on storybooks. It has a detailed version of the Toltec kingdom under the influence of "Topilci," who is the son of a murdered lord whose bones he recovers. He builds a ceremonial center and makes Tula a great capital. A controversy about human sacrifice disturbs his kingdom because he is in favor of sacrificing snakes and butterflies, but not human beings. Forced out of his kingdom, he arrives in Tlapallan, where he dies. The account notes that he dressed in the manner of the Spaniards and continues with a discussion of subsequent dynasties focusing on Culhuacán.

A fifth source, the *Histoyre du Mechique*, completed by 1543, contains at least two chapters of sacred history originating from central Mexico. It is a French copy, in the hand of André Thevet, of a lost Spanish original based on pre- and post-conquest storybooks. Quetzalcoatl of the Toltecs appears here after a description of the creation of the world. His parents are the deities Camaxtli and Chimalman. His mother dies in childbirth. Details of his family struggle emphasize the problem of finding a successor for his murdered father. Quetzalcoatl, worshiped as a god, reigns in Tollan until the god Tezcatlipoca

comes and brings about the god-king's downfall. The source records
the important migration of the Quetzalcoatl cult to Cholula, where
a great temple is built, and shows once again that this tradition was
important in at least one other pre-Aztec city-state. Finally, the hero
is cremated and the smoke from his body becomes the Morning Star.[58]

From these transitional prose sources we see the confirmation of
the storybook testimony—Quetzalcoatl is remembered as a creator-
god who is intimately related to a human figure named Ce Acatl
Topiltzin Quetzalcoatl. The deity creates human life and is a central
figure in the cosmogony. We get the general impression that the rulers
of Aztec Tenochtitlán traced their power in some form to the Quetzalcoatl tradition of Tollan. This tradition emphasizes the recovery of
the hero's father's bones, his experience as a warrior, ecstatic priest,
ruler, and builder of ceremonial centers which are usually organized
around one or four temples. We see new detail concerning the priest-
king's idyllic realm: his defeat by enemies, his flight through Cholula
to Tlapallan, and his transformation into the Morning Star.

Mestizo Sources

A fourth category of evidence consists of those manuscripts authored by descendants of preconquest royalty who, like their most
celebrated example, Alvarado Tezozomoc, had access to extant picture writings, oral informants, and some written narratives containing
information about pre-Columbian religion and life. We include here
Tezozomoc's *Cronica Mexicana*, Diego Muñoz Camargo' s *Historia de
Tlaxcala*, and Juan Bautista Pomar's *Relación de Tezcoco*.

Generally, these histories represent what I call a mestizo point of
view, marked by striking cultural ambivalences and an obvious mix-
ture of motives and goals. While only two of these writers were
mestizos, all wrote their works combining Indian and European points
of view. On the one hand they display a tendency to glorify their
respective Indian families, ties, and towns with nostalgic appreciation
of "the good old days," while on the other hand they praise Spanish
Christianity and condemn the pagan system of human sacrifice and
sometimes Indian morality in general. In one case, we see an author
embellish stories to justify the massacre of Indians by Spaniards.

Alvarado Tezozomoc was of full-blooded Indian royalty, the son
of a postconquest *tlatoani* and Moctezuma's daughter. His rustic narrative displays a sensitive pride in the feats and life-styles of Aztec
warrior-kings, but he rigorously criticizes Aztec sacrifice and shows
a warm appreciation for some aspects of Spanish Christianity. Completed in 1598, the *Cronica Mexicana* is filled with references to the
deity Quetzalcoatl and the Toltec priest-king Quetzalcoatl which cannot be fully summarized here. Suffice it to note that Quetzalcoatl

appears in relationship to kingly prestige and power. In a rare reference to the foundation of the Aztec city, we are told that the Mexica built their first shrine to Huitzilopochtli, but it was made of materials associated with Quetzalcoatl.[59] Also, Quetzalcoatl is mentioned as the first king to have his image carved in the gardens of Chapultepec, a royal custom repeated up to the time of Moctezuma Xocoyotzin.[60] At least one king is reminded at his coronation that Zenacatl y nacxitl Quetzalcoatl was the first lord to sit on the throne.[61] The throne, he is told, is on loan to the new king, but will someday be returned to the one it belongs to. Finally, Tezozomoc clearly recounts the story of Moctezuma's fear that Quetzalcoatl has returned to rule in Tollan when word of the advancing Spaniards reached Tenochtitlán.[62] The fuller accounts of these events will appear in the interpretive sections to follow.

Juan Pomar, a mestizo, was the great-grandson of Tezcoco's famous philosopher-king Nezahualcoyotl on one side and a Spaniard on the other. He was well-educated and he consulted Indian elders, ancient sayings, and extant storybooks in order to present a glorious image of his ancestors' kingdom as a golden age of art, politics, and religion in the *Relación de Tezcoco*. At least one authority has claimed that Pomar's work is "by far the richest ethnographic description that is known."[63] While this is true, it must be noted that his work is also marked by a search for Christian parallels in the illustrious events of his family's past and sustained criticism of paganism as false religion. He reported that his famous ancestor's religious revolution of the middle fifteenth century had similarities to Christianity, which from his viewpoint, living in sixteenth-century New Spain, made Nezahualcoyotl a unique genius indeed. In this regard he argued that the cities of Tenochtitlán and Tlacopán borrowed the superior laws and cultural forms of Tezcoco but invented the terrible ritual of human sacrifice themselves and imposed it on the great cultural capital of the Nahua world.

In a small but significant reference, Pomar discusses the priesthood of Tezcoco and notes that the high priests, called "Quetzalcoatls," opened the chests of sacrificial victims. These ritual specialists were respected like great lords and his discussion of the priestly lifestyle suggests that Topiltzin Quetzalcoatl was apparently the priestly archetype for more than one city in the Valley of Mexico.[64]

Diego Muñoz Camargo was the mestizo son of a Spanish conquistador and an Indian woman. He married into Tlaxcalan nobility and held a number of powerful administrative posts in the Spanish government in Tlaxcala. He was aggressive in his treatment of Indians and his periodic cruelty did not go unnoticed by Spanish authorities. Benjamin Keen writes, "His involvement in the factional struggles of the Indian community resulted in a royal order demanding the expulsion from Tlaxcala of Muñoz Camargo and some other mestizos 'for their abuse of the Indians and for setting a bad example,' but evidently the order was not carried out."[65]

Muñoz Camargo tells us that a Tlaxcalan deity, Quetzalcoatl, was revered throughout New Spain. We also read that a human Quetzalcoatl, born to Coatlicue and Mixcoatl Camaxtli, became a great leader and was respected like a god. Later we find that the Toltecs established two sacred cities—one at Teotihuacán, dedicated to the sun and moon, and one at Cholula dedicated to the evening star Quetzalcoatl.[66] In the second book, we see Muñoz Camargo's feelings about the Indians and Quetzalcoatl come clear, when he discusses the Spanish massacre of Indians at Cholula. He notes that the Indians of Cholula had great faith and confidence in the great deity Quetzalcoatl, but that this bloodthirsty deity, especially hungry for the blood of children, failed miserably to help his people when faced with the true god of the Spaniards.[67] In his description of the massacre that ensued, he invented a vicious attack by the Cholulans on a messenger from Cortes as a means of justifying the terrible slaughter of Indians that followed.

The additional information that appears in these sources strengthens the link between Aztec kings and Quetzalcoatl of Tollan. Specifically, we have another reference that Moctezuma thought that Quetzalcoatl might be returning in the guise of the Spaniards. Moreover, Quetzalcoatl's significance in Tezcoco as the title of the priestly office is established and we find another mention of his powerful position in Cholula. We see the intimate relationship between Quetzalcoatl the god and Quetzalcoatl the man throughout the *Historia de Tlaxcala*.

Spanish Letters and Descriptions

An indispensable though suspect group of sources includes some of the letters, histories, and accounts written by Spaniards who were witnesses of the conquest and members of the early colonial society. Rarely were these documents based on storybooks, and they demonstrate, in their focus and attitude, the extent of Spanish intervention in Aztec society and its sixteenth-century image. Yet, that Hernán Cortes, Bernal Díaz del Castillo, and Andrés de Tapia were eyewitnesses of the city, religion, and society they conquered makes them unusually valuable sources for reconstructing late Aztec religion and the meaning that Quetzalcoatl held at the time of the conquest. Between the seeing and the telling, however, they injected complex political and literary agendas such as the desire, in the case of Cortes, to aggrandize himself before the king; or the attempt, in the case of

Díaz del Castillo, to establish himself as the most accurate and brilliant scribe of the conquest; or the effort, in the case of local magistrates, to fulfill through the *Relaciónes* the requirements of Philip II's questionnaires.

The earliest conquest reference to Quetzalcoatl appears in the celebrated Second Letter that Cortes wrote to King Charles I in 1520. For us its principal value lies in Cortes' report of two nearly identical speeches by Moctezuma, who, following a direct reference to his own storybook tradition, welcomed Cortes as the representative of an ancient Indian hero, "our natural lord," who created Indian culture, left the land, and returned years later, only to be rejected by his people. The hero departed, but the people expected his descendants to return and establish his rule again.[68] In these speeches, the Spanish king is identified as the true lord of the land and the people are invited to obey Cortes. Though Quetzalcoatl's name is not mentioned, it seems likely that Moctezuma is referring to the Topiltzin Quetzalcoatl tradition. This letter is a strong basis for the argument that the Toltec hero was appreciated as a paradigm of rulership in Tenochtitlán and that this paradigm influenced the Aztec's initial reception of the Spaniards.

Andrés de Tapia, one of Cortes's captains, wrote the *Relación sobre la conquista de Mexico* sometime before 1552.[69] As an official in Cholula immediately following the conquest, this rugged soldier is probably reflecting a Cholulan perspective. In his account we are told that "Quetzalcoate" was the founder of that great city and was remembered and appreciated for having refused to sacrifice human beings. He was also famous for having built wonderful ceremonial structures, including temple pyramids, and for ordering peaceful coexistence.

The importance of Quetzalcoatl in Cholula is elaborated in Gabriel de Rojas's composition *Relación de Cholula* of 1581. It is reported, in response to various questions, that "Quecalcoatl" founded the city, which was called "Tullam Cholullan Tlachuihaltepetl." Further, the principal rulers lived in the central temple called "Quecalcoatl," which was revered throughout the land. The supreme importance of this center and Quetzalcoatl is reflected in the statement, "the Indians from all parts of the land came for their devotions on pilgrimages to visit the temple of Quetzalcoatl—because this was the city that was venerated like that of Rome in Christianity and Mecca to the Moors."[70]

These three sources, although filled with Spanish mischief, have enriched our picture of Quetzalcoatl. The impact on Moctezuma of the prophecy of Quetzalcoatl's return is elaborated in a full and flowing narrative. Furthermore, we have the reference to Quetzalcoatl's prohibition of human sacrifice, his cult in Cholula, and the statement that Cholollan was also called Tollan.

Priestly Writings

In his comments on ancient Mesopotamian literary sources, Leo Oppenheim writes,

> references to literary *topoi*, historical facts, and historical situations are so densely interwoven that the historian is not only faced with philological difficulties but also with the far more complex problems of style and literary influence as they mold and distort the report for specific purposes.[71]

A similar situation faces the historian of religions working in the ancient Mesoamerican society where, as we have seen, the authors of most of our primary sources, "manipulate the evidence, consciously or not, for specific political and artistic purposes."[72] Nowhere is this clearer than in the final category of written texts, the priestly writings, of which Sahagún's encyclopedia is the finest example. In all the texts by Mendicants, we see the strong influence that a foreign world view, with its set of ideological requirements, had on the different reformulations of an ancient indigenous world view. The final stage in the transformation from storybook to encyclopedia was set, not just by the individual genius of Sahagún, but by a handful of priest-historians whose evangelical commitments, linguistic abilities, and personal interaction with Indians and their surviving traditions encouraged the refinement of a systematic method for gathering information and the application of European principles of ordering that information. Sahagún's monumental twelve-volume work, which carries important accounts of the Quetzalcoatl tradition, can best be understood and appreciated if we survey first the other priestly historians who preceded him, worked alongside him, and followed him. In this section I will discuss the invaluable works of the Franciscan "school" of writers, including Motolinía and Andrés de Olmos, before focusing on Sahagún's *Florentine Codex* and finally reviewing the works of the Dominicans Diego Durán and Diego de Landa.

The earliest extant document produced by the Franciscans was authored by Fray Toribio de Benavente (hereafter referred to as Motolinía, the Indian name he adopted), one of the original twelve Franciscans who arrived in Mexico in 1524. Motolinía's ministry was characterized by an intimate association with Indian communities in many key parts of New Spain during the heyday of New World evangelization. In fact, he participated in the initial plans to build a uniquely integrated farming community near Cholula which would restore the Christian faith to its original purity and purpose. He held important administrative posts in various communities including the office of *ministro provincial* in Mexico from 1548 to 1551. Commissioned in 1536 to write a history of notable things concerning the Indians and the Franciscan mission in the New World, he produced an important original document, now lost, of which we have two versions, the *Historia de los Indios de Nueva España* and the *Memoriales*.

In a sense, Motolinía is the founder of the Franciscan ethnographic tradition. To collect his information, he used sustained and careful personal observations of Indian life, for which he felt a combination of disdain and admiration. He held interviews with the most informed Indians in his parishes and attempted to record these interviews carefully. Whenever he could, he interviewed the owners of storybooks or individuals who understood the paintings. He was greatly admired by later writers, at least six of whom used large sections of his works in their accounts. Johanna Broda has summarized his contribution accurately: "Above all, the great value of his work consists not so much in the systematic summary of material but in the originality and authenticity of his data, collected at an early date by a man intimately familiar with the Mexican conditions of the first colonial period."[73]

Motolinía's works present a summary of Topiltzin Quetzalcoatl's early life in Tollan, emphasizing his innovative ritual bloodlettings, preaching, chastity, and fasts. He was appreciated as a model by his people, "for since that time many in this land began to fast." The narrative relates the episodes of Quetzalcoatl's death, transformation into the Morning Star, and the fact that his prophesied return led to his identification with the Spaniards. At another point in the text, Quetzalcoatl's temples are again important, only now in an intriguing new way. The text reads:

> This god of air, they called in their language Quetzalcoatl . . . he was a native of Tollan, and from there he set out to build up certain provinces. But he disappeared and the Indians always hoped that he would return. Hence, on the arrival of the ships of the Marques del Valle, Don Hernando Cortes, who conquered this New Spain, the Indians seeing them in the distance, coming by boat, they said their god was coming and when they saw the white and high sails, they said their god was bringing his *teocallis* [temples] over the sea.[74]

Earlier, in Motolinía's Introductory Letter, there is a direct reference to Quetzalcoatl's paradigmatic relationship to the rulers of Mexico. Speaking of Quetzalcoatl, he says, "From him, they say, descended the people of Colhua, the ancestors of Moteuczoma, lords of Mexico and Colhuacán. It is said that the Indians considered Quetzalcoatl one of their principal gods, calling him god of the air. Everywhere they erected innumerable temples in his honor, set up his image and painted his figure."[75] Elsewhere it is noted that Quetzalcoatl had special influence in Cholula, a city "like Rome" where great and long rituals were performed in his honor. We also find references to To-piltzin's or Quetzalcoatl's transformation into the Morning Star.[76]

Motolinía's work is especially significant for the identification of Cortes's ships with those four buildings that have been part of our survey ever since the *Codex Vienna* pictures and the direct tie of the Toltec hero to the rulers of Tenochtitlán. Again, Cholula appears to have been a religious capital.

The process of sensitively researching the Indian world view begun by Motolinía was carried forward by the methodological research of his colleague Andrés de Olmos. Olmos, whose specific works are still difficult to identify, applied his humanistic training, with his deep interest in classical languages, to the task of understanding Indian life. He became known as the best Nahuatl student of his day. Commissioned in 1533 to write about the antiquities of Mexico, Tezcoco, and Tlaxcala, he described the ritual and political beliefs, practices, and institutions of many different cities and towns. His concern for method is reflected in the personal interviews he held with Indians whom he encouraged to report on the meanings of their artworks and storybooks. He produced a protoencyclopedia which systematically described a wide range of elements in pre-Columbian life and thought. The original work and at least three copies were sent to Spain and were subsequently lost. Later he wrote a great summary of his work, using old rough drafts and memory. Parts of this summary appear in the *Histoyre du Mechique* and the *Historia de los Mexicanós por sus pinturas,* and in the *Codex Tudela* before it was also lost. Olmos's influence on others has been great and he served as a source for writers like Bartolomé de las Casas, Geronimo de Mendieta, and many others. He knew Sahagún well; they taught together at the Colegio de la Santa Cruz.

The material concerning Quetzalcoatl which can be attributed to Olmos's research (not including the works just mentioned) is reflected in the borrowed material found in the works of Las Casas and Mendieta.[77] Abstracting his works from those sources, we see that Quetzalcoatl is the greatest deity of Cholula because of the wonderful actions of the human being Quetzalcoatl, who taught the populace metallurgy, forbade human sacrifice, and preached a peaceful existence. His city Cholula was a truce center for all peoples, including enemies. Although other rulers were invited to set up their shrines in this central city, Quetzalcoatl was clearly recognized as the greatest "Lord" of all. There is also a reference to Quetzalcoatl's flight to his original homeland with four leaders and his promise to return in the future with bearded white men who would rule Mexico. It should be stated that when evaluating Olmos's contribution to our picture of Quetzalcoatl, we must express appreciation for the wonderful ma-

terial which appears in all documents which he authored in part or
as a whole.

Sahagún's Encyclopedia

In order to make an accurate general evaluation of the relevant
testimony in the *Florentine Codex*, it is necessary to consider the social
and religious atmosphere in which Sahagún worked, his specific purposes, the methods he used, and his results. Such a task would take
volumes, and numerous studies have been and are being carried out.
In what follows, we summarize the best research on Sahagún, with
special gratitude to Alfredo López Austin for his unique essay, "The
Research Method of Fray Bernardino de Sahagún: The Questionnaires."[78]

All of the religious orders working in New Spain tended to see
the land and the natives as the setting for a grandiose drama of
evangelization. They hoped, in different degrees, to convert souls as
well as take control of the traditions in the storybooks in order to
accomplish the greatest conversion in world history. This commitment
is summarized by J. L. Phelan in his fascinating study *Millennial Kingdom of the Franciscans:*

> But before the age of Discovery, Christianity was geographi-
> cally parochial, confined to a rather small part of the world.
> Under the impact of this realization in the sixteenth century, a
> dazzling vista opened up. Christianity for the first time could
> implement its universal claims on a world-wide basis. The gos-
> pel could be brought to all peoples and all races. It could be
> global as well as universal. To those of mystical temperament
> this possibility appeared as a vision which was so blinding and
> radiant that its fulfillment must inevitably foreshadow the rap-
> idly approaching end of the world. It seemed to these mystics
> that after all the races of mankind had been converted, nothing
> further could happen in this world; for anything else would be
> an anticlimax.[79]

Bernardino de Sahagún's view of his apostolic responsibilities was
less millennial than most, but conversion of the natives was still his
central goal. He felt strongly that in order to cure the Indians of their
"sins of idolatry, idolatrous rites and beliefs, omens and supersti-
tions," it was absolutely necessary to know "from what disposition
and cause the sickness proceeds . . . the preacher should know the
vices of the republic in order to direct his teaching against them."[80]
Therefore, he set out to write a grand handbook, or encyclopedia,
that would inform Christian priests of the nature and character of
pagan religious practices. He also hoped to encourage a young generation of Indians to reject the teachings of their forefathers as well

as the life-style of the corrupt Spanish conquistadors and embrace a true Christian existence. In order to bring this about, he set out to do three things: (a) to know as much as possible about Indian religions, (b) to create a Nahuatl vocabulary to assist in the effective preaching of the Gospel, and (c) to lay the documentary basis for an accurate appraisal of the character of Nahuatl culture. His sniping Christian eyes were always aimed at the falsehoods of indigenous religion and the "great carelessness and culpable ignorance" displayed by his fellow priests toward Indian religion. For instance, in his appendix to book 4, *The Soothsayers*, he presents an extended and harsh critique of Motolinía's "very great lie" concerning the Indian calendar. Picking out lines, sentences, and paragraphs from Motolinía's description of the calendar, Sahagún works to demolish the tolerant attitude toward the Indian's "Count of Years" found in his predecessor's books. Elsewhere, at the end of book 5, *The Omens*, he cannot constrain himself from adding a final word of condemnation—

> These superstitions harm the Faith, and therefore it is well to recognize them. Only these few have been recorded, though there are many more. But diligent preachers and confessors should seek them out, in order to understand them in confessions and to preach against them; for they are like a mange which sickeneth the Faith.[81]

Sahagún's rare accomplishments were enhanced by the students he taught at the Colegio de la Santa Cruz. In Tlatelolco a generation of elite Indian youngsters were taught the classics of the Greco-Roman tradition, Latin and Nahuatl script, and were initiated into the doctrines and mysteries of Spanish Christianity. These students also became Sahagún's informants and his collaborators in research. The crucial research elements of storybooks, Indian interpreters, and Spanish priests utilized by Motolinía and Olmos were now strengthened by the addition of trilingual Christian Indian students who could assist in the verbatim transmission of knowledge from storybook to encyclopedia.

The Method. Sahagún's *Historia General* was guided by the organizing principles set forth in ancient and medieval encyclopedias. Apparently inspired by Flavius Josephus's *Antiquities*, Aristotle's *History of Animals and the Parts of Animals*, and principally Pliny's *Natural History* and Bartholemew de Glanville's *On the Properties of Things*, the Franciscan used the precedent of medieval hierarchies, which ordered knowledge by beginning with divine things, descending to consider humans and animals, and ending with plants and minerals. He researched the Mexican world according to the European model and

FIG. 4. The colonial image of Tenochtitlán's foundation reveals the influence of European styles and attitudes on the native pictorial tradition. From Diego Durán's *Historia*.

made his own shifts in this hierarchy in his final manuscripts. As his research progressed, he realized the immensity of what was being lost and he encouraged the natives to speak in their own fashion about their world view. This encouragement led to treasures of information, but also to his occasional loss of control of the project.

Sahagún developed what is called today the "Interview round table agreement method" and used it in all the sites of his research.[82] This method depended on two types of documents and three kinds of people. The documents were a guiding questionnaire, now lost, constructed by Sahagún, and native pre- and postconquest storybooks brought to the interviews by the informants. The participants at the sessions were Sahagún, his native trilingual students, and elderly native informants and interpreters who had lived in preconquest society and could articulate the older traditions. Sahagún's questions, knowledge of the language, and attitude, along with the presence of bicultural students, evoked the expression of the native concepts and nuances. He used this approach in three different centers over a decade. He worked first in Tepepulco, second in Tlatelolco, and finally in Mexico City. In each location the interpretations of the storybooks were recorded in Nahuatl. When it came time to compile the evidence from these three centers, he cross-checked and compared the responses to discover consensus and incongruity. Thus, the direction of information went from Sahagún's questions to native informants interpreting the storybooks speaking in Nahuatl to colonized Indian scribes recording the responses in Nahuatl which were later translated into Spanish. He remarked about native participation, "The Mexicans added and amended many things in the twelve books as they were being copied." The multiple sites of research produced a series of documents and versions of documents that were finally integrated after complex evolution into the *Historia General*, consisting of thirteen volumes, completed in Nahuatl in 1569. This first complete document was lost, but fortunately two bilingual copies in Spanish and Nahuatl were made before the disappearance of this first version.

The results of Sahagún's work are both marvelous and uneven. On the one hand, he can justly be called the "leading pioneer in American ethnography"[83] and be deeply appreciated for transcending the trends of his time and training. On the other hand, his work contains limitations, distortions, and failures. The great praise due this indefatigable priest should not deflect us from noting several limitations of his work, because this will help us develop the accurate and balanced picture necessary for any effective hermeneutics of suspicion. We know, for instance, that some of his sources were inadequately informed about such topics as Indian cosmology and cosmography, and it is possible that this was deliberately the case. López Austin's analysis of the questionnaires and the resulting dialogues and monologues reveals that on occasion Sahagún meddled with some native responses in a limiting way and also failed to pursue obviously important lines of information. For instance, it appears that in the gathering of the sacred hymns from the elders, Sahagún gave them great freedom of expression. But unlike many other situations where he probed and asked for clarification, he failed to explore the meaning of these important statements. López Austin notes that this "may be due in part to his inexperience as a text collector, but undoubtedly he was strongly motivated by his aversion to material he judged diabolical." The priest had a difficult time in his research on natural astrology, which resulted in book 7, a volume that Lopez Austin calls a "personal failure." Sahagún probed the Indian understanding of astronomy from his European point of view and was clearly upset when the Indians responded with statements about sun worship, celestial monsters, and that "the star arrow worms dogs and rabbits." In the text, Sahagún made disparaging remarks about the vulgarity of the Indian view of astrology causing López Austin to write:

> He could not be more unjust. This book is a personal
> failure. . . . If he attacks the Indians for their low level of un-
> derstanding, they must have felt the same way about his intel-
> ligence when confronted with questions they considered
> ingenuous in their lack of knowledge. If Sahagún had under-

stood something about the clash of ideas, perhaps his book
would be one of the best sources on the cosmic vision of the
Nahuas, discussing the upper to lower floors, the course of the
stars through them, the supporting trees, information that is
seldom available from other sources.[84]

Sahagún's Quetzalcoatl. But this and other scattered failures are
admirably balanced by a string of successes; for example, the material
in relation to Quetzalcoatl is both rare and comprehensive. Sahagún's
work uncovered stories and traditions about Quetzalcoatl that involve
almost all the themes and roles we have seen in the other works. To
name just three important entries, to be used in detail later, Quetzalcoatl's role as creator deity and his part in the drama of the creation
of the fifth sun are described in fine detail. References to Quetzalcoatl's relation to the priesthood, childbirth, and the *calmecacs* are
found in different parts of the codex.[85] Sahagún's persistent probes
also uncovered one of the most complete accounts of the Toltec tradition about Quetzalcoatl in Tollan.[86] Perhaps most important for our
study is the detailed identification of Cortes with Quetzalcoatl found
in the twelfth book, "The Conquest."[87] Not enough can be said here
about the relevant material on the feathered serpent, but it will be
used thoroughly on the pages that follow.

A comment is needed concerning the references in book 12 which
show that Moctezuma thought Cortes was Quetzalcoatl. This extremely important account was collected decades after the events
described. Sahagún and his trilingual students apparently gathered
this version from the elders of Tlatelolco. These elders, while clearly
within the Aztec hegemony, represented a position somewhat critical
of the Aztec elite who conquered them nearly a century before. This
has led some scholars to argue that this identification of Quetzalcoatl
may have been a *post eventum* fabrication by rivals to expose a hys-
terical Moctezuma's failure of nerve. If we follow this reasoning, what
are we to make of the almost identical picture appearing in Cortes's
letters, written long before this account was gathered? In my view,
what we have is not a politically motivated fabrication, but a *post
eventum* elaboration of the actual identification of Cortes with Quetzalcoatl by members of the Aztec elite in 1519. The belief in Quetzalcoatl's return, as shown in a number of other sources, had such
a strong grip on the Aztec mind that even decades after the events
described, it was used to communicate the persistence of the Aztec
commitment to certain cosmological patterns of destiny. While it is
possible that the Tlatelolcans may have elaborated this belief, I do not
think they could have fabricated it.

Diego Durán

The apostolic strategy of conquering the Indian spirit by first knowing its attachments was pursued with particular fervor by the Dominican priest and writer, Diego Durán. Durán's evangelical research efforts produced three works of lasting value, *History of the Indians of New Spain*, *Book of the Gods and Rites*, and *The Ancient Calendar*. His intense commitment to change Indian beliefs is reflected in these comments from his works. In *Book of the Gods and Rites*, we read:

> I am moved, O Christian reader, to begin the task of [writing this work] with the realization that we who have been chosen to instruct the Indians, will never reveal the True God to them until the heathen ceremonies and false cults of their counterfeit deities are extinguished, erased. Here I shall set down a written account of the ancient idolatries and false religion with which the devil was worshiped until the Holy Gospel was brought to this land. Fields of grain and fruit trees do not prosper on uncultivated rocky soil, covered with brambles and brush, unless all roots and stumps are eradicated.[88]

And in his *Ancient Calendar*:

> Not only today but in the past we have known of old men who were proselytizers, soothsayers, wise in the old law, who taught and are still teaching the young folk, who are now being educated. They instruct them in the count of days, and of the years, and of the ceremonies and ancient rites. . . . Owing to this suspicion I was encouraged to produce this work, moved only by the zeal of informing and illuminating our ministers so that their task may not be in vain, worthless. . . . In order to administer the sacraments, one needs more knowledge of the language, customs, and weaknesses of these people than most people think.[89]

Like his Franciscan counterparts, Durán sought out surviving elders and their picture books and made strenuous efforts to talk with anyone who had some understanding of pre-Columbian traditions. Yet his descriptions of Aztec life are riddled with Christian polemics and attacks on Indian idolatries. Still, his works contain some vital information concerning Quetzalcoatl's significance for the Aztec dynasties. Among the many references to Topiltzin Quetzalcoatl and Quetzalcoatl we find the intriguing story (also found in Tezozomoc's *Cronica Mexicana*) of Moctezuma's visit to Chapultepec to view his carved effigy. He is told that this custom began with Quetzalcoatl and the suggestion is that a direct link existed between the Toltec king and Aztec royalty.[90] The *Book of the Gods and Rites* begins with a chapter on Topiltzin where we are informed that the Aztecs derived their ceremonial order from the great king in Tula.[91] Topiltzin's wonderful reputation as preacher and his miraculous acts led the Dominican to suggest that he was possibly an ancient Christian apostle who carried the Gospel to the New World centuries before the Spaniards came. Moreover, we find in his *History* elaborate references to the identification of the Spaniards as Quetzalcoatl by Moctezuma plus the fascinating detail that when the Spaniards sent biscuits for the Aztec king to eat, he had them sent to be buried in the temple of Quetzalcoatl in Tula.[92]

Brief mention must be made of Diego de Landa's invaluable work, *Relación de las Cosas de Yucatan,* which carries information about the Quetzalcoatl tradition in the Mayan region.[93] Diego de Landa worked in Yucatan from 1549 to 1563 and had excellent exposure to the native traditions, which he violently tried to stamp out. In 1563, he was summoned to Spain to defend his harsh inquisitorial treatment of Indians. Acquitted of all charges, he returned to Yucatan as its bishop in 1573 and remained there until 1579. His work is the most valuable we have for this region and is often compared with Sahagún's *Historia,* although it has nothing of the depth and breadth of that work. The principal value of this study lies in the description of a conquering Toltec Quetzalcoatl, who established himself as the ruler of Chichén Itzá and built a magnificent ceremonial temple to the feathered serpent deity. A small kingdom was organized under the guidance of this priest-king who introduced heart sacrifice into the region. In a confusing set of references, we are also told of another Toltec invasion, probably several hundred years later, also led by Quetzalcoatl, who established his capital in Mayapan.

Comments on the Archaeological Evidence

Paul Westheim, in his important book, *The Art of Ancient Mexico,* makes an interesting archaeological interpretation. He notes that the main pyramid at Tenayuca, located near Mexico City, is circled by interwoven bands of serpents and fifty-two gaping serpent heads. The image implies that the pyramidal structure is generated out of the body of the serpent, as though it is "magically sprouting from the earth."[94] Although this interpretation can be challenged, there is no doubt that serpent symbolism and more specifically feathered serpent symbolism is spread throughout the architecture of ceremonial centers in Mesoamerica. Carved and painted images of Quetzalcoatl appear on murals and monoliths, accompanying deities, priestly figures, warriors, and astronomical glyphs. Apparently, some of the round pyramids of the Classic and Post-Classic centers are representations of this dynamic sacred being. Fray Motolinía, in a section called "Temples of the Demon," notes:

> There were also some houses or temples of the demon which were round, some large and others smaller, according to the size of the town. The entrance was like that of a cave and on it was painted the mouth of a frightening serpent with terrible fangs and teeth. . . . These houses . . . were round and low and had a sunken floor. . . . They were dedicated to the god of wind, who was called Quetzalcoatl.[95]

In the six urban centers to be examined, we find the meaningful coincidence of Quetzalcoatl's image ornamenting the central pyramid temple complexes of the ceremonial centers. The implication of this coincidence is that not just the pyramidal structure, but also the institutions that gave these cities their authority and coherence were in various degrees generated by Quetzalcoatl. In these initial comments on the archaeological evidence, I will briefly describe the feathered serpent images carved on the pivotal shrines of these cities.

Serious and significant archaeological research did not begin in Mexican cities until the second decade of this century with Manuel Gamio's controlled excavations of Teotihuacán during the Mexican Revolution. Since those early excavations, powerful strides have been made by several generations of Mexican, German, French, and American teams. They have worked at major and minor sites throughout Mesoamerica using coordinated field excavation techniques and literary evidence to fill in the static picture that archaeology yields. As a result of these advances it is possible to identify artistic sequences, trace the origins and flow of sculptural styles, recognize urban building innovations, and discuss the evolution of deity representations, especially in the Classic and Post-Classic periods. When we turn to the archaeological record concerning the Quetzalcoatl tradition, the evidence is spectacular; nowhere is this more striking than in Teotihuacán, the earliest of our great ceremonial centers and the subject of a stunning publication, *Urbanization at Teotihuacán, Mexico: The Teotihuacán Map.*[96] This imperial center of the high plateau, which developed and flourished between around 100 B.C. and A.D. 750, is' known to us almost totally through the archaeological record, and the feathered serpent's fantastic zoomorphic image not only impresses but also confronts the observer. This confrontation is most evident in the Pyramid of the Feathered Serpent located in the middle of the Ciudadela, where Quetzalcoatl's image shares the architectural stage with another deity, probably Tlaloc. The magnificent strength of the feathered serpent cult reflected in this image has inspired the anthropologist Charles Margain to admire this pyramid as an example of "aesthetic factor" at work in the construction of a "significative and valuable world" that was crucial to human life in Teotihuacán. Apparently, the artists, engineers, and architects of Teotihuacán cooperated to express their refined visions and exquisite sensitivity in making this building; it is a fine example of "complete integration. True plastic integration exists when no single element of its composition, pictorial, sculptural, architectural—can be added or subtracted. The Temple of Quetzalcoatl demonstrates this, even in its present ruined state."[97]

A frieze consisting of alternating giant carved stone heads of Quetzalcoatl and possibly an early version of Tlaloc adorns the structure. Quetzalcoatl's head deserves added comments because in it we see the divine grin of this ancient deity, a grin flashed in other centers, as we shall see. It is a monumental, jutting visage with open jaws displaying thick, white, carved teeth beneath what were once obsidian eyes. The head emerges from a bouquet of feathers that join it to the body. A thickly stylized body undulates horizontally along the pyramid over and under various shell figures. In this earliest of great capital cities, perhaps the original Tollan of the sources, Quetzalcoatl was clearly appreciated as a great sacred power. We shall return to this structure and its wonderful ornaments in chapter 3.

While the same exuberant claim for "true plastic integration" cannot be made for the Quetzalcoatl temples in the "other" Tollans, it does appear that each ceremonial center is symbolically integrated by shrines adorned with plumed serpent imagery. A similar coincidence of plumed serpent and central shrine appears in Xochicalco, where Quetzalcoatl's image almost totally dominates the pivotal structure. In this much smaller tenth-century site, which was probably a significant part of Teotihuacán's empire, we find Quetzalcoatl related to a surprising variety of artistic motifs and styles from Monte Alban, Teotihuacán, El Tajin, and lowland Mayan cities. The iconography on the numerous stone structures of this hilltop fortress suggests that Xochicalco was at least an aesthetic crossroads in Mesoamerica and achieved a distinct sense of cultural integration. This accomplishment is partially reflected in the rare and astonishing Temple of Quetzalcoatl, which crowns the highest terrace of the city. Surrounding this temple is a magnificent feathered serpent frieze, consisting of a huge, tense undulating feathered serpent, again with his divine grin, passing over and under the bodies of Mayan priests and calendar signs, symbolically weaving together and supporting the figures and their meanings. In this case, Quetzalcoatl functions as a dominant leitmotif.

In Tula, we have a more complex relationship between Quetzalcoatl and ceremonial center. The controversy surrounding this city's identification with the grand Tollan described in the *Anales de Cuauhti-*

tlán reflects some of the difficulties of understanding Quetzalcoatl's role in Mesoamerican urban traditions. The feathered serpent's image does not dominate the iconography of Tula, but there are Quetzalcoatl images on some of the major buildings and sculptured figures in and near the primary ceremonial center. In the written sources, however, it is abundantly clear that the main temples were associated with both the deity Quetzalcoatl and the ruler Topiltzin Quetzalcoatl. One of the more elaborate temple pyramids in Tula's main plaza apparently has images of Quetzalcoatl's role as the morning star, causing Ignacio Marquina to name it the Temple of Tlahuizcalpantecuhtli. Feathered serpents also appear on the small heelcap decorations of the sandals worn by the great stone Atlantean warriors that stood on top of one pyramid. In the nearby Burnt Palace, small colorful, feathered and cloud serpents decorate cornices and banquet friezes. Moreover, the east altar of Mound 3 contains the feathered serpent in the apparent position of a patron deity to warrior figures. A pottery vessel from Tula, now located in the Vienna naturhistoriches Museum, has a similar image. Desiré Charney reported that he saw a feathered serpent image on the ball-game ring during his work in Tula. There are two possible images of the historical priest-king Topiltzin Quetzalcoatl appearing at the site. One is on a pillar discovered by Jorge Acosta in the 1941 excavations, where we have a warrior with an unusual helmet mask decorated with an eagle head and a full beard. The name glyph above the figure appears to be the feathered serpent, leading H. B. Nicholson to conjecture that this may be a carving of the historical individual who bore the title Quetzalcoatl. The second image appears on the Cerro de la Malinche about a mile from the main center. High on a hillside, on a rock wall facing the ceremonial center, is a finely carved figure of what appears to be a priest or warrior (partly defaced) who is drawing blood from his ear. A magnificent undulating serpent appears vertically behind and above the human figure. The date 1 Reed appears to the right of the figure. Although it seems that this figure was carved later than the apogee of Tollan by Aztec artists, this in no way detracts from the possibility that it may be an effigy of Topiltzin Quetzalcoatl.

Recently, Eloise Quiñones Keber, impressed with the possibility that the Aztecs had this image carved long after the fall of Tula, has come up with the suggestion that this effigy "might be seen as part of the attempt on the part of Aztec rulers to provide their youthful dynasty with a historical validation of political legitimacy by connecting it to Toltec forebears."[98] This seems quite possible when we remember that the Aztec custom of carving effigies of rulers at Chapultepec originated with Quetzalcoatl. In this case, the suggestion is that they returned to the archetypal city to sacralize their dynasty. Regardless of whether Tula is the Tollan of the sources, it is evident that the feathered serpent was important enough to be embedded in stone throughout the ceremonial center.

The Toltec colonial capital of Chichén Itzá located far to the southeast is a refined version of Tula's artistic style mixed with indigenous Mayan architectural features. Among the many stunning buildings of this marvelous center, at least three buildings, the small Temple of the Jaguars on the east side of the mammoth ball court, the great Temple of the Warriors, and El Castillo or the Temple of Kukulcan, contain significant images of the feathered serpent. The latter structure dominates the center of the sacred enclave where the feathered serpent grins at the bottom of the stairways leading up to the shrine. Within view of this commanding pyramid is the Temple of the Warriors, which has the unusual characteristic of being decorated with numerous upside-down feathered serpents guarding the great doorway. These carvings and other smaller images of the feathered serpent found throughout the center demonstrate that Toltec culture, with its fascination for Quetzalcoatl, reestablished itself in this Mayan center and they will prove to be valuable data for our analysis of Quetzalcoatl's power at the periphery of the Mexican urban tradition.

These traces are also found, in much less impressive fashion, in Cholollan, the religious capital of Mesoamerica, where the archaeological record has suffered from ill-planned and poorly organized excavations. Yet in the major ceremonial courtyard at the base of the largest pyramid in the world, we find what appear to be prominent feathered serpent images on two altars.[99] In our discussion of this longest inhabited center in America we will rely much more heavily on the testimony of the written records.

The shattered ruins and reconstructed models of Tenochtitlán's great ceremonial compound suggest that the feathered serpent tradition was effectively intermeshed with the symbolic landscape of Aztec syncretism. Quetzalcoatl was honored by a fine round pyramid, referred to earlier by Motolinía. It was apparently situated directly in front of the Templo Mayor, where the shrines of Tlaloc and Huitzilopochtli towered above the sacred landscape. As we will suggest later, the spatial relationship of these three shrines demonstrates that the power and meaning of Quetzalcoatl for the Aztec capital, while persistent, has changed. Quetzalcoatls are also found on the central shrine in the form of great grinning serpent heads guarding the base of the stairways leading up to the shrine of Huitzilopochtli. Further, it appears that the entire ceremonial precinct, occupying a square space of about 440 meters on each side, was surrounded by a *coatepantli* or serpent wall, which according to Jorge Hardoy was decorated with hundreds of feathered serpent heads. The feathered serpent images found on Aztec stones are too numerous to discuss at this point, but they will receive further attention, particularly at strategic points in chapter 4.

DESIGNS OF QUETZALCOATL

Ce Acatl Topiltzin Quetzalcoatl, son of Iztacmixcoatl and Chil-malma, was born, at least to human beings, in the Central High Plateau of Mexico in the year 843 or in 895 or in 935 or in 947 or in 1156. . . . Born? Well, following detailed studies of the sources, it is possible to negate his existence or affirm that he died in Uxmal, in the Pyramid of the Advino on the 4th of April in 1208, at six in the evening, Yucatan time.[100]

The intriguing array of evidence described here suggests that the painted, carved, and written images of Quetzalcoatl reflect certain major cosmological concepts, cultural paradigms, and historical events that had significance during a long period of pre-Columbian history. The puzzling arrangements of powers and meanings which characterize the tales, myths, and stories of Quetzalcoatl are perhaps accurately represented in the feathered serpent's distilled artistic image, the stepped fret with its antagonism, striking ambivalence, and flowing arcs. It seems clear that we are faced with a situation similar to the one summarized by Clifford Geertz as a "multiplicity of conceptual structures, many of them superimposed upon or knotted into one another, that are at once strange, irregular and inexplicit, and that the ethnographer must contrive somehow to grasp and then render."[101]

When dealing with the Quetzalcoatl tradition of ancient Mexico, scholars are in a similar position to the one exclaimed upon by Sherlock Holmes:

HOLMES: My dear Watson, this is a most unique case!
WATSON: Unique? How's that Holmes?
HOLMES: Most unique indeed! Instead of being faced with too few clues, we are given too many. We have a puzzle with too many pieces in it.

This ancient Mexican conundrum has led scholars to interpret and redesign its shape and meaning in marvelous, insightful, confused, and sometimes laughable ways. It must be stated that these scholarly designs of the feathered serpent reflect the intellectual ingenuity of scholars as much as the sybilline power of the pre-Columbian symbol. It is rare indeed when we feel, with exhilaration, that the two expressions are close together. The scholarship on Quetzalcoatl is full of inventiveness, contrivance, and fabrication, and the studies of Quetzalcoatl are a fascinating topic in themselves. Intellectual paradigms, artistic intuition, and schools of thought have been applied to the evidence, resulting in strikingly divergent portraits of this major Mexican symbol. It is necessary, in the face of this meeting of intellectual paradigm and indigenous data, to be both suspicious and appreciative of the major studies on this figure. The following short summary of three dominant streams of interpretation will describe the general outline of each approach and focus briefly on the finest renditions of its lines. We will benefit from previous discussions by Alfonso Caso and Alfredo López Austin, who organized the major studies on the Toltecs and Quetzalcoatl into three categories:[102] the diffusionist, symbolic, and historical designs of this ancient, fantastic figure.

The diffusionist design is the picture that has Quetzalcoatl originating outside ancient Mexico in a Christian, oriental, or other foreign culture. Special reference will be made to the scientific diffusionist approach of Alexander von Humboldt, whose expansive and ornate work helped set the stage for later scholars impressed with the possibility of transoceanic connections.

The symbolic design is an attempt to understand the category of myth as testimony to the religious imagination. Quetzalcoatl was a mental creation symbolizing (a) human perceptions and interactions with forces of nature or (b) the conscious and sometimes unconscious search for spiritual wholeness and integration. Special reference will be made to the works of Eduard Seler, Laurette Séjourné, and Miguel León-Portilla.

In the historical design scholars propose that Quetzalcoatl of Tollan was a historical individual whose biography can be discerned by stripping away miraculous elements in the evidence. Detailed versions of the historical approach appear in the writings of Jiménez Moreno, Paul Kirchhoff, H. B. Nicholson, and Alfredo López Austin.

Diffusionist Design

The most persistent and popular interpretation of Quetzalcoatl speculates that the culture hero and his deity migrated to ancient America from a foreign country. This earliest of interpretations was generated in response to the crisis of knowledge felt in European countries and transplanted European communities resulting from the discovery and conquest of America. Faced with lands and peoples never mentioned in the authoritative, geographical and theological works of the Old World, scholars, clergy, and citizens alike made strenuous attempts to place the age of discovery within the context of meaning provided by the biblical, Greek, and Renaissance classics. Writing of these efforts, Lewis Hanke notes that "even before the first decade had passed, these plumed and painted peoples, so erroneously called Indians, had become the principal mystery which perplexed the Spanish nation, conquistadores, ecclesiastics, crown, and common citizens alike. Who were they? Whence came they?"[103] The first waves of Spaniards were intrigued by the presence of Indian crosses, rituals of confession and baptism, and stories of an ancient lord who preached a wonderful message in the land, gave the people a new religion, left, and promised to return. When versions of this story suggested the preconquest presence of a religious genius who made a marvelous impact on cities and towns, two theories arose concerning his significance. Either clerics were faced with proof of evil supernatural influences of the devil who had misled the Indians into their false and terrible beliefs, practices, and idolatries, or they had proof of a redeeming contact from early Christianity in the form of an apostle whose missionary activities were recorded in the stories.

Consider the hopes of the Dominican priest Diego Durán, who, upon hearing of a mysterious ancient book in the possession of a village near Popocatepetl, hurried to the spot in hopes that he would find "the Holy Gospel in Hebrew." He was told that the book was originally given to the villagers by Topiltzin Quetzalcoatl, but that it had been destroyed a few years earlier because the Indians could not read it. Distraught at this loss, Fray Durán held out the belief to the end of his life that Quetzalcoatl was most likely the wandering Saint Thomas and that he had visited the New World centuries before. This interpretation of a foreign missionary, Quetzalcoatl, was elaborately developed during the seventeenth century in such books as *Pluma Rica Nueva Fenix de America* by Manuel Duarte and *Finix de Occidente: Santo Tomás Apóstol hallado con el numbre de Quetzalcoatl entre las cenizas de antiquas tradiciones conservadas en piedra, teoamoxtles tultecos y en cantares teo chichimecos y mexicanos* by Sigüenza y Góngora.

The idea that some of the attractive elements in pre-Columbian religion had been disseminated from the Old World was eventually refined and changed by the amazing work of Alexander von Humboldt, whose theories and conclusions influenced generations of natural scientists and opened new intellectual channels for students of Mexican culture. His influence can be seen in such important scholars as William Prescott, Walter Krickeberg, and Robert Heine Geldern.

Between 1794 and 1804, Humboldt traveled six thousand miles throughout the Americas in order to study the natural and cultural history of the New World. This robust genius applied the scientific method in the best manner of the German intellectual tradition to describe and understand the artifacts and peoples he encountered. Partially inspired by the writings of Johann Wolfgang von Herder, he made connections and traced relationships between different cultures within and beyond the New World. His splendidly illustrated *Vues de cordilleres et monuments de peuples indigenes de l'Amerique* recorded the presence of pyramids, picture books, pottery, ceremonial centers, plus stories of Quetzalcoatl that suggested to him that some ancient contact had been made between Asian cultures and the Indians.[104] While Humboldt was not sure that the great ruler Quetzalcoatl was a foreigner, it seemed to him likely that some of the wonderful elements of that marvelous kingdom were transmitted from Asia. A careful look at Humboldt's work reveals that he was debating with himself the idea of cultural diffusion against the notion of independent invention of these civilizational elements. Humboldt's genius—for he was called an academy in himself—provided some of the tools and legitimation for later studies of cultural diffusion, most recently articulated by the Vienna school of ethnology.

Symbolic Design

The scholarly designs of Quetzalcoatl took a celestial turn in the dense and intricate works of the so-called German school, which appeared toward the end of the nineteenth century. Led by the genius of Eduard Seler, this group of thinkers argued that the category of myth could not be reduced to historical events and transoceanic journeys. Rather, myths were symbolic expressions of the ancient imagination, and the Quetzalcoatl myths reflected the ancient appreciation of the dynamics and beauty of natural phenomena. This antihistorical approach was forcefully stated by Daniel Brinton in his essay, "Myths Are Not History": "Let it be understood, hereafter, that whoever uses these names (Itzamna, Quetzalcoatl) in a historical sense betrays an ignorance of the subject he handles, which were it in a better known field of Aryan or Egyptian lore, would at once convict him of not deserving the name of scholar."[105]

Brinton argued that myths were "spontaneous productions of the mind, not reminiscences of historic events" and that Quetzalcoatl's story was one example of a widespread Indian hero myth personifying the luminous scenarios of nature which impressed archaic peoples in their appearance, movement, contrasts, disappearance, and continual return. Translating Quetzalcoatl as "Admirable Twin," he suggested that the colors and elements of Quetzalcoatl's costume were symbols for the dazzling lights that inspired the beholder. The splendid Tollan was certainly not "the little town of Tula" but the brilliant object and motion of the glowing sun.

Eduard Seler, a genius who did broad studies on Mesoamerica, developed this perspective by using the methods gleaned from his knowledge of comparative linguistics, ethnography, and archaeology. Part of Seler's great contribution lies in his skillful and often successful analysis of storybooks such as the *Tonalamatl Aubin, Codex Borgia,* and the *Codex Vaticanus A,* and his pioneer translations of Sahagún's early Nahuatl manuscripts. His rigorous comparative approach resulted in the first serious opening of the West to the meanings and figures in the pre-Columbian pictorial tradition.[106]

For Seler, Quetzalcoatl's meaning is rooted in natural phenomena, especially water. The pictures he analyzed suggested that the ancient priesthoods proclaimed Quetzalcoatl to be the primordial creator of the world and the maker of human life. This grandiose concept sprang from a more archaic notion about *quetzalcoatls*—mythical serpent beings who symbolized the moisture and life produced by the new rains that poured after the long dry season. Quetzalcoatl's original mythical meaning was as the active agent of water that gave life in its most basic forms. This mediating capacity between drought and fertility was elaborated in Mexican thought when Quetzalcoatl took the form of Ehécatl, the god of wind who precedes the coming of rain. Seler saw the theme of religious mediation elaborated in the stories of Quetzalcoatl's manifestation as the great priest-king who initiated civilization and mediated between the gods and man. Thus, there was a historical dimension to the stories about the great ruler, but they also contained metaphorical statements about creativity at natural and cultural levels. While other deities, such as Tlaloc, the rain god, remained natural forces throughout Mesoamerican religion, Quetzalcoatl became a special human being with social and cultural significance, making this deity a very distinctive one. A rain-dispensing god and a rain-making priest were joined in a special combination to become the center of Mesoamerican civilized life.

The advances of Seler and his students have never been matched in Mesoamerican studies. But another group of scholars has developed the view that the myths about Quetzalcoatl and the archaeological images of the feathered serpent represent the spiritual and psychological genius of ancient Mexican culture. In particular, Laurette Séjourné argues that Mesoamerican history was highlighted by a poetic age of creativity which was centered in Teotihuacán. She believes that ancient Mexican culture suffered a great anxiety of transcendence which led to the degraded Aztec practice of terror through massive human sacrifice. This degradation was preceded by a beautiful spiritual vision of the human being achieving liberation through heroic self-sacrifice, a vision embodied in the Quetzalcoatl tradition. Séjourné feels that the two Quetzalcoatls, the priest-king and the creator-deity, represent the majestic lines of an archetype of spiritual liberation acted out in Topiltzin Quetzalcoatl's self-sacrifice in Tlapallan and in Quetzalcoatl's cosmic dive into the underworld to reclaim the bones of ancestors to create human life once more.

Quetzalcoatl's career was a metaphor of transcendence and a model of liberation that guided the golden age of ancient American civilization.[107]

A similar spiritualist approach has been articulated by Miguel León-Portilla, who portrays Quetzalcoatl as the personification of wisdom. This magnificent role was achieved by both the god Quetzalcoatl and the culture hero Quetzalcoatl. The latter penetrated the heavens in a great ecstasy and established the ritual means for the religious virtuosi to commune with the highest forces of the universe, realizing the title of *tlamantinimi*. The deity Quetzalcoatl constantly revealed the high gods' creative intentions in giving life to the universe in its various forms. Quetzalcoatl was the creative spirit who originated agricultural and human life as well as the cultural spirit that discovered the profound meanings of life.[108]

Historical Design

The third and dominant scholarly design is the historical one that focuses on the outline of Topiltzin Quetzalcoatl's biography and the identification of the earthly city where he reigned. Most of these scholars benefit from the euhemeristic theory of religion, that gods were once kings or heroes whose great achievements encouraged their deification in myth. Myths, in this approach, were considered reminiscences of human events and even historical stages. Vigorously antidiffusionist in their approach, these historians have attempted to find the historical Quetzalcoatl camouflaged in myth.

Among the early exponents of this design were the Jesuit Francisco Clavigero, Orozco y Berra, and Alfredo Chavero. All three saw Quetzalcoatl as a human being who represented indigenous cultural values and articulated religious meanings during a pivotal period of Mesoamerican history. Orozco y Berra, called the first scientist of Mexican civilization, saw the mythical conflicts of Tezcatlipoca and Quetzalcoatl in Tollan as accounts of the struggle between two religious traditions. Alfredo Chavero went so far as to construct the first decent detailed biography of the Toltec king. Amazingly, both Chavero and Orozco y Berra arrived at their insights without the Sahagúntine corpus, which had not yet been rediscovered.

These insights and methods have been used with unusual skill by H. B. Nicholson, whose amazing source analysis has yielded a reasonably clear picture of the biography of Topiltzin Quetzalcoatl. This biography, embedded in sources from all over Mesoamerica, is likened to a seven-act play including the birth, childhood, rise to power, reign, downfall, death, and promised return of the Toltec hero. According to Nicholson, Quetzalcoatl's significance for subsequent cultures was as a religious innovator. Forced to leave his city, he disappeared from history, but his fame led to his transformation into a priestly archetype. In time and memory he was confused with several preexistent deities, primarily Ehécatl.

Twentieth-century historians received the benefit of Paul Radin's *The Sources and Authenticity of the History of the Ancient Mexicans*, in which he demonstrates that the scribes and rulers of ancient Mexico had a pronounced historical sense expressed in a variety of types of history. Not only were the ancient Mexicans aware of change, said Radin, but they actively and consciously produced it. Their culture underwent profound social developments including the transformations from a nomadic tribal culture to an urban civilization, and these changes were recorded in their writings and oral traditions. Radin's proof of an authentic historical sense in ancient Mexico marked the beginning of an era of confidence in the task of reconstructing Mesoamerican history on the basis of documents.

Within this context, historians and anthropologists took up the problem of identifying Tollan in geographical space. The problem they faced most directly was the tremendous disparity between the archaeological evidence at Tula and the marvelous descriptions of the great Tollan. The Sociedad Mexicana de Antropología organized a six-year study of the evidence culminating in a conference highlighted by a debate between parties arguing for Tollan Xicocotitlán and Tollan Teotihuacán. While some voiced their vote for Teotihuacán (and the issue has not been finally settled), the majority of scholars favor the position articulated by Wigberto Jiménez Moreno, who studied all types of evidence, including folklore in contemporary Mexico, to reconstruct the life of Topiltzin Quetzalcoatl and to identify his city. He identified places and natural settings near Tula that were described in myths and demonstrated the similarities in the ceramic styles between Chichén Itzá and Tula. This elder statesman of Mesoamerican studies also made the wise suggestion that Tula was a synonym for "metropolis."[109]

Jiménez Moreno and Paul Kirchhoff, working from the same sources, carried the debate to a more detailed level when they attempted to identify exactly when Topiltzin Quetzalcoatl's reign in Tollan took place. Jiménez Moreno argued that Quetzalcoatl was the founder of Tollan, while Kirchhoff favored the position that he was the last ruler and that, further, the historical record goes back only to the end of Tollan in the eleventh century.[110] It is clear that this question will never be settled, given the present evidence.[111]

The splitting of the historical Quetzalcoatl from the mythical Quetzalcoatl has been shrewdly reversed in the illuminating work of Alfredo López Austin, who discusses Quetzalcoatl as the quintessential Hombre-Dios of Mexico. Hombre-Dioses, says López Austin, were extraordinary individuals whose religious ecstasies and knowledge, which included the power to carry, keep, and speak for the tribal god, made them living authorities in the many migrating communities. With the development of Classic cities, these figures mediated the social, economic, and spiritual transformations characteristic of the urban process and became the rulers of civilized centers. Topiltzin Quetzalcoatl was a sterling example of this transformed Hombre-Dios and was appreciated as the paradigm of new leadership. He was the keeper and spokesman for the Quetzalcoatl deity whose existence had been significant since the time of Teotihuacán.

Recently, the historical significance of the Quetzalcoatl tradition has received a vibrant and compelling interpretation by Jacques Lafaye, whose *Quetzalcoatl and Guadalupe: The Formation of Mexican National Consciousness, 1531–1813* focuses on the colonial sources about Quetzalcoatl and the uŝes that priest and *campesino* made of the Aztec god-hero during the critical years when Mexico was striving for its own identity as a nation. What is particularly valuable in this work. is the way in which the author shows how historical memory and myth-making processes were woven together to make Quetzalcoatl a symbol for political and social legitimacy. It is an essay in what Lafaye calls "intra-history" and shows how both Quetzalcoatl and the image of Guadalupe have a persistent relevance in the modern Mexican imagination.[112]

Remembering that a line can be understood as a point that moves, we have attempted to identify the original points of Quetzalcoatl in the different scholarly sketches of this symbol and then trace whatever movement was most clearly described in the major studies. The diffusionists saw Quetzalcoatl's point of origin outside of America, moving across the ancient landscape into Mexico. The symbolists located Quetzalcoatl's origin either in the rhythms of the sky or in the depth of the human spirit. This original inspiration moves brilliantly through the celestial and terrestrial landscapes or through the spiritual universes of human beings in quest of liberation. The historicists identify Quetzalcoatl originally in Mexican events when he moves gallantly in the drama of social development and change before being swept up into an imaginary flight along the arc of the morning star. As we turn to the present interpretation, it is clear that the full meaning of this mesmerizing design and figure eludes us still.

Two

Quetzalcoatl and the
Foundation of Tollan

INTRODUCTION

A selection of Aztec lore contains the following lament:

In Tollan stood the house of beams, where still the
    serpent columns stand deserted.
Gone away is Nacxitl Topiltzin.
Departing, he is wept for by our princes.
He goes away; goes to where he rests, in Tlapallan.
Now he leaves them in Cholollan, traveling
    through the land of Poyauhtecatl, going to
    Acallan. . . .
Ah, but no! Your palace, your temple—these you
    leave behind you here in Tollan
    Nonohualco . . .
Your palace, your temple—these you leave behind
    you here in Tollan Nonohualco. The painted
    stones, the beams, you left them here behind
    you, in Tollan where you came to rule.
Nacxitl Topiltzin! Never can your name be lost, for
    your people will be weeping.
The turquoise house, the serpent house, you built
    them here in Tollan where you came to rule.
Nacxitl Topiltzin! Never can your name be lost, for
    your people will be weeping.[1]

This lament, sung and written down a full three
hundred years after the events it describes, is a helpful
point at which to begin our exploration of the meaning
Quetzalcoatl had for the pre-Columbian city. Within
the song's ambiguous complexities we find references
to one of the most prominent heroes and prominent
ceremonial centers of ancient Mexican culture. More
important, perhaps, we see the basis of the relationship between the culture hero and special space.

63

At first glance it appears that the singers who chanted this lament are remembering the departure and loss of Nacxitl Topiltzin, "Our Prince the Four Fold," which we know from source analysis to be another name for Topiltzin Quetzalcoatl.[2] He has gone away to Tlapallan leaving the people in tears as they cry, "Never can your name be lost." But the song also laments that the "house of beams" stands deserted in Tollan. In the repeated references to the place of Tollan, now in a ruined state, much more than a hero is lamented; the loss of a vital living space is also apparent. The passage suggests that the loss of Topiltzin Quetzalcoatl also means the loss of Tollan. Although it is not referred to directly as a city, the phrases, "in Tollan stood the house of beams, where still the serpent columns stand deserted . . . the painted stones, the beams, you left them here behind you, in Tollan . . . the turquoise house, the serpent house . . . you built them here in Tollan," show that what is truly lamented is the separation of a leader from his ceremonial city, a separation which empties that city of life and people. But there is still more in this fragment. Twice it states, "in Tollan where you came to rule." The basic relationship between this figure and the city is one of sovereignty. The repeated reference to this power suggests that the passage laments not only the loss of a king, but also the loss of a *kingly* place.

To open the discussion of the Toltec paradigm, we surmise that this fragment contains an indigenous view of the ideal city and sovereign ruler in Mesoamerica and that this view unites Quetzalcoatl to the city of Tollan through the *exercise of supreme authority*. This coincidence of Quetzalcoatl and Tollan is repeated through the primary sources from central Mesoamerica, giving us an important hint about the social and religious significance the symbol of Quetzalcoatl has throughout a long period of Mesoamerican urban history. The meaning of Quetzalcoatl, expressed in references to the priest-king of Tollan or in references to the sky-creator deity, formed and elaborated by priestly elites, is firmly grounded in the urban situation and can be more fully understood within this context. The human Quetzalcoatl is the founder, organizer, and ruler of an ideal type of city, whereas the deity Quetzalcoatl is the occasional creator, organizer, and sometimes ruler of the cosmos, which undergirded city and state. Both figures function as creative orderers of the world.

While the two elements of Quetzalcoatl and Tollan are often discussed in relation to one another, no one has adequately focused on the significance of Tollan as a symbolic city in a context to help reveal the meaning of the feathered serpent tradition. Tollan has been identified by archaeologists and historians as an actual earthly site. But the primary sources suggest rather clearly that this historical place was also understood as a "symbolic center": a center symbolic of the achievement of an elaborate level of social and cosmological integration, "the painted stones, the beams . . . your palaces, your temples, the turquoise house, the serpent house," an achievement crystallized by that institution known as the traditional city.

In this chapter I will strive to test the hypothesis that the sources contain historical references, mythology, and a sacred history portraying a paradigm of primordial order which eventually inspired and was used by subsequent capital cities. The stories about Quetzalcoatl and Tollan are accounts of a great king and his city and constitute an account of the crucial shift between the world of the gods and the world of men in the history of the cosmos. Tollan is portrayed as the original earthly city that derives its power from celestial forces and sets the example for human existence. This paradigm has three major components: (a) the cosmological/earthly setting for (b) the organization of a ceremonial city by (c) the hero. The Toltec paradigm contains the models of sacred kingship and ceremonial city, sovereign leadership and the effective organization of space as they were understood, revered and developed by Toltec and Aztec elites. In this chapter I will examine the outlines and content of the Great Tradition of the Toltecs which contains these models, locating them loosely with the evidence from Tula Xicocotitlan. I also attempt to understand the mythological role Quetzalcoatl had within the cosmological setting of Mesoamerican society. The following chapter, "Other Tollans," examines four city-states that used, altered, and were guided by these models. Chapter 4 focuses on the last Tollan, Tenochtitlán, where these valued traditions were applied with special dexterity by Aztec elites who, in the end, were subverted by this primordium.

THE URBAN SETTING

Recently, the character of the traditional city has been explicated by a number of scholars, especially by the urban geographer Paul Wheatley. In his two most recent books, *The Pivot of the Four Quarters* and *From Court to Capital*, Wheatley developed the model of the ideal type of ceremonial center to elucidate the complex processes of social-cultural interaction that gave substance to ancient cities. While the traditional city often functioned as marketplace, military citadel, and administrative center, it is clear that, in its pristine form at least, "the predominantly religious focus to the schedule of social activities associated with them leaves no room to doubt that we are dealing primarily with centers of ritual and ceremonial."[3] To develop his perspective, Wheatley examined a rich variety of cultural expressions from seven areas of primary urban generation, abstracting what he calls a "generalized integrative pattern of functional relationships." The model of urban generation and character that emerges postulates a dramatic interaction between the priestly elites of the ceremonial center and an "ecological complex" resulting in population control and use, environmental exploitation, technological advances, and developments in social structure.[4] The dramatic interaction between priestly elites and the ecological complex results in, to borrow Jonathan Friedmann's fine phrase, the "effective organization of space." In Wheatley's view, the control mechanism of the traditional city is religion. The effective order of the city is validated by systems of sanctification which regulated city and state affairs. A system of thought and action that synchronized the cycles and rhythms of human life with the patterns and power of heaven and the cosmic structure is crucial to the development and maintenance of ancient urban life. Wheatley calls this synchronization or parallelism "cosmo-magical thought."[5] This religious attitude and its application to the social processes in traditional urban societies emanates from the ceremonial precincts in the center of the settlement. The ancient city is perceived as the pivot of the world, a center-oriented construct.

Historical evidence has led Wheatley to argue that as the urban traditions evolved, cities were revitalized through processes of internal differentiation resulting in competing religious cults and in the necessary sharing of power between religious and so-called secular elites. Yet, even in this revitalized urban setting, cosmo-magical thought and the ceremonial center still validated, guided, and sanctified all traditional processes and developments.

During the last three decades, Mesoamerican scholarship has expressed the growing awareness that cities in the traditional mode were the social and symbolic centers of life between at least A.D. 100 and 1521. This realization was the outgrowth of long-term debates on the "nature" of pre-Columbian peoples and the eventual rejection of the anthropological theory that "the pueblo of Mexico" was, according to Lewis H. Morgan, peopled by "ragged Indians" living in the "middle status of Barbarism."[6] The Aztecs, said Morgan, were the Iroquois of the south, and their loose and democratic institutions were proof of "how distant yet were the conceptions of a state or nation among the aboriginies of Mexico." A new, less Europocentric perspective, which began in part with the Marxist studies and grand conceptual schemes of V. Gordon Childe and Karl Wittfogel, who articulated theories of urban revolutions and specialized bureaucratic elites, has been applied and tested with surprising results by Americanists concerned with reconstructing the Aztec image. In more recent times, it was Paul Kirchhoff who illuminated Aztec studies by talking of Mesoamerica as an urban civilization.[7] Research in this direction was highlighted by Pedro Armillas's pioneering work, *Program of the History of American Indians*, and by the more precise study of Philip Phillips and Gordon Willey, *Method and Theory in American Archaeology*, both of which describe the urban character of Mexican civilization as ancient and pervasive. One of the most sophisticated discussions of the native city in the New World is Robert McC. Adams's *The Evolution of Urban Society*, where he compares the growth and development of the Mesopotamian and pre-Hispanic urban cultures, focusing on processes contributing to the intensification of social stratification. Significantly, Adams recognizes the presence and importance of religious forms and discusses the persistence of religious convictions through the great transformation from the "theocratic stage" to the "militaristic stage." René Millon has added depth to our perspective of these processes by his stunning work, *Urbanization at Teotihuacán*, which explores the origin, structure, and development of this first central Mexican city containing a mammoth and marvelous ceremonial center. He postulates the critical interaction between economic and religious institutions as the core of the Pax Teotihuacána.[8] It seems that the accumulated picture emerging from recent scholarship on the Mexican urban tradition allows us to discuss Quetzalcoatl and Tollan from the point of view expressed by Wheatley's model. All of the settlements that dominated social and cultural life during Pre-Classic, Classic, and Post-Classic periods were organized around and by ceremonial centers. Reading the evidence shows that the Toltec tradition in stone, picture, and prose depicts a creative era when a ceremonial city and its leader expressed cosmomagical formulas contributing to that site's prestige as the paradigm for many subsequent regional and interregional capitals. To illuminate this paradigm we describe in more detail the ideal type of ceremonial city and then turn to the archaeological and literary evidence concerning Tollan.

In Wheatley's model, urban society is generated and maintained through rigorous interaction between certain social processes and the built forms of the ceremonial center. This interaction is characterized by centripetal and centrifugal forces which draw all manner of goods and powers into the ceremonial city and dispense them outward into society's enclaves. This interaction is focused in areas of population control, the development of social surpluses, the redistribution of goods, specialization in craft industries, and social stratification.

Ceremonial cities, especially those that developed into the ideal type of settlement, stimulated population increases and attracted more people into the city's sphere of influence. This population explosion tended to stimulate increased building activity, intensification of agriculture, abundance of craft activities. More personnel were able to care for, exploit, and organize the resources from the regional environment. The priestly elite who controlled these growing zones of continued settlement manifested their power not only in the exploitation of these potentials, but also in the organized construction of monumental architecture which usually covered large tracts of land in strategic locations. These ceremonial and administrative structures required large numbers of laborers expending large units of time and effort in the transportation, shaping, construction, and ornamentation of buildings. The evidence of the organized control of population attests to the exercise of centralized, superabundant authority. For instance, Eric Wolf suggests that the construction of the Pyramid of the Sun in Teotihuacán required something like ten thousand workmen for twenty years. Perhaps more important than the bulk form as an indicator of centralized power was the sophisticated orientation, layout, and ornamentation of the principal structures in these ceremonial centers. In Teotihuacán, Chichén Itzá, Cholollan, and Tenochtitlán, for example, the conceptually intricate organization of ball courts, palaces, major roads, and sacrificial temples reflected the sophisticated concentration of power in the hands of an elite. In these examples, minimally touched upon here, human populations were attracted to and nurtured by the ceremonial core of the city, which used their labor and skills to extend its influence outward for greater control.

A second and related ecological component integrated by the ceremonial center was the natural environment. The traditional city in general and the Mesoamerican city in particular developed and redeveloped systems of resource exploitation, specialization, and redistribution. It is clear that in Aztec times and perhaps as far back as Teotihuacán times, farming activities reached such intensity that they required sophisticated management by elites in whose hands food distribution rested. Managerial responsibilities involved institutions that controlled workers' schedules, organized building and repair projects, administered the appropriate rituals, and managed irrigation flows. This exploitation of fertility potentials resulted in the rise of social surpluses[9] and the intensification of complex relationships among different segments of society, specialized occupations, trading centers, and the temple complex that controlled these surpluses. According to Robert McC. Adams, this intensification took a special form in Mesoamerica, where the interdependency of different ecological zones extended to distant regions and included crucial exchange patterns between highland and lowland centers. The ceremonial centers of Mesoamerica were forced to develop mechanisms to collect and redistribute agricultural goods and craft items over short and long distances.

The magnetic and redistributive powers of Mesoamerican ceremonial centers is certainly clear in the Aztec case where the elites under Moctezuma II's direction controlled a tribute network involving over four hundred towns and cities within and beyond the central plateau. The capital of Tenochtitlán was the end and center point of a steady stream of porters delivering specific types and quantities of goods according to a tightly organized schedule. Sixteenth-century prose records and at least two storybooks reveal

> that the bulk foodstuffs of Tenochtitlán alone are calculated to have amounted to 52,800 tons, or enough for more than 360,-000 people at the estimated mean annual consumption. Moreover, the enormous flow of cacao beans, cloth mantles and other goods serving as media of exchange placed additional instruments of economic superiority not only in the hands of the palace but in those of the nobility and even of the capital population at large. Centrally distributed through the palace, this wealth not only strengthened the autocratic features of the political structure but also heightened class stratification and urban-rural differences.[10]

A third area of centralized control was technology. While the earlier tendency to place enormous importance on the contribution of technology to urban origins has been seriously undermined, it was clear that technological competence accompanied and also triggered social surpluses and enhanced the powers of the central place. It appears that some traditional cities depended in part on the strength of particular craft institutions for their successful participation in and periodic control of trade relationships, architectural superiority, and the transportation of regional commodities. The craftsmen and merchants who used the best developed tools and crafts were themselves major tools of the priestly elite, who managed all technological development.

Perhaps the most important component in the cohesiveness of the ancient city was the social structure. In Wheatley's model, social differentiation was not only the key to the generation of urban settlements but also the critical, if delicate, link that bound the city-state together throughout its history. Following Eisenstadt, who held that the most important breakthrough of ancient social history consisted of the emergence of a religio-political elite controlling all institutions, Wheatley noted that

> it signified for the first time in the history of the world the sundering of the populace at large from direct access to supernatural power, at the same time as it deprived the people en masse of participation in political decision making. In other words the populace had been alienated from the loci of both sacred and secular power.[11]

It appears that while the first elites were exclusively specialized priests, social stratification was further differentiated through the secularization of the ceremonial center; this means simply that the apex of society was inhabited by a military sovereign as well as an ecclesiastical authority. But the notion of secularization is misleading because it is clear that the new types of leadership were as deeply compelled by their religious thought as the incense keepers and high priests. At all levels of leadership, religious ideas sanctified and guided the achievement of goals.

CITY AS SYMBOL

The generation of effective space summarized in the preceding paragraphs depends on a frame of mind which can be called cosmomagical thought. In his elaboration of insights provided by René Berthelot and Mircea Eliade, Wheatley notes that urban elites who devised and expressed the symbolic models for their societies were motivated by a complex of ideas,

> which presupposed an intimate parallelism between the regular and mathematically expressible regimes of the heavens and the biologically determined rhythms of life on earth as manifested in the succession of the seasons, the annual cycles of plant regeneration, and, within the compass of an individual life, birth, growth, procreation and death.[12]

This drive toward an intricate and tight parallelism between planes of reality developed concomitantly with the new levels of social and cultural integration that characterized the traditional city. An earlier phase of social integration was dominated by what Berthelot calls *bio-astrale* thought, "in which the numerical regularities observable in the motions of the heavenly bodies had not yet been adapted to the biological cycles on earth."[13] This achievement of synchronization led to the confidence that perfect harmony could be achieved between heaven and earth through ritual and ceremony which remembered, marked, celebrated and regulated cosmic events. Cosmomagical thought, then, guided a style of life which saw that the

> 'real' world transcended the pragmatic realm of textures and geometrical spaces, and was perceived schematically in terms of extra-mundane, sacred experience. Only the sacred was 'real,' and the purely secular,—if it could be said to exist at all—could never be more than trivial . . . in those religions which held that human order was brought into being at the creation of the world, there was a pervasive tendency to dramatize the cosmogony by constructing on earth, a reduced version of the cosmos, usually in the form of a state capital. In

other words, Reality was achieved through the imitation of a celestial archetype, by giving material expression to that parallellism between macrocosm and microcosm without which there could be no prosperity in the world of men.[14]

In concrete terms, this attitude was manifested in at least three dimensions (two of which we shall examine in this chapter): (a) the spatial ordering of the sacred enclave and its surrounding precincts, (b) the elevation of leaders to the level of supreme rulers whose actions insured the harmony of heaven and earth, and (c) the creation of calendar systems that periodically celebrated the cosmogonic events that created the world.

In the terms of Mircea Eliade, the ancient ideal type of city was a sacred space oriented around a quintessentially sacred center in the form of a temple or temple pyramid. This pivot of the community partook of the "symbolism of the center," meaning that it was believed to be the center of the world, the point of intersection of all the world's paths, both terrestrial and celestial. The central structure was an *axis mundi*, "regarded as the meeting point of heaven, earth, and hell," or "the point of ontological transition between the spheres."[15] The priestly elites who planned and directed the construction of their ceremonial centers often attempted to align their causeways, sections of city, or major buildings with the cardinal compass directions of the universe, "thus assimilating the groups' territory to the cosmic order and constructing a sanctified living space or *habitabilis* within the continuum of profane space."[16] These four highways, sections, or structures enforcing the sanctification of the central place were centripetal and centrifugal guides, pulling the sacred and social energies into the center and diffusing the supernatural and royal powers outward into the kingdom. Another aspect of urban sacred space was manifested when a ceremonial center, or one or more of its major buildings, represented through the image, design, and interrelationship of parts a cosmological concept or mythological episode. In this instance, a correspondence between stone image and celestial pattern was achieved in the appearance of a ceremonial building.

It appears that the evolution in religious thought that guided the style of life in traditional cities was accompanied by an evolution in leadership. The new systems of hierarchy and coordination regulating social and cosmic processes were administered by leaders who shared generously in the hierarchy and prestige of the deities they served and the capitals they ruled. In other words, rulers appeared who emphasized their elite status through an intensification of communication and identification with the divinities and sacred forces of the cosmos. These sovereigns were regarded as the prime movers in the crucial processes of human existence including the fertility of the realm, the redistribution of goods, and the harmony of the heavens. The traditional city was the theater for the intensification of cult activity designed to clarify human-divine relationships through the "elaboration of a communication system mediated through worship and sacrifice." These priestly elites, the human pivots of the four quarters, claimed a superior religious status materialized in their noble families who were descended from the deities who originally established the order of the world.

It is important at the end of this brief summary of Wheatley's model to remind ourselves that it was abstracted from a review of evidence from more than seven examples of primary urban generation. Wheatley noted that specific cases, in order to be more fully understood, may require alterations in the pattern summarized here. Still, this model affords us a general awareness that cosmo-magical thought "brought the city into being, sustained it and was imprinted on its physiognomy." And it serves the larger purpose of demonstrating that not only were these traditional capitals organized around centers of symbol, ritual, and ceremony, but that they were, in their totalities, vital centers of masses of people and also centers of the organization of effective sacred space. The traditional capital is at the heart of the pathos that flows through the lament we heard at the beginning of this chapter.

The Historicity of Tollan

One of the most significant "style centers" in Mesoamerican history is referred to in the sources as Tollan. For instance, in Sahagún's book 3, *The Gods,* the city inhabited by the great priest Quetzalcoatl is called "the regimen of Tollan." A recurrent claim made in the sources that the Spaniards burned, copied, and transformed was that Tenochtitlán inherited the great cultural traditions of Toltec Tollan, which was remembered as the original cultural hearth. One of the "official" creation myths in the Aztec records tells that the universe had passed through a series of eras, each ending in a cataclysm, before the present "Sun" or "Age" was created and that "this was the Sun of our Lord Quetzalcoatl in Tula."[17] (Tula is a corrupted form of Tollan.) As one reads accounts of this place and its lord Quetzalcoatl, it appears to have existed far back, at the dawn of time and civilized life. The language and character of the multiple versions of Tollan's history have made it possible to claim that these stories fall into the category of mythical geographies; that is, they refer to no historical place or have no fundamental historical significance. This judgment seems quite possible when we find in the *Annals of the Cakchiquels,* for instance, a reference to "four Tulans" coinciding with four positions in the cosmos and the sources of human life.

> From the four places the people came to Tulan. In the east is one Tulan; another in Xibalbay; another in the west, for there we came ourselves, from the west; and another is where God is. Therefore, there were four Tulans, "oh our sons," so they said. "From the west we came to Tulan, from across the sea; and it was at Tulan where we arrived, to be engendered and brought forth by our mothers and fathers. . . ."
>
> And setting out, we arrived at the gates of Tulan. Only a bat guarded the gates of Tulan. And there we were engendered and given birth.[18]

In this instance, Tulan was the name given to the generative points in the universe from which life in its various forms flowed.

But we also have ample evidence that Tollan refers in some way to the historical Tula of the Toltecs, who governed the capital of a unified society between the tenth and twelfth centuries. The present consensus, articulated by members of the Sociedad Mexicana de Antropología, is that the archaeological ruins near present-day Tula are the remains of the city referred to in the sources. This issue may never be settled in a strict, literal sense because the Tollan described in the storybooks and prose works does not refer to just one historical kingdom but to an archetypal kingdom that contained the buildings, heroes, achievements, and memories of several illustrious effective spaces. What is recorded in the primary sources about Tollan is, to borrow a phrase from Richard Diehl, "the native model for the exercise of religious and political power."[19]

It would be a critical mistake to reduce these references by claiming that they are really confused historical narratives—that instead of mythical geography, we have mythicized geography. Yet in order to acquire a sound understanding of the Toltec tradition, which served as the primary focus of the Great Tradition, it is necessary to present a brief historical picture of Tollan through reference to the archaeological evidence and the accepted opinion concerning the Toltec ecological complex.

TOLLAN (XICOTITLAN): THE SITE AND ITS PERIPHERIES

The significant but puzzling ceremonial center at Tula has been periodically excavated since Desiré Charnay's work in the 1890s. The present consensus concerning the historical nature of the site holds that during its heyday, the main settlement covered about twelve square kilometers around the confluence of the Tula and Rosa rivers. At this strategic control point were two sizable groups of buildings, the major ceremonial center or acropolis and Tula Chico, located 2 kilometers to the north. Other smaller architectural precincts were settled in nearby areas. Although no overall plan is discernible at Tula, it is evident that attached houses of adobe and stone were built around large patio complexes which included small *adoratorios*. It appears that this settlement rose to prominence with the waning and fall of Tenochtitlán and eventually dominated a population of 50,-000–60,000 people.

The main ceremonial center, in and near which the Quetzalcoatl images described in chapter 1 appear, was constructed on a high treeless hill which had been artificially leveled to resemble a broad, basically square platform. On this space were constructed two sizable plazas known today as the Central Plaza and the North Plaza. The Central Plaza was about 120 meters wide and was obviously the location of great and small ceremonies, affairs of state, and sacred games. This spacious plaza was bounded on the north by a series of impressive palaces, known to us as the Burnt Palaces, each arranged around a central interior courtyard. In these palaces were found sculptured and painted benches lined with colored cloud serpents and feathered serpents among other figures. The palaces were situated just west of a finely worked pyramid called the pyramid temple of Quetzalcoatl-Tlahuizcalpantecuhtli, which supported a series of huge, erect stone warriors who once held up the main temple.

In front of the Burnt Palaces and the Pyramid of Quetzalcoatl was a hall named the Great Vestibule, which was supported by a series of fifty-four pillars. Then, higher than any other structure in the city, rose a second pyramid perpendicular to the Great Vestibule on its eastern end. The two pyramids, the vestibule, and the palaces formed the north side and the northeast corner of the central courtyard. Across the spacious plaza to the west was a large and finely constructed ball court. In the center of the plaza stood a small square structure about 4 feet high with a stairway on each of the four sides. When looking north, east, or west from this vantage point, one had the impression of being securely enclosed.

One of the unique Toltec forms, the *coatepantli*, or serpent wall, separates this plaza from the North Plaza. The *coatepantli*, which became a major feature of Aztec ceremonial centers, is a high wall, lined with the repeated motif of a gaping feathered serpent and a human skull in juxtaposition. Each dynamic figure seems to be emerging from the other. This series of symbols is interrupted by a passageway leading to the North Plaza, which is a largely undefined space dominated by an older ball court running east to west.

In spite of the small size of this ceremonial center, scholars are convinced that during its apogee Tula dominated and organized the

FIG. 5. The pyramid of Tlahuizcalpantecuhtli in Tula. This structure, according to archaeologists, was dedicated to Quetzalcoatl as the morning star. Tula (A.D. 900–1100) was the capital of the Toltec Empire. Courtesy of Lawrence G. Desmond.

northern parts of Mesoamerica and several scattered sections in the south. The *Historia Tolteca-Chichimeca* describes the "Great Tollan" as including twenty settlements, and Ixtlixochitl eulogizes the Toltec kingdom as extending "from one sea to another." While Tula apparently shared the power with other cities like Cholollan, Tajin, and Xochicalco, perhaps for a time it was the dominant political center in the group. Archaeological evidence shows that it was the first central Mexican settlement following the fall of Teotihuacán to foster and maintain relationships with both western Mexico and the Gulf coastal region to the northeast.

Tula's ecological complex included refined craft industries, long-distance trading patterns, a sizable population, and monumental architecture. Although researchers have not found clear-cut evidence of intensive large-scale agriculture, it is likely that some form of hydraulic management existed. A sizable number of artisans supported a variety of handicraft workshops as witnessed in the variety of wares found throughout the site, including pulque cups, braziers, censers, bowls, cylinder jars, jewelry. Craft developments used in the monumental sculpture, painted relief work, large ceremonial buildings, and great walls led one archaeologist to exclaim, "Toltec architecture acquired new contrasts and patterns, becoming one of the finest expressions of artistic integration among Indian culture."[20] Art historians have recognized that the architectural style, craft patterns, and religious traditions represented in Tula had widespread influence throughout central Mexico and beyond. Furthermore, there is evidence that the Toltec trade routes extended not only into northeastern and western Mexico, but also south through Chiapas, Guatemala, central Vera Cruz, and into Costa Rica and Nicaragua. It also appears that a sustained relationship existed between Tula and the culture around Lake Patzcuaro. The Toltec elites apparently extended the trade routes established by Teotihuacán, an extension that resulted in a marvelous prosperity, eventually spreading into the Mayan city of Chichén Itzá.

This memorable achievement was translated into the term *toltecatl*. Derived from Tollan, which means variously, "place of reeds," "among the reeds, rushes, cattails," or "toponomy of great city, city in general," this word referred to a refined person who had great knowledge and artistic abilities. An urban significance is obviously communicated in the third referent to Tollan: "great city," "a place of abundant culture" or "an authoritative center of cultural order." Combined with the notion of a *toltecayotl*, "wonderful artist," Tollan was appreciated as the place of creativity. This paradigmatic significance is supported by Robert A. Diehl's observation that Tollan was not only "the capital of a major new political system," but also "that it articulated a similar mode of political order as the Aztecs." As we will see, Tollan, Toltec, and *toltecatl* referred to the culture that flourished at Tula Xicocotitlan as well as to a variety of places where abundance, creativity and authority were combined.[21]

Historical research has dimly discerned that the prosperity and influence this dispersed ceremonial city had did not last long. The fall of Teotihuacán, which Tula had overthrown in the eighth century, was repeated after a handful of calendar rounds. Tula as a center collapsed in the twelfth century after it had expanded its religious and social influence south beyond the Valley of Mexico into the Yucatan area. Tula's collapse is recorded again and again in the sources, and in more than a few cases Quetzalcoatl is central to the story. Other Tollans were developed and new variations on this effective space were created.

THE LITERARY TESTIMONY
The Toltec Great Tradition contains the earliest record of a Mexican traditional city and is full of stories about Quetzalcoatl and Tollan. H. B. Nicholson has thoroughly analyzed more than seventy-five sources that contain full versions, supplementary accounts, or fragments of a tradition he calls the "Topiltzin Quetzalcoatl of Tollan Tale."

His analysis included material on the deity Quetzalcoatl-Ehécatl, who was intertwined with the Toltec hero. The Tollan tale was apparently taught in the *calmecacs,* schools of higher learning located in the cities and towns of the Valley of Mexico, the Puebla region, and other parts of central Mesoamerica in Aztec and pre-Aztec times. These schools taught the theology, ethics, divine songs, and history of the realm to the children of the wealthy who usually became the priests and high officials of society. I contend that the Topiltzin Quetzalcoatl of Tollan tale is the central thread of a genre of archaic historical thought called sacred history. This special form of archaic wisdom has been described by the historian of religions Mircea Eliade in his important article "Cosmogonic Myth and Sacred History."[22] Following his discussion of the power and prestige cosmogonic myths hold in archaic cultures because they tell of the transformation from primordial chaos into the original order of the world, Eliade described another kind of mythical language characteristic of the "thought of the people who played an important role in ancient history." This second type of mythical thought takes the form of sacred histories, which are influenced by the great cosmogonic myths but have an intentionality and value of their own. A "sacred history" of a people tells of a "process representing a more radical incarnation of the sacred in life and in human existence"[23] by illuminating the ancestral labors that gave form to the preexistent *materia prima*. Often, the sacred history of a particular culture presents an image of a fabulous epoch constructed or achieved by the ancestors, in which nature, animals, and humans appear to be free of inhibitions and limits. This image is, to adapt one of Eliade's formulations, a "terrestrial primordiality." This epoch is understood and portrayed as the time and space in which human life as it now exists was brought into being.

It appears that a dominant characteristic of Toltec and Aztec sacred histories was a prophetic emphasis, that is, the view that human experience was patterned by a sequence of events that linked past, present, and future together in some detailed meaningful pattern. Through the songs, poems, ethics, calendars, and histories, a world view was pointed in which present situations were understood as having been set in motion in a remembered mythic past by a prophetic event or figure and which would move into a "known" or prophesied future. All significant contemporary conditions originated in a primordial series of actions that would continue through the present and be terminated or recreated in some future, but measurable time. In Mesoamerican capital cities from the eleventh century on just such a sacred history was taught; it represented the great moments when the sacred was incarnated in the life of the city of Tollan through the heroic and inspired career of Quetzalcoatl. Further, it seems possible

that the Toltec sacred history contained the closest thing we have to
a Mexican aretalogy: it focused on a remarkable hero whose potency
and achievements stemmed from his relationship with a divine coun-
terpart enabling him to work wonders, to face enemies, and to lose
his city but then gain a final victory through his transformation at
death.[24] Let us now turn to the Toltec sacred history and examine
these dimensions. It should be understood that the names Ce Acatl,
Naxcitl, refer to the human Quetzalcoatl, sometimes referred to as
Topiltzin Quetzalcoatl.

The literary image of the Toltec urban tradition is outlined in this
passage from the *Historia Tolteca-Chichimeca*. "These are the nations
who were allies of the Toltecs in the Great Tollan. Twenty were the
inhabited places which formed its hands and feet. The waters, the
mountains were of the Toltec. Only when the Great Tollan dispersed,
did they obtain their kingdom."[25] The general impression is clear. The
"Great Tollan" was not merely one city among many, but an organized
political space, a city-state which encapsulated twenty other settlements that formed its hands and feet, and constituted its order. The
power of this kingdom extended to include the water, the mountains,
and the earthly places in between. This unified kingdom, centered
in the capital city, finally dissolved or dispersed, resulting in the
fragmentation and autonomy of the different settlements. Elsewhere
we are told that the Toltec kingdom's influence as well as dismemberment was guided by Quetzalcoatl.

> The Tolteca were spread over all parts and although they were
> very rich, they departed, they moved; they left their houses,
> their lands, their cities, their wealth . . . and as they had great
> faith in Quetzalcoatl . . . no one failed to obey: all moved when
> Topiltzin Quetzalcoatl went to enter into the water at Tlapallan,
> where he went to disappear.[26]

The collapse of the Great Tollan was tied up with the life of Topiltzin
Quetzalcoatl, and it is apparent that the "biography" of Quetzalcoatl
was one of the threads running through the Toltec testimony. We plan
to follow that thread as a strategy to present the image of space and
leadership crucial to an understanding of Tollan's significance.

While it is obvious that Tula was not the first traditional city to
order the social complexities of central Mesoamerican culture, the
literary record, at least in some of the most respectable accounts,
places Quetzalcoatl's career at a critical turning point in the cosmological dramas in which Tollan ushers in human history. In several
sources, Topiltzin Quetzalcoatl and Tollan appear at the end of great
cosmogonic sequences, as in the already mentioned *Leyenda de los
Soles* version where the creation of the fifth age of the universe initiates

Quetzalcoatl's kingdom. While Topiltzin Quetzalcoatl and Tollan sometimes appear together as fully formed realities, a number of sources begin the story of Quetzalcoatl prior to and outside of the city with references to a miraculous birth and a family feud involving divine and semidivine relatives. This dimension of the tradition and the subsequent developments suggest that the union of hero and ceremonial city was appreciated as the turning point between the creation of the cosmos and the history of the human community.

Quetzalcoatl is usually portrayed as a "sacred human being," by which we mean that his life manifests the presence, again and again, of divine and celestial forces and appearances which determine and drive his destiny toward an archetypal model. Almost all the core sources that carry birth accounts state that his parents were divinities or semidivine beings, or that something unusual or miraculous happened at his birth. The best example of miraculous influence appears in the *Anales de Cuauhtitlán*, where it is recorded: "In the year 1 Reed, it is told, they say, in its time in that year—Quetzalcoatl was born— called Topiltzin Priest One Reed Quetzalcoatl, and his mother was called Chimalma, and they say that this was the manner in which Quetzalcoatl was placed in his mother's belly; she swallowed an emerald."[27] Mircea Eliade has shown how, in the history of religions, the texture, color, grandeur, shape of certain stones results in their being considered "hierophanies," that is, manifestations of the sacred which bestow value, power, and meaning on the human life that comes in contact with them. One of the ideas associated with sacred stones is that they have the power to fertilize women, a power emanating from the spirit that animates the stone.[28] Just such a complex of ideas is at work in this reference to Quetzalcoatl's miraculous birth, a motif which also appeared in the birth of 9 Wind in the *Codex Vienna* when he and his sixteen attributes are born from a stone. When Quetzalcoatl's mother swallows an emerald and conceives, the sacred stone manifested the power to create a special human being, who in that culture's terms is a precious being himself, the emerald of the Toltecs. Elsewhere, Quetzalcoatl's birth results in the death of his mother, "And in coming forth he greatly afflicted his mother for the duration of 4 days. Thereupon, by that time and in this manner, Ce Acatl was born. But as he was born, then already his mother was dead."[29] Ce Acatl is a posthumous child, a child without a mother, a child whose situation in one source leads to his adoption by an earth goddess. In another case, his father dies during the pregnancy, and in yet another case we are told that his father dies seven years before he is born!

Elsewhere, Quetzalcoatl's mother is Coatlicue, "Lady of the Serpent Skirt," the earth mother deity. Divine mother status is reflected elsewhere when Chimalman ("Prostrate Shield") is referred to by the commentator as "a mother of the people" or great mother figure. While it appears that these episodes are about a human being, it is clear that the child is divinely engendered.

The accounts of Quetzalcoatl's beginnings have further important dimensions. For instance, a number of sources relate important information concerning his existence prior to birth, conditions that affect his birth and life. Quetzalcoatl is born into a world of ferocious warfare and in some cases his parents are on opposite sides in the fighting. In the *Historia de los Mexicanos por sus pinturas*, the gods create the Chichimec people for the purpose of gaining sacrificial blood through warfare. An opposing warrior, Mixcoatl, is defeated in battle and meets a Chichimec woman, a relative of the god Tezcatlipoca, and they produce the illustrious child Quetzalcoatl. The joining of opposing groups and suggested resolution appears even more dramatically in another account where an elaborate and magical courtship between the antagonist Mixcoatl (now a Chichimec) and the woman Chimalman takes place. She appears in the nude and entices the warrior. He shoots arrows at her which she dodges, catches, and pulls from between her legs. A chase through the forest and into a cave ensues. The female warrior Chimalman is eventually taken and impregnated, and she gives birth to Quetzalcoatl.

The point is that Quetzalcoatl's birth is not only timely (it follows the creation of the fifth age) and miraculous (divine dimensions of the birth), but it also represents the union of warring opposites (male and female, warring tribes). Before Tollan appears we thus have a new beginning in terms of the cosmic creation, birth of the sacred hero, and the suggestion that the social order is changing. This change is intensified in the next episode of the story. Two of the earliest sources tell us that the orphaned Quetzalcoatl is raised by grandparents and in one case the grandmother appears to be an earth mother goddess. Then, and this is often overlooked by scholars, Quetzalcoatl begins a career as a warrior and conqueror. In one of the earliest documents, the young Quetzalcoatl undergoes seven years of penance during which he bleeds himself and seeks divine aid for becoming a great warrior. His quest is rewarded and he displays extraordinary skill before being chosen as the ruler of Tula. In the *Leyenda de los Soles*, he fights gallantly alongside his father, who is killed by Quetzalcoatl's paternal uncles.

> But when he had grown, then he went and made war with his father. And as a warrior he proved himself in a place called Xihuacan such that he took captives there. But there in that place were Ce Acatl's uncles, the four hundred Mixmixcoa.

Now they hated and therefore killed his father. And when they had killed him, they covered him up in the sand.[30]

Quetzalcoatl recovers the body of his father and buries him on Cloud Serpent Mountain. An argument over sacrificial victims develops between the nephew and his uncles. A magical combat takes place in which Quetzalcoatl slays the uncles.

And the uncles were very angry then, and they started at once. Apanecatl led the way, hurriedly scaling the temple. But immediately Ce Acatl rose up, and striking him full in the face sent him tumbling down, and he fell to the base of the mountain. Next he seized Zolton and Cuilton and as the animals blew on the fire, then he put them to death; he spread them with chili and slashed their flesh; and when he had tortured them, then he cut open their breasts. And then once again Ce Acatl set out to make conquests.[31]

It should be clear from these episodes that the life situation prior to Tollan was a world of combat, human sacrifice, and conflict. The Tollan tale is not only about the creation, existence, and fall of an ideal state that existed in the beginning, but it is also about an achievement that interrupted the warring world of the ancestors. Tollan begins to appear in the narrative immediately following the episode between Quetzalcoatl and his uncles.

Quetzalcoatl's appearance in Tollan follows two basic patterns. In one he is a native of Tollan, appearing to be its first ruler. He builds the major ceremonial structures. His military achievements and religious piety cause his elevation to the position of ruler. In the other pattern of Quetzalcoatl's linkage to Tollan, he either travels to the site or is brought there to rule on the basis of his reputation. In the *Juan Cano Relaciones*, his victory over his brothers results in his rulership of Teoculhuacán, where peace and tranquility are established. He then moves his people to the city of Tollantzinco. On the advice of the gods he travels to Tollan to become the ruler of the city. In another source his building and religious activities in another city result in his invitation to become king in Tollan.

[In the year] 2 Rabbit it was, when Quetzalcoatl came to Tollantzinco. There he remained four years and built his house of penance, his turquoise house of beams. From there he passed on to Cuextlan. . . . In the year 5 House the Toltecs came for Quetzalcoatl to install him as king in Tollan, and he was their priest.[32]

TOLLAN THE MARVELOUS "CENTER"

The world of Tollan appears as an ideal social and natural order when we turn to the fullest descriptions in the *Florentine Codex* and the *Anales de Cuauhtitlán*. The dynamic relationship between the ceremonial center and the surrounding world has created a state of plentitude and harmony. The Aztecs remembered Tollan as the original city-state where the systems of farming, craft productivity, and religious ritual were effectively integrated with cosmological forces.

The Sacred Traces

Working with the controversial chapter 29 of book 10, "The People," in the *Florentine Codex*, we read that the purpose of the chapter is to tell "who came to cause the cities to be founded." Most prominent among the founders of cities were the Tolteca, "the first who settled here in the land." This prestige of origins is tied directly to the Aztecs, referred to here as the Mexica. "First those named the Tolteca, so called; these first came to live here in the land, called land of the Mexica, land of the Chichimeca." Although these founders passed away, they "left many of their traces, which they had fashioned," traces which are still visible. Consider the spatial character of these ancient imprints.

> And these the traces of the Tolteca, their pyramids, their mounds, etc., not only appear there at a place called Tula [and] Xicocotitlan, but practically everywhere they rest covered; for their potsherds, their ollas, their pestles, their figures, their armbands appear everywhere, because the Tolteca were dispersed all over.[33]

These traces, such as Tollan's house of beams, are appreciated for their longevity: "today it stands, today it exists, considering that it is indestructible, for it is of rock, of stone." The persistence of these forms is in part due to Aztec digging. "Tolteca bowls, Tolteca ollas are taken from the earth. And many times the Tolteca jewels—arm bands, esteemed green stones, fine turquoise, emerald green jade— are taken from the earth."[34] Our initial impression from this text is that the Toltecs are the founders of cities whose ruins carry a high prestige, whose jewelry is sought after, whose buildings are indestructible—and all this is spread throughout the landscape.

This creativity was centered in Tollan where great structures still cause amazement. "They went to dwell on the bank of a river at Xicocotitlan, now called Tula. . . . they there resided together . . . they left behind . . . the so-called serpent column, the round stone pillar made into a serpent. And the Tolteca pyramids, the mounds, and the surfaces of Tolteca [temples] . . . are there to be seen."[35]

All these traces are prized, not merely because they survived, but because of the creative excellence of Toltec life. Consider this crescendo of superlatives: "The Tolteca were wise. Their works were all good, all perfect, all wonderful, all miraculous; their houses beautiful, tiled in mosaics, smoothed, stuccoed, very marvelous."[36]

Plentitude

The superb style, expressed in the ceremonial buildings that formed the center of the Great Tollan, was accompanied by the fruitful agricultural endeavors of the Toltecs. Harmony and abundance characterized their farming, perhaps eliminating the need for emergency subsistence efforts. In the third book of the *Florentine Codex*, we are told that the wealth of the Toltecs resided in their fields, where "all the squashes were very large, and some quite round. And the ears of maize were as large as hand grinding stones, and long. They could hardly be embraced in ones arms."[37] Not only were the corn stalks like small tree trunks, but the amaranth plants were as tall as trees. "And the amaranth plants—verily they climbed up them; they could be climbed." The plants were so plentiful that the smaller ears of corn, which in another age would have been valued, were hardly needed. In Toltec times, "the small ears of maize were of no use to them; they only [burned them to] heat the sweat baths."

This ancient Findhorn included incredible types of cotton farming. The cotton fields were miraculously colored—"burnt red, yellow, rose colored, violet, green, azure, verdigris color, whitish, brown, shadowy, rose red, and coyote colored. All different [colored cottons] were this way; so they grew; they did not dye them."[38] This abundance was accompanied by an array of "birds of precious feathers—the blue cotinga, the quetzal, the trupial, and red spoonbill, and all the different birds, which spoke very well; which sang right sweetly." These references demonstrate that going "to dwell" at Tula meant living in a place of superabundant reality.

This environmental plenitude was the proper setting for the Toltecs to show their technological excellence and artistic perfection. Toltec prestige derived from the belief that these archaic craftsmen originated the crafts and perfected them. Again in book 10, we are told not only that the Toltecs were serenaded by wonderful birds but that the people

> were feather workers. . . . In ancient times they took charge of the gluing of feathers; and it really was their discovery, their exclusive property. . . . In truth they invented all the wonderful, precious, marvelous things which they made, including . . . that which pertained to herbs, to the nature of their es-

sence; which ones were good, which esteemed, and which of
them were just plants, which ones bad, evil, harmful, rather
deadly.

They invented the art of medicine. . . . So learned were they
that they were the ones who for the first time, discovered,
found, and for the first time used green stones, fine turquoise,
[common] turquoise, the common obsidian, the emerald green
jade—all kinds of wondrous precious stones.[39]

It is stated almost obsessively that Toltec technology was the original
technology of ancient culture. The text lists the great occupations of
the Toltecs: "many of them were scribes, lapidaries, carpenters, stone
cutters, masons, feather workers, feather gluers, potters, spinners,
weavers," and miners of the most important quarries.

These feats of discovery, invention, and skill, repeated in the
record almost as a ritual gesture, show that the Toltecs were considered the prototypes of cultural creativity and that their kingdom was
an abundant source of food and goods. In at least these two ways,
Tollan was the "center," the original place of value, power, and substance.

Cosmo-Magical Discoveries

The record shows that the Aztec nostalgia dwelt not only on the
Toltec landscape and the uses made of it, but also on the Toltec discovery of the shape of celestial space and time and their significance
to people. The Toltecs were esteemed as the ancestors who realized
and designed the cosmo-magical thought that underpinned and
guided society's life. The Toltecs were "thinkers, for they originated
the year count, the day count, they established the way in which the
night, the day would work . . . which day sign was good, favorable;
and which was evil, the day sign of wild beasts. All their discoveries
formed the book for interpreting dreams."[40] This important reference
suggests that the Toltecs were considered the inventors of at least
part of the storybook tradition having to do with divination and calendrical calculation. The Toltec commitment to establishing heaven-
earth parallels was elaborated:

And so wise were they that they understood the stars which
were in the heavens; they gave them names and understood
their influence. And they understood well the movement of the
heavens. Their orbits they learned from the stars. And they
understood that there were many divisions of the heavens,
they said there were 12 divisions.[41]

This passage suggests just the complex model of synchronization that
we have identified as typical of thought systems in the traditional

city. Parallelism between the spheres, in the form of identifying co-incidences between heavenly regularities and human processes are reflected in such phrases as, "they established the way in which the day would work" and "they understood the movements of the heavens." This knowledge of celestial influences and the layers of the universe, translated into the book of dreams, was joined to an intimate awareness of the Creative Pair who presided over all living things. (Toltec discoveries and understanding included a journey through these heavenly divisions to the place where the Supreme Being resides.) The relevant passage portrays divine-human connections in the form of the divine conception of human beings.

> [In the 12 divisions] there existed, there dwelt, the true god and his consort. The name of the god of the heavens was Ome tecutli, and the name of his consort, the woman of the heavens, was Ome cihuatl; that is to say they were lords, they were rulers, over the 12 heavens. It was said that there were we, the common people created; thence came our souls. When babies were conceived, when they dropped [from heaven] their souls came from there, they entered into their mother's womb. Ome tecutli sent them.[42]

At the center of this abundant creativity and sacred knowledge lived Quetzalcoatl, whose role as the source of creativity is clearly stated: "Truly with him it began—truly from him it flowed out, All Art and Knowledge."[43]

Quetzalcoatl: Ecstasy and the Center

Quetzalcoatl is the hero and living source of this amazing kingdom and his presence is revealed in the monumental architecture of the city. The elites of Tollan, under the influence of Quetzalcoatl, utilized their version of cosmo-magical thought to guide the construction of their ceremonial precinct. Consider one of several references to Quetzalcoatl's temples, which we remember were heavenly gifts given to 9 Wind in the *Codex Vienna*:

> Wherefore was it called a Tolteca house? It was built with consummate care, majestically designed; it was the place of worship of their priest whose name was Quetzalcoatl; it was quite marvelous. It consisted of four [abodes]. One was facing east; this was the house of gold; for this reason it was called house of gold; that which served as the stucco was gold plate applied, joined to it. One was facing west, toward the setting sun; this was the house of green stone, the house of fine turquoise. For this reason was it called the house of green stone, the house of fine turquoise, what served as an inlay of green stone of fine turquoise. One was facing south, toward the irrigated lands,

this was the house of shells or of silver. That which served as
the stucco, the interior of the walls, seemed as if made of these
shells inlaid. One was facing north, toward the plains, toward
the spear house, this [was] the red house; red because red
shells were inlaid in the interior walls, as those stones which
were precious stones were red.[44]

The majestic houses of worship glimmering with their marvelous
jewelled facades were laid out along lines of cardinal axiality reflecting
the Toltec commitment to the imitation of celestial order and influence.
    Within this ceremonial order stood Quetzalcoatl's special temple,
which functioned as the Toltec cosmic mountain.

Quetzalcoatl was looked upon as a god. He was worshiped and
prayed to in former times in Tollan, and there his temple stood;
very high, very tall. Extremely tall, extremely high. Very many
were its steps and close together, hardly wide but narrow.
Upon each step indeed one's foot could not be straightened.[45]

Still another reference suggests that the ceremonial center had abundant buildings and that a human Quetzalcoatl dwelt there.

Very many were the marvelous houses which they made. The
house of Quetzalcoatl which was his place of worship, stood
on the water; a large river passed by it; the river which passed
by Tula. There stood that which was the bathing place of Quetzalcoatl, called 'in the waters of Green Stone' (Chalchiuapa).
Many houses stood with the earth where the Tolteca left many
things buried.[46]

It appears that the ceremonial center was ruled by the human
Quetzalcoatl, whose activities became the model for subsequent ceremonial structures and rituals. Consider Diego Durán's discovery of
Topiltzin Quetzalcoatl's reputation during his research on sixteenth-
century Mexico:

However, he [the Indian informant] added material telling me
that all the ceremonies and rites, building temples and altars
and placing idols in them, fasting, going nude and sleeping on
. . . the floor, climbing mountains to preach the law there, kiss-
ing the earth, eating it with one's fingers, and blowing trumpets and conch shells and flutes on the great feast days—all
these things imitated the ways of that holy man (Topiltzin
Quetzalcoatl).[47]

Throughout the different sources are references to the ritual activities
and paraphernalia of Quetzalcoatl and perhaps in this area he made
his greatest mark on Mesoamerican religious tradition. Pictures of his
bloodletting ritual appear in the *Florentine Codex* and one source notes

that his offerings included "snakes, birds and butterflies." One ritual episode is described in some detail, no doubt because of its contribution to Quetzalcoatl's prestige as the priestly archetype. A religious breakthrough into the world of the gods is described after Topiltzin Ce Acatl Quetzalcoatl had been installed as king in Tollan. The text tells that in the year 2 Reed he built a special temple in conformity with the cardinal directions and began intense ritual activity. "There he worshiped, did his penance and also fasted. And even at midnight, he went down to the streams, to the place called Edge of the Water. . . . And he set thorns into his flesh on the summit of Xicocotl also on Huitzco, also on Tzincoc, also on Mt. Nonohualco. And he made his thorns of jade-stone."[48] Following this elaboration of ritual space and the sacrifices on the four sacred mountains, Quetzalcoatl goes into a supreme ecstasy which reveals to him the layers of heaven and the Creative Pair who dwell at the top.

> And it is related, they say that he sent up his prayers, his supplications, into the heart of the sky and he called out to Skirt-of-Stars, Light-of-Day, Lady-of-Sustenance, Wrapped-in-Coal, Wrapped-in-Black, She who endows the earth with solidity, He who covers the earth with cotton. And they knew that he was crying out to the place of Duality which lies above the ninefold heavens. And thus they knew, they who dwell there, that he called upon them and petitioned them most humbly and contritely.[49]

Now, Quetzalcoatl is more than the source of art, craft, and knowledge. He is the human link to the great divinities of the Toltec heaven which he visits in an ecstatic experience. These are the deities who "dropped" into the wombs of all mothers to insure the presence of continued human life.

Hombre-Dios

The significance of Quetzalcoatl's centrality in this landscape is clarified in another passage which illuminates where the human Quetzalcoatl ends and the divine Quetzalcoatl begins. It shows that the source of Tollan's abundance and authority is a duality. There are two Quetzalcoatls in Tollan. Consider the following:

> They were very devout. Only one was their god; they showed all attention to, they called upon, they prayed to one by the name of Quetzalcoatl. The name of one who was their minister, their priest, [was] also Quetzalcoatl. This one was very devout. That which the priest of Quetzalcoatl required of them, they did well. They did not err, for he said to them, he admonished them; "There is only one god; [he is] named Quetzalcoatl. He

requireth nothing; you shall offer him, you shall sacrifice before him only serpents, only butterflies." All people obeyed the divine command of their priest. And they had very great faith in the priest of Quetzalcoatl . . . for all obeyed, all had faith in Quetzalcoatl.[50]

The first Quetzalcoatl in this passage is the patron deity of Tollan, the most creative offspring of the Creative Pair. Among his powers are the creation of human life, the ability to blow the sun into motion, the sovereignty over one of the cosmic eras, the creation of corn and pulque, and the organization of the universe. It appears that this Quetzalcoatl holds a special position in the Toltec pantheon of being the Supreme Being's double, the active agent of the high god. This is what is reflected in the claim that Quetzalcoatl is the one god. The second Quetzalcoatl, or Topiltzin Quetzalcoatl as he is alternately called, is a type of religious personality who directed social life in Mesoamerican societies, called Hombre-Dios. In his excellent book, *Hombre-Dios*, on religious specialists in Mesoamerican society, Alfredo López Austin uncovered the following pre-Columbian beliefs about the Hombre-Dios. All human beings receive, when they are born, a divine force that animates them and allows them to know something of the gods. In some individuals, this divine force is more intense and these persons often become the sacred specialists who mediate between the gods and the people. Such an Hombre-Dios (or Mujera-Diosa) is a special personality type who has extraordinary powers of transformation which derive from the tribal deity. This figure is capable of guiding and governing the tribe during migrations, commanding war, and offering ritual; most important, he communicates with the major deity, known in the sources as the "corazon del pueblo." This communication with the god is of a highly specialized nature in which the priest, through ritual preparation and a unique temperament, was understood to acquire the power of the deity and to be converted into the *nahual* or spokesman of the god. This means that the *hombre* had the capacity to "be possessed, to have inside his body" the god, thereby becoming the man-god.[51]

Following Lopez Austin, it appears that the confusion of Quetzalcoatl as god and man in the sources is not just the result of mistranslation of names of Quetzalcoatl, but of a living configuration in which the human and the god, Topiltzin Quetzalcoatl and Quetzalcoatl, are united at their point of similarity, the point where the god's powers are found in man. Topiltzin Quetzalcoatl is renowned as the *nahual* of the great deity Quetzalcoatl. While this type of leadership is common in Mesoamerica, it seems possible that both the god Quetzalcoatl and the leader Topiltzin Quetzalcoatl came to be figures of special prestige. Quetzalcoatl, the deity, came to be "a captain of creators" while Topiltzin Quetzalcoatl became the paradigmatic Hombre-Dios, the exemplary human representative of the deity's power and authority on earth. The two together became a unique model of authority for ritual and political life in Tollan and in other centers claiming its heritage. It is important to remember that the significance of this fusion of powerful figures and symbols was not restricted to temple rituals. Quetzalcoatl was a religious structure whose power reached all realms of Toltec and Toltec-derived dynasties. That this paradigm operated beyond the ceremonial requirements of Tollan's dynasties was clear in statements about Toltec laws.:

> [For Quetzalcoatl's] vassals, the Toltecs, nothing with which they dealt was too distant. Very quickly they could arrive whither they went. And because they were fleet, they were named Tlanquacemilihume (those who walked the whole day without tiring). And there was a hill called Tzatzitpetl. Just so it is named today. It is said that there a crier stationed himself: [for] that which was required he placed himself there in order to announce [it]. He was heard clearly in distant places. Everywhere was heard what was said, the laws that were made. Swiftly all would come forth to learn what Quetzalcoatl had commanded.[52]

The centrifugal-centripetal pattern of Quetzalcoatl's influence was vividly reported in this important passage about "Crying out Mountain." Quetzalcoatl was a lawgiver and these laws diffused into the kingdom, drawing the attention of the masses to Quetzalcoatl's commands. Quetzalcoatl's total importance for the Toltec urban tradition is succinctly stated in this passage: "Him the fire priests imitated, and the [other] priests, and the priests took their manner of conduct from the life of Quetzalcoatl."[53] Here we see the indigenous affirmation that Quetzalcoatl was the model for the priesthood. But his influence included the so-called secular realm, too; as the passage continued, "by it they ordained the law of Tula. Thus were customs established here in Mexico."[54] We could hardly find a clearer indication of Quetzalcoatl's creativity and legitimizing power. It was by Quetzalcoatl's life that the laws were ordained and applied, the rituals practiced, and the customs established in Mexico.

It is obvious that Quetzalcoatl is remembered as the giver of all that mattered in Tollan's great florescence. This sacred history, telling of the great era of the ancestors, where abundance and majesty crystallized to form a model kingdom, portrays Quetzalcoatl as the pivot of Tollan. Quetzalcoatl lives at the center of those elements which constituted what we earlier referred to as the ecological complex. In the horizontal sphere, all developments emanate from him as man-god and god. His "divine commands" and laws spread out to a king-dom organized around a ceremonial center where his temples repli-cated the cardinal directions and where the social complexities of the Toltec world were administered. Quetzalcoatl is also at the center of vertical space, the keeper of the terrestrial pivot, where, as the in-carnation of the creator-god Quetzalcoatl, he penetrates the levels of heaven and communes with the high god, establishing the patterns for the celestial flights of later priesthoods. The symbolism of the center in Tollan is multilayered, like the heavens. For the site at Tula Xicocotitlan is the center of the Great Tollan, which is the center of a sacred history about the traditional city. Eventually, Quetzalcoatl is led to a symbolic abdication of his authority through the deceptions of enemies and he flees the city for the land of Tlapallan where, according to different traditions, he is cremated and transforms into the morning star or he disappears on a raft of serpents after promising to return and restore his kingdom. We shall see the significance of the abdication and promised return in chapter 4. Long after the golden day of Quetzalcoatl's Tollan ended in humiliation and conflict, this paradigm lives on in stone sculptures, oral history, and storybooks.

QUETZALCOATL AND THE MYTHIC-COSMIC SETTING

Mircea Eliade, in a brilliant array of essays and books, has illu-minated the archetypal relationship between cosmos and city. In his essay, "The World, the City, the House," he writes:

> So it is clear to what a great degree the discovery—that is, the revelation—of a sacred space possesses existential value for reli-gious man; for nothing can begin, nothing can be done, with-out a previous orientation—and any orientation implies acquiring a fixed point. It is for this reason that religious man has always sought to fix his abode at the "center of the world." If the world is to be lived in, it must be founded—and no world can be born in the chaos of the homogeneity and relativ-ity of profane space. The discovery or projection of a fixed point—the center—is equivalent to the creation of the world. Ritual orientation and construction of sacred space has a cos-mogonic value; for the ritual by which man constructs a sacred space is efficacious in the measure in which it reproduces the work of the gods, i.e., the cosmogony.[55]

The founding of a world, in our case the founding of Tollan, can only take place within a mythic-cosmic setting, that is, within the cos-mological order established by the gods during the creation of the world. In other words, the creative acts of Topiltzin Quetzalcoatl in founding the primordial city of Tollan reflect a prior foundation, the foundation of the cosmic order which is exemplified in the creation myths of the Toltecs and the Aztecs. Recently, Cornelius Loew, a scholar working in the Mediterranean and Near East, labeled this attitude, "a cosmological conviction," which means "the conviction that the meaning of life is rooted in an encompassing cosmic order in which man, society, and the gods all participate."[56] This conviction includes the belief that a cosmic order created by the gods permeates every level of reality and that the acts and relationships of the divine society of the gods reveals the character of the cosmos and its pattern of destiny. Loew notes that this great pattern and setting may be invaded by tension and threats of disorder, but it is believed that the cosmic structure will prevail against the forces of chaos. In Mesoamerica we find a strikingly similar attitude about the relationship of cosmogony to city. The concern of the next section is the character of the Mesoamerican mythic-cosmic setting and the role the deity Quetzalcoatl had in the creation and maintenance of that order. This will enable us to understand the relationship that existed between the cosmos and ideal type of city in Mesoamerica as well as between the deity Quetzalcoatl and the culture hero Quetzalcoatl.

The Mesoamerican cosmos had several distinctive qualities, including the fact that the cosmic setting was a dynamic, unstable, destructive one distinguished by sharp alternations between order and disorder, cosmic life and cosmic death. The cosmic order was marked by combats, sacrifice, and rebellion, as well as by harmony, cooperation, and stability. But the former actions always seemed to overcome the latter. Also, it was clear that this extraordinary cosmos demanded extraordinary ritual responses from the keepers of the four quarters, including elaborately planned human sacrifices. Further, a general and fascinating parallel existed between Quetzalcoatl's divine career as creator of human life, arranger of the cosmos, ruler of an age, and the creativity of Topiltzin Quetzalcoatl's ritual building, action, and rule. In an unstable and destructive cosmos, Quetzalcoatl as god and god-man was a creative figure. Although Quetzalcoatl participated in the destructive cosmic patterns, he represented a principle of creative order and ordering of time, space, and culture. It was partly from this creativity, which originated in the supernatural sphere, that Quetzalcoatl became the symbol of sovereignty. In the brief review of cosmogony that follows, we will make some tentative interpretations of these distinct characteristics.

In his important summary of religion in pre-Hispanic central Mexico, H. B. Nicholson outlined the "basic cosmological sequential pattern" discernible in the creation myths.[57] "Ten major episodes stand out with particular clarity," he claims, the last one being the "quasi-historical" traditions about the Toltecs. But prior to this last

creative sequence, according to Nicholson's scheme, the history of
the cosmos passed through nine stages of creation. It is important for
us to note that these ten "episodes" do not appear as such in any
one or even several indigenous documents as "episodes" or as a
unity. What Nicholson has done is survey the many creation myths
and extract ten different incidents of divine creative activity. While
we are aware that this radical decision may change the actual intent
of the myths themselves, his division and sequences can be utilized
to demonstrate the Mesoamerican cosmic pattern and several important characteristics about Quetzalcoatl's role, without reducing these
patterns to a twentieth-century analytic structure. As we have already
demonstrated, sequence and story are an important part of the indigenous culture. And by following this scheme we can see more
clearly that the myths portray not just ten sequences but also a sequential descent of the Supreme Being, represented sometimes in
Quetzalcoatl, into the earthly existence of the ancient culture.

A quick perusal of the mythical sequences reveals that Quetzalcoatl is a very active deity. He is one of the four sons of the Creative
Pair, he generates the world alongside his brother Huitzilopochtli or
Tezcatlipoca, rules over one of the cosmological eras, creates the present fifth age, creates present mankind with the help of his consort,
assists in the discovery of corn and pulque, creates the sun of the fifth
age, creates fire, and participates in the sacrifice of the gods. He does
not play any part in the creation of human sacrifice and universal
warfare. Whether we accept Nicholson's divisions or not, Quetzalcoatl's dimension as a cosmic creator seems well established.

It seems much more difficult than has been admitted to identify
the "typical" cosmogonic myth in Mesoamerican religion. While it is
often suggested that Mexican cosmogony begins with the myth of the
four suns, the *Historia de los Mexicanos por sus pinturas,* which is
considered by scholars to reflect the "official" traditions about religion
for the Aztec elites of Tenochtitlan, begins at an earlier point in cosmic
history and presents a kind of précis of the cosmogony. We will constantly refer to this important account when viewing some of the
other myths. According to the *Pinturas* account, the history of the
cosmos begins with a divine pair in the thirteenth heaven. This pair
generates four children: Red Tezcatlipoca, Black Tezcatlipoca, Quetzalcoatl, and Huitzilopochtli. The divine family lives without moving
for six hundred years. Then the four sons assemble "to arrange what
was to be done and to establish the law to be followed." From among
these sons, Quetzalcoatl and Huitzilopochtli are chosen to arrange
the universe. They proceed to make fire, half the sun ("not fully
lighted, but a little"), and man and woman who are ordered to cul-
tivate the earth. From these two people are born the human race. The

woman is ordered to weave and the gods give her maize with which to heal and do magic. The two brothers create the calendar by dividing time into eighteen months of twenty days, create hell and the lords of hell, and then make the two heavens. The four brothers reassemble to create water and its divine beings.

This description of the creation of the cosmos is short and concise. The *Pinturas* cosmogony is a single, rapid and full arrangement.

At this point in the history of the cosmos, the creation of the four ages begins, a process recorded in other sources which carry the widespread myth of the suns. This mythical sequence appears in twenty-three extant sources including the calendar stone, shell ornaments, bowls, and eighteen written documents.[58] The most complete account is found in the *Leyenda de los Soles*, which rates as one of the "canonical" versions of the cosmogony along with the *Pinturas* document. Both documents tell of repeated foundations of the universe, each foundation having a different duration and ending in a terrible cataclysm. The mood of these accounts is dynamic instability actualized in a series of total cosmic destructions balanced by cosmic regenerations. In the summary that follows we combine the details that appear in these two documents. In brief, the first foundation (in the Leyenda) was the sun "4 Tiger," in which (according to the *Pinturas* account) the god Tezcatlipoca was in charge. Giants who ate acorns lived in this age. They were devoured by jaguars after a period of 676 years. (In the *Pinturas* account, the lines of combat between Tezcatlipoca and Quetzalcoatl are immediately drawn when Quetzalcoatl strikes Tezcatlipoca with a club, knocking him into the water, where he becomes a tiger.) Quetzalcoatl became the reigning deity of this second age. The second foundation or era was the sun "4 Wind," with Quetzalcoatl presiding. People subsisting during this era on piñon nuts were swept away by a great hurricane and changed into monkeys. In another version, enemies of Quetzalcoatl kicked him out of heaven and Tlaloc's age began. The third age was "4 Rain," with Tlaloc presiding, when people subsisted on a wild aquatic seed plant and were destroyed by a mighty rain of fire. (In the *Pinturas* account, the conflict is more direct—Quetzalcoatl rains fire from the sky and places Chalchiuhtlicue as the next sun.) The people were transformed into butterflies, dogs, and turkeys. The fourth age was "4 Water," presided over by Chalchiuhtlicue, when people lived on another seed plant and were swept away by a great flood and turned into frogs. The sky then fell and there was darkness and flatness between heaven and earth.

As Wayne Elzey notes, the different versions of these important sequences have caused much discussion among scholars.[59] The number of ages are given variously as three, four, five, and six in the primary sources. The duration of a given age is 23 years in the *Histoyre du Mechique*, 676 years in *Leyenda* and 5,042 in the *Codex Vaticanus*. In the last source, the length of the ages gradually increases from the first to the last while in others the lengths of the ages sometimes increase and decrease randomly, while in still others they remain constant. It appears that someone has been altering the cosmic stage a bit.

But a "consensus" emerges that the universe passed through four suns or eras, that all durations are multiples of fifty-two–year cycles, and that each sun is associated with colors, directions, and qualities. What is outstanding about these myths is the cataclysm that ends each age. The significance of this should not be passed over lightly, for although it is not unique to Mesoamerican cosmo-magical thought, it is an important fact that each age takes its name and "character" from its destructive elements, not from its creations. In one sense, the myths of the suns are not so much stories of repeated creations but are narrations of repeated disruptions, destructions, and holocausts. When reading these first mythical accounts, one recalls phrases like A. J. L. Wensinck's "dramatic conception of nature" and Henri Frankfort's comments on the "deep uncertainty" and "anxiety" in Mesopotamian views of time.[60] The cosmological conviction in Mesoamerica fills out with each new sequence, but a dynamic, unstable, destructive pattern has already appeared in these scenarios of insecurity. Each beginning is sure to result in a catastrophe and there appears to be no end in sight to this divine antagonism, these rains of fire, vigilante jaguars, deluges, and hurricanes. The forces of nature collapse with violent totality upon the little populations. In this cosmogonic tradition even the gods appear as less than totally secure, as each is ejected from his seat of dominance by a rhythm that permeates the entire cosmos and is more powerful than the suns themselves. It is a rhythm that threatens stability. It is the stepped fret turned into a story of time, a story of the universe's repeated death, a pattern that will become more terrestrial and forceful and intimidating to human life as the creation proceeds.

It is important to ask who generated and utilized this mythical pattern, but it is impossible to discern clearly the source of the tradition. Although it is claimed and generally accepted that the cultures of Teotihuacán and Tula generated many of these traditions, the sources we have limit us, for the most part, to the last half of the fifteenth century. However, the geographical spread of these conceptions about the repeated creations and destructions of the cosmos indicate that the myths of world ages were believed during the Classic Period. As we will demonstrate in chapter 3, evidence of these ideas appears in the archaeological structures of Teotihuacán, Xochicalco,

Chichén Itzá, and Cholollan. And there is no doubt that the later urban communities of the central plateau readapted the myths. An obvious example is found in the *Pinturas* account, where Huitzilopochtli, clearly a latecomer to the central plateau and the tribal god of the Mexica, becomes one of the four original sons of the high god and is named as Quetzalcoatl's co-creator. It is likely that this widespread formula of cosmic time was worked and reworked for centuries before the Spaniards came.

Quetzalcoatl's shared creative activity becomes even more dramatic in the *Pinturas* account of the creation of the fifth age. Again with a brother, this time Tezcatlipoca, Quetzalcoatl revives the broken universe and establishes the fifth age. In the darkness the four gods disperse the waters and restore the dry land. Four roads are carved to the center of the earth in order to raise the sky once more and create living space. Here we have the cosmogonic model for Tollan's axially constructed temples and the establishment of the sacred center. The four sons are aided by four beings who were created for this specific purpose. Quetzalcoatl and Tezcatlipoca lift the sky with its stars. (The parallel with the world creation episode in the *Codex Vienna* is striking.) The account of divine weight lifters is even more vivid in the *Histoyre du Mechique's* two accounts of this creative act. In one version the two brothers enter the body of an earth monster—one through the navel, the other through the mouth—and they meet at the heart of the earth. There, with the help of the other gods, they heave the monster apart and the sky is lifted and held up. In the second account, the brothers descend from heaven and transform themselves into a giant water snake in order to rip apart a great primeval water monster. Splitting the monster in half, they form the earth and the sky. Quetzalcoatl's cosmological acts reflect the great cosmic pattern of creation and destruction. With his three great brothers he builds and destroys the cosmic ages. But he has already displayed a special creative energy in his arranging of the cosmos and lifting the sky—acts that decisively provide the setting for human existence.

At this point we break away from Nicholson's chronology as it moves on to consider the creation of present mankind. This may not be the correct order, especially if we follow the earliest accounts in the *Historia de los Mexicanos* or the events as presented in the *Leyenda de los Soles*, which focus on the completion of creation of the present sun before the appearance of mankind. The central theme of the cosmological conviction as we have examined it consists of the story of the ages, and the fifth age has not yet been completed. The transformation from the unit of four previous suns into the fifth age is brought about by a great sacrifice of two pairs of deities. Unlike the creative acts of the first four suns, which consisted of divine battles in the air, the Fifth Sun, according to Sahagún, is created at Teotihuacán in a sacrificial fire. It is an episode of great significance for the daily life and ideology of the cultures using this myth.

In the *Pinturas* account, 26 years pass after the earth and sky are separated and Quetzalcoatl wants his son to be a new sun. He fasts, bleeds himself from the ears, prays, and sacrifices. Then he takes his son and hurls him into a great fire. From it emerges the sun to light the earth. Then Tlaloc throws his son into the ashes and the moon is born ashen and dark, forever following the sun, never catching it, walking across the air without ever arriving in heaven.

This creation of the sun and moon through the sacrifice of deities takes on extra significance in the account of Sahagún, which justifies even more our juggling Nicholson's sequence. It is clear here that the fifth age is being set apart from the previous ages and that it is also a continuation of the former pattern.

For 52 years following the end of the four ages, the world was in darkness. "When no sun had shown and no dawn had broken," the gods gathered at Teotihuacán so they could create a new age. They asked, "Who will carry the burden? Who will take it upon himself to be the sun, to bring the dawn?" Following four days of penance and ritual, all the gods gathered around a divine hearth where a fire had been burning for the duration. Two gods, Nanauatzin, "The Pimply One," and Tecuciztecatl, "Lord of Snails," prepared to create the new sun by hurling themselves into the fire. After they dressed themselves for the ceremonial suicide, Tecuciztecatl approached the fire several times but became frightened. Then Nanauatzin was ordered to try.

> "Onward thou, O Nanauatzin! Take heart!" And Nanauatzin, daring all at once, determined-resolved-hardened his heart, and shut firmly his eyes. He had no fear; he did not stop short; he did not falter in fright. . . . All at once he quickly threw and cast himself into the fire; once and for all he went. Thereupon he burned; his body crackled and sizzled. . . . Tecuciztecatl . . . cast himself upon [the fire]. . . . It is told that then flew up an eagle, [which] followed them. It threw itself suddenly into the flames, it cast itself into them. . . . Therefore its feathers are scorched looking and blackened. And afterwards followed an ocelot . . . he was only blackened—smutted—in various places, and singed by the fire. . . . From this [event] it is said, they took . . . the custom whereby was called and named one who was valiant, a warrior . . . then the gods sat waiting [to see] where Nanauatzin would come to rise—he who fell first into the fire—in order that he might shine [as the sun]; in order that dawn might break.

When the gods had sat and been waiting for a long time, thereupon began the reddening of the dawn; in all directions, all
around, the dawn and light extended. And so, they say, thereupon the gods fell upon their knees in order to await where he
who had become the sun would come to rise. In all directions
they looked; everywhere they peered and kept turning about.
Uncertain were those whom they asked. Some thought that it
would be from the north that [the sun] would come to rise,
and placed themselves to look there; some [did so] to the west;
some placed themselves to look south. They expected [that he
might rise] in all directions, because the light was everywhere.
And some placed themselves so that they could watch there to
the east. . . . Thus they say [that] those who looked there [to
the east] were Quetzalcoatl: the name of the second was Ecatl:
and Totec . . . and the red Tezcatlipoca. . . . And when the sun
came to rise, when he burst forth, he appeared to be red; he
kept swaying from side to side. It was impossible to look into
his face; he blinded one with his light. Intensely did he shine.
He issued rays of light from himself; his rays reached in all directions; his brilliant rays penetrated everywhere.[61]

This is the cosmic condition facing men in "the time of our Lord
Quetzalcoatl in Tula." The sun is "swaying from side to side," an
unstable, threatening cosmic orb born out of the self-sacrifice of the
gods, a world of faltering magnificence penetrating the universe. The
fifth age is marked by the promise of cosmic order thwarted by the
imbalanced fixture of the sun. Significantly, it is Quetzalcoatl who
first knows that the new age will dawn in the east. He orients himself
properly and witnesses the result of the magnificent exertions of the
gods. But the unstable and threatening situation demands still more
exertion from the gods because the sun and moon "could only remain
still and motionless." The gods then commit themselves to a course
of action that will have a terrible paradigmatic influence on the Toltec
and Aztec societies: They decide to sacrifice themselves to insure the
motion of the sun. "Let this be, that through us the sun may be
revived. Let all of us die." Then Ecatl, apparently one of Quetzalcoatl's
forms, is chosen to "deal death" to the gods and slay them all.
Amazingly, this group sacrifice fails to move the sun; "even then the
sun god could not move and follow his path." Faced with this immense cosmic crisis, Ecatl the wind god, a guise of Quetzalcoatl,
"arose and exerted himself fiercely and violently as he blew. At once
he could move him, who thereupon went on his way." Again, the
creative powers of Quetzalcoatl are manifested as he moves the sun
into its orbit and initiates the fifth age of the world.

Quetzalcoatl's identity as the wind is well attested, but it is important to emphasize here the aspects of cosmo-magical thought that

elaborate this identity. One reliable source notes the cardinal-point nature of Quetzalcoatl as the wind, supporting once more the cosmic legitimacy for the layout of many Mesoamerican ceremonial centers. "That which was known as the wind was addressed as Quetzalcoatl. From four directions it traveled. The first place where it came was the place from which the sun arose, which they named Tlalocan. . . . The second place . . . was called Mictlampa . . . the land of the dead . . . the third place was . . . Ciuatlampa . . . the fourth place was . . . Uitzlampa."[62] In the storybook images of Quetzalcoatl, he is often adorned with the wind jewel and mask, and in several prose works it is stated that as the wind he was the bringer of rain and fertility, the carrier of Tlaloc in the fields.

One cannot help but be impressed by the persistence of the motif of change, sacrifice, death, and destruction, followed by Quetzalcoatl's creativity in this story and its related information. This cosmogony is not just a drama of one large transformation of chaos and immobility into order and motion, but of the repeated attempts to insure a foundation, an order, a sun in motion, a place in which man and the gods could securely stand. And, at least in this great myth, the motion that finally insures a foundation emanates from Quetzalcoatl. Quetzalcoatl knows the direction of the rising sun; then, Ecatl, the wind aspect of Quetzalcoatl, performs a creative murder of the other divinities. Finally, this deity blows the cosmos into motion. Still, the myths give the impression that the creation of order is never complete, never fully accomplished, never consummated, if left up to the gods alone. A "divine doubt" or doubt in the divine exists in the message of these myths. The cosmos is not so much a ballet of great rhythms in which order is accomplished against the forces of chaos, but a revolutionary pattern of ferocious attack by one part of the cosmos against another. The cosmic plan that appears so peaceful and balanced at the beginning of the *Pinturas* manuscript has dissolved into a periodically rotating kaleidoscope in which the loose and colorful bits of the Supreme Being fall apart and out of each other, forming temporary order, which impresses and calms the world with structure. Then the motion starts again, a wave of rushing deities runs before the eye, colors change, and the world is in motion. The Aztec elites reworked this cosmic formula in a shrewd manner, which we will examine in chapter 4.

Quetzalcoatl's role as creator is significantly elaborated in the myths of man's creation recorded in the *Leyenda de los Soles*. In this anthropogonic myth, which has at least three basic versions, the plumed serpent restores human life through a heroic journey to the land of the dead, where he is forced to use his shrewdness and regenerative powers to overcome the forces of death.

As in the previous episode, the gods gather to answer the question, "Who shall live on earth?" They choose Quetzalcoatl for a special mission. He travels to the land of the dead and announces to the lord there (Mictlantecuhtli) that he has come for the precious bones of the ancestors to make a new humanity. Quetzalcoatl is given the impossible task: "Blow my trumpet shell and circle four times round my emerald realm"; but the shell given him by the lord of death is not hollow, it has no holes and is impossible to blow. Faced with this trick, Quetzalcoatl calls on two natural creatures, worms who make holes in the shell and bees who fly through and make the shell sing. Quetzalcoatl wins the first round. But the struggle continues when the lord of the underworld consents to have Quetzalcoatl take the bones away as he secretly turns to the beings of the underworld, telling them that Quetzalcoatl must be stopped. Now a struggle ensues within Quetzalcoatl as he develops his strategy. Initially he attempts to defy the lord of the dead verbally. Then his double tells him merely to answer, "I do but relinquish them." Of course, Quetzalcoatl plans to slip out of the underworld with the bones, but is sighted by the demons who prepare an abyss into which he falls when frightened by quail. Quetzalcoatl falls dead and the bones he was carrying are broken and nibbled by the quail (thus accounting for men's different sizes). After Quetzalcoatl's double regenerates him, he breaks out of the abyss and flees to Tamoanchan with the broken bones. He gives them to his consort Cihuacoatl-Quilaztli, who places them in her jadestone bowl and grinds them up. Then Quetzalcoatl bleeds his penis into this bowl. After the gods do penance, a male child is born, followed in four more days by a female child. From these children all mankind are descended.

In comparison to cosmogonies we have already related, this struggle for the creation of man takes place in more concrete, human terms. Conversations take place, tricks are set and overcome—conspiracy is in the air—and the hero dies and is reborn before giving his fluid to the ancestral remains. The many antagonisms are more subtle and life-size.

The pattern of the cosmological conviction takes sharper lines in this episode. The collection of myths so far examined demonstrates that creation takes place (a) through the coincidence of opposites—when dualities struggle against each other or cooperate. Each age is created by a pair in combat or sacrifice. Tezcatlipoca and Quetzalcoatl are the creative agents, or Huitzilopochtli and Quetzalcoatl take this balanced role; the high god is a duality, lord and lady of the innermost heaven; Quetzalcoatl and his double struggle against the lord and lady of the underworld to find the ancestral bones. Or creation takes place through (b) a cosmic dive. Quetzalcoatl descended from one sphere of the cosmos into another sphere, in this case into the region of the dead, in another case into the primeval waters or into the earth. In this important creation myth of the ancestral bones, Quetzalcoatl goes even deeper into the earth mother's vessel. This theme of descent is important in understanding Quetzalcoatl's meaning because he appears closer to the human condition than any of the other major deities. This pattern of divine descent fits with the Toltec belief that human "souls dropped from heaven" into mothers' wombs. It is as if Quetzalcoatl himself is the divine semen whose dive into the underworld and fall into the abyss, from which he is reborn, is the model for the generative process in which his blood falls into the divine vessel from which man is born.

But this creation, like the others, has serious flaws. When Quetzalcoatl is revived, he says to his nahualli, "What shall I do now?" and is answered, "Since things have turned out badly, let them turn out as they may." This curious comment sets a tone we have witnessed before, one that repeats itself vividly in the subsequent sections of the Tollan tale where "things turn out quite badly" and Tollan falls into ruin. Each example is an expression of the "divine doubt" alluded to, the instability expressed throughout these myths, which is a problem that plagues and motivates Mesoamerican religious elites. It is one more example of the sun "swaying from side to side." It also reveals that Quetzalcoatl is an incomplete creator. For although he represents the engendering power, he is frail and limited, and he creates through an interdependence with other divinities.

Quetzalcoatl's limited creativity appears in two of the three major versions of the creation of food. In the *Leyendas* account, which includes the creation of man just reviewed, Quetzalcoatl confronts a red ant who is bringing corn kernels from Food Mountain. "Where did you find it, tell me," he asks. After repeated attempts to gain the secret, Quetzalcoatl is pointed the way, so he turns himself into a black ant, obtains corn kernels, and takes them to Tamoanchan, where the gods have a taste and decide to give it to mankind. Quetzalcoatl sets out to bring Food Mountain to Tamoanchan by carrying it on his back. He fails. Then the primeval couple Oxomoco and Cipactonal divine the maize kernels and announce that it is "Nanahuatl who must break upon Food Mountain." Before this happens, four groups of rain gods come forth—"blue rain gods, white rain gods, yellow rain gods, red rain gods." Nanahuatl breaks open the mountain and white, black, yellow, and red corn, as well as other foods, are made available to man.

A rather different account appears in the *Histoyre du Mechique* where Ehecatl Quetzalcoatl steals Mayahuel, a young maiden goddess, from the celestial guardian monster and carries her to earth, where the two are transformed into one tree—each becoming great branches. The monster guardian discovers the theft and chases them to earth. The tree splits in two and the Mayahuel branch is attacked and torn to pieces by the monsters. Ehecatl Quetzalcoatl is unharmed and gathers up the bones of Mayahuel and buries them. From her grave grows the maguey plant, which gives man his intoxicating pulque.

In both of these myths concerning the appearance of food, one can almost say that Quetzalcoatl is a potent bystander whose actions are secondary, but important, to the acquisition of food. In the first case, it is the red ant who discovers and reluctantly makes available the discovery of Food Mountain. Quetzalcoatl's power then becomes operative and he is the go-between, a dramatic mediator between the gods and the food. But he fails in his comic-heroic attempt to tie up the mountain and carry it on his back. Other, presumably less powerful, beings acquire food for man.

In the second case Quetzalcoatl's theft and union with the goddess do not create the pulque. Again, Quetzalcoatl participates in the creative act but is not the creator himself; in this case he is split away from his partner, whom he discovered is broken apart and then buries her. It is not Quetzalcoatl who brings forth the fruit, but he is credited with having followed the correct procedure in burying her. However, it is the union of bones and earth that generates the plants.

There is a final cosmogonic sequence that takes place before the meaningful events in Tollan. The divine blood sacrificed in Teotihuacán at the beginning of the fifth age is not sufficient to energize the sun across its path, although it is blown by the mighty wind from Ecatl. In at least two sources we are told that it was necessary for the gods to institute warfare and human sacrifice among human beings in order to keep the cosmos in working order. In different versions, four hundred men are created to capture, kill, and sacrifice each other. War is instituted on earth and human sacrifice becomes the way of man. It is following this series of cosmogonic acts that the Toltec era appears in the central Mexican accounts of history. They provide the setting for the achievements of Quetzalcoatl, the man-god of Tollan.

QUETZALCOATL THE CREATOR

The Mesoamerican city is doomed to exist in a cosmic crisis that demanded more than just human action to renew and repair the cosmos. Human beings are required to sustain the cosmos through blood sacrifice. Here we have another example of the distinct character of the Mesoamerican cosmological conviction, or mood of ancient

Mexican civilization. As in all traditional urban societies, the priestly attitude toward the structure and dynamics of the universe is one of conforming to the pattern of the cosmogony and the destiny of the world. If we compare the Mesoamerican mood with the Egyptian and Mesopotamian examples analyzed by Thorkild Jacobsen, we would have to say that there is a close affinity here with the dynamic-tense world of the city-states of Mesopotamia that depend on the unreliable schedules of the Euphrates and the Tigris rivers and the extreme seasonal changes. But there is an important distinction as well. If Thorkild Jacobsen is correct, Mesopotamian society is plagued with the sense that its citizens are "but mere man—his days are numbered; whatever he may do, he is but wind."[63] In Mesoamerica human beings live with a more ambiguous destiny. They were not faced with a world that is clearly doomed, but they live with a sense of extreme anxiety about their role in sustaining a cosmic order which *might* be prolonged by their ritual strategies. In the face of this threatening cosmological destiny, they devise the political and ritual strategies of war and heart sacrifice in order not only to repeat the cosmogony but also to delay its destruction. In a sense, their wars and sacrifices are forms of self-affirmation in a world of doubt and tension. The weight of the creative task, "who will carry the burden," crossed from the divine realm into the human realm partly because the gods did not have sufficient power to maintain it themselves. The divine need descended into mankind whose job is not merely to conform, repair, and repeat, but to complete the universe and to insure its survival.

Perhaps these last comments illuminate in a small way the depth of loss expressed in the lament that opens this chapter. The human Quetzalcoatl of Tollan not only constructed a marvelous ceremonial city, where disruption was replaced by harmony, abundance, and creativity, but he was remembered as devising ritual practices which did not emphasize human sacrifice. There was a divine source for this special creativity, and it gave the Toltec tradition the quality of authority which influenced subsequent capital cities. The deity Quetzalcoatl was also exceptionally creative. Within the unstable, dynamic, and destructive cosmic-mythic setting, which appears at times to be filled with desperate and aggressive forces, Quetzalcoatl manifested the power of creation and creative ordering. Quetzalcoatl was instrumental in the creation of the universe and the establishment of the four-quartered cosmos. Quetzalcoatl participated in the creation of human life, corn, and pulque. He was part of the dynamic that created and destroyed the ages of the world. Although this deity also had limits, his creative quality was outstanding. The character of this creativity permeated the career of Topiltzin Quetzalcoatl, who acquired his power on earth. So, Tollan was remembered as an original creative time inspired by both the god and the god-man. It was the loss of this intricate combination of city–king–creator diety–authority that was lamented, recreated, and repeated in a series of "other" Tollans to which we now turn.

Three

Other Tollans

The story of ancient Mexico is the story of places and visions of places. Mexican storybooks, chronicles, histories, and encyclopedias are filled with place signs and place references of cities and towns which were founded, visited on pilgrimages and trading expeditions, celebrated, and conquered. The most prominent place in Aztec memory is Tollan of Quetzalcoatl and Topiltzin Quetzalcoatl. In chapter 2 this place is portrayed as a dazzling, expanding, integrated landscape. *Tollan*, which originally meant "place of reeds," grew to signify "great city," with the prestige of the sacred capital of ancestors where nature, agriculture, human creativity, and cosmic order flowed together, for a time, in a paradise of exuberance. Its renowned monumental architecture, glistening like a rainbow in some wonderful past, its cosmological orientation, its paradigmatic ritual tradition, and its prestige as the place par excellence of human genius made Tollan the true center of central Mexico.

The Aztec nostalgia for Tollan contains more than a description of a place; it also contains a "vision of a place" that inspired and legitimated a number of capital cities during the Classic and Post-Classic period. It is a vision of a divinely ordained, original capital which sets the pattern for subsequent societies. The Toltec tradition provides a picture of a general way of life, an orientation for later peoples to build upon and expand. This is a crucial point, for, as Jonathan Z. Smith has noted, "The question of the character of the place on which one stands is the fundamental symbolic and social question. Once an individual or culture has expressed its vision of its place, a whole language of symbols and social structure will follow."[1] The Tollan of Quetzalcoatl is a

vision of the original achievement of the capital city which founds
and organizes social life in central Mexico.

Tollan was not only the center of the world for its contemporaries,
but also the archetypal city of power and authority for many subsequent city-states. Tollan was the place through which later people had
to pass, as pedestrians enriched socially and culturally, or as members
of genealogies invigorated by Toltec blood, in order to be accepted as
civilized leaders. To be human in a cultural sense, or to be a ruler in
a legitimate sense, one has to pass through Tollan or descend from
someone who had lived or ruled in Tollan.

The vision of place that influenced the Aztecs in the fourteenth
through the sixteenth centuries referred, in a cumulative sense, to
much more than the settlement, inhabitants, and symbols of Tula
Xicocotitlan. Tollan, like all symbolic places grasped and expressed
by the archaic mind, was multivocal. It had material, spiritual, political, and other meanings. But the real complexity and richness of this
vision derives in part from the fact that it was multilocal: there were
other Tollans, inspired by the original Tollan, which elaborated the
vision and passed it on. The great image of Tollan, which challenged
and worried the Aztecs, was inspired by different places and peoples
who enriched it during the erratic history of the Classic and Post-
Classic world. Following the fall of Teotihuacán in the eighth century,
the city-states of Cholollan, Xochicalco, Culhuacan and eventually
Tenochtitlan enjoyed periods of regional and interregional dominance. Each of these capitals drew some of its legitimacy from the
vision of Tollan's stability, creativity, expansion, and power, which
they claimed to inherit. The records show that a number of city-states
striving to achieve stability in a world of periodic fragmentation added
the title of Tollan to their place names and revitalized the Quetzalcoatl
tradition in their ceremonial centers as a means of legitimating their
authority.

We ask, "Why does Quetzalcoatl appear in so many cities over
the great span of Mesoamerican history?" Complicating the problem,
the meanings, conventions, and attributes of Quetzalcoatl as god and
as god-man change significantly through time. The Quetzalcoatls of
Teotihuacán are somewhat different from the Quetzalcoatls of Cholollan, Tula, Xochicalco, Chichén Itzá, and Tenochtitlán. Yet in each
of these capitals Quetzalcoatl is a prominent symbol associated with
the regulation of the society and the maximal expression of the sacred.
He appears on the main temple pyramids, on emblems of the high
priesthood, in some instances as the name of the ruler and he also
appears as the creator god and god of wind. Certainly the answer to
this puzzle of change and continuity is difficult to discern. In my
view, the persistence and diversity of Quetzalcoatl are in part the

result of the fact that, in the minds of sacerdotal and royal elites, he symbolizes the origin and essence of the mode of existence identified with the city. Quetzalcoatl is a symbol of something essential to the continuity of Mesoamerican culture. He is the symbol of the sanctification of authority, the paradigm of legitimate rule and order.

In order to see this pattern, a change in perspective is necessary. It is not enough to see that Quetzalcoatl appears within the iconography of different capitals—many deities do. It is a question of how he appears within these cities. The ceremonial center and Quetzalcoatl appear together at the origins of, throughout the history of, and at the end of the urban process. And in all instances, there is an apparent association with authority. This is why in this discourse we focus on the image of Tollan and the symbol of Quetzalcoatl together. Tollan and Quetzalcoatl were organizing principles identified with the origin and substance of a general way of life crystallized in the image of Toltec Tollan. Together they constitute a paradigm of primordial order for society, religion and authority of the city. The Toltec tradition is revered, not because it portrayed a mode of being, but because it symbolized a sanctified mode of being in the form of the primordial city.

The other Tollans that organized parts of central Mesoamerica were ruled by elites who utilized this paradigm of primordial order as a means of sanctifying their own authority. As I will argue in this chapter, the rulers of Xochicalco, Cholollan, and Chichén Itzá elaborated the Toltec vision of place; that is, they recast it in terms of their own conditions, to validate their own historical circumstances. I will also show here why I think Teotihuacán was the first Tollan.

The flexibility of this tradition can be partly understood by reference to what Mircea Eliade calls the dialectic of the sacred.[2] Eliade shows how, within the history of religions, almost everything, at one time or another, has been considered sacred. New expressions of culture, especially those that have exceptional power, will tend to be sacralized by the existing tradition. The capacity of the sacred to transform the status of profane or secular elements has been illuminated recently by the anthropologist Roy Rappaport. According to him, it is sanctity that assists a society in adapting to new social circumstances without weakening the cherished cultural conceptions. We have long known, he contends, that sanctity supports and conserves the social order. Traditionally, scholars have viewed adaptations and innovations as signs of secular advances and the break with conventional theologies and ideologies. Rappaport, however, uses Hockett and Ascher's formulation of "Romer's Rule" to argue a different approach. This formulation "proposes that the initial effect of an evolutionary change is conservative in that it makes it possible for a previously existing way of life to persist in the face of changed conditions."[3] Rappaport argues that the sacred can actually enhance the flexibility in social structure and symbolic expression because sanctification permits previous modes of social and symbolic organization to persist in the face of innovation and change. In other words, the threatening aspects of changed conditions can be somewhat neutralized by being incorporated into sacred tradition. This ability to combine flexibility and rigidity derives from the fact that some elements of the sacred are not restricted in their meaning to specific social goals or institutions.

> They can therefore, not only sanctify any institution while being bound by none but can also sanctify changes in institutions. Continuity can be maintained while allowing change to take place, for the association of particular institutions or conventions with ultimate sacred postulates is a matter of interpretation, and that which must be interpreted can also be reinterpreted without being challenged. So, gods may remain unchanged while the conventions they sanctify are transformed through reinterpretation in response to changing conditions.[4]

Rappaport shows that sacred concepts communicate much more than information about temple activity. They convey information about the political arrangements and the regulation of society, and they imbue these arrangements with an aura of the sacred. Sanctity is infused in all systems and subsystems of society in order to maintain the fundamental order of social life. Sanctity allows the persistence of traditional forms in the face of "structural threats and environmental fluctuations." This approach provides a framework within which to understand the continuity and change manifested in the other Tollans. In this chapter I will examine the extent of Tollan's fame and the elaborations of this major paradigm by the elites of regional capitals. In each case we see how the model of a divinely ordained urban order is expanded in order to sanctify a specific city. As the evidence shows, there are "other" Tollans and "other" Quetzalcoatls, but there is always Tollan and always Quetzalcoatl.

TEOTIHUACÁN: THE IMPERIAL CAPITAL

Teotihuacán began in a cave. The greatest of Classic cities, with its immense towering pyramids, elaborate ceremonial courtyards, and residential palaces, began underground at the mouth of a well. Recent excavations have revealed that directly under the Pyramid of the Sun lie the remains of an ancient shrine area which was the sacred center for rituals and perhaps the goal of pilgrimages. A natural tunnel 103 meters long, formed by subterranean volcanic activity, led into a series of chambers shaped like a flower. Like the city that was to spread out above it, this cave was artistically reshaped and decorated by the Teotihuacános, who used it until around A.D. 450, three centuries after the pyramid was built over it. The tunnel was reshaped, roofed, plastered, and divided into thirty sections which ended at the ceremonial chamber containing the spring. There can be little doubt that the ancient shrine had a profound religious significance in the early development of Teotihuacán. The place glyph for Teotihuacán, found in the *Codex Xólotl*, was two pyramids over a cave. Clara Millon, who has worked intimately with the Teotihuacán Mapping Project, said about the cave, "This may have been the beginning of everything."[5]

Research in the history of religions teaches us that religious shrines and monuments inevitably point to some marvelous sacred event or hierophany which took place at that spot in the past. These sacred locations are considered the receptacles of ontological forces which become forever accessible to the pilgrim and priest. Throughout ancient Mexican history, caves are appreciated as sacred places where the creations of gods, human beings, and celestial bodies took place. Caves are the places of communication with the underworld and places for humans to travel into the spiritual realms to meet supernatural beings. In some instances, caves represent the womb of the earth mother who gave birth to life in its myriad forms.[6] We find accounts of the sun and moon and even the sky emerging from caves, and in one example a text tells that the moon was born in a cave of Teotihuacán. Doris Heyden illuminates the sacred significance of caves, noting that Teotihuacán's prestige as a place of origins derives in part from the importance and attraction of the cave beneath the Pyramid of the Sun.

The cave's specific religious character may be represented by its shape, which resembles a four-petaled flower. In some of the later primary written sources, the Mesoamerican cosmos is symbolized by a four-petaled flower representing the division of cosmic space into four cardinal regions and a center. It is possible that the cave was Teotihuacán's earliest *imago mundi* or sacred image of the cosmos. The symbolism of cardinal-point orientation and the center are duplicated in the city which developed above and around the cave.[7]

Evidence of ritual activity found in the cave makes it apparent that this shrine had strong attraction for religious pilgrims who not only worshiped there but also exchanged goods, information, and ideas, contributing in a variety of ways to the expansion of the shrine into a large ceremonial center. René Millon, the director of the Teotihuacán Mapping Project, demonstrates that the city arose out of the interaction of "intertwined circumstances," including religion and trade. It appears that this cave is the original nexus of these circumstances.

In an enigmatic sense, Teotihuacán was the first Tollan. We have no way of knowing whether or not it was called Tollan during its heyday. Tollan, as interpreted here, referred not only to Tula of tenth-century Mexico, but to a vision of a place that transcended and inspired specific historical sites. This vision probably had its birth in Teotihuacán. When we contemplate the truly extraordinary size, longevity, widespread influence, and artistic brilliance of Teotihuacán, realizing that it was the first great capital on the highland, it is obvious that it affected the character and style of contemporary settlements and subsequent capitals. One source gives the name of the city as Tollan Teotihuacán,[8] and in several works Toltec buildings and peoples were associated with this capital. The creation of the Fifth Sun, as reported in Sahagún, took place in Teotihuacán, but the text reads that this was the origin of the era of Quetzalcoatl, who ruled in Tula. These are not so much historical references as archetypal ones. They suggest that the general vision and character of cities which dominated the central plateau emerged during the rise, heyday, and fall of Teotihuacán, whose imperial domain was ordered and inspired by cosmo-magical thinking. Although Teotihuacán was not the Tollan the Aztecs had in mind when they eulogized it, the great Classic city must have contributed in a vibrant way to the ideas and symbols that formed the urban process. It is likely that this place and the vision it reflected carried a prestige and content which permeated later conceptions of spatial order and sacred authority. Significantly, evidence suggests that the Temple of Quetzalcoatl integrated the spatial order of the city and that the rulers were inspired and sanctified by the deity's creative power. Like the cave beneath the pyramid, which gave religious and economic impetus to the city that covered it up, the memory of Teotihuacán became an obscure and confused vision, and yet it remained a brilliant vision of space, creativity, and authority, which helped later capitals face the cultural storms and changes. Teotihuacán's imperial character transcended its own historical era by providing powerful models which were used by other cities until the end of pre-Columbian history.

Teotihuacán: The Center of the World

This majestic ancient capital is located in the semiarid northeastern part of the Valley of Mexico in what is known today as the valley of Teotihuacán. Known to most people as "the pyramids," Teotihuacán, which means the "abode of the gods," is the most frequently visited archaeological site in the Americas. Its size as well as its significance in Mesoamerican history have lured generations of scientists from around the world to come and seek out evidence of its origin and developments, social structure, and religious system, as well as to unravel the mystery of its abrupt collapse. Once thought to be mainly a ceremonial center inhabited by priests who controlled life in the surrounding countryside, it is now clear that Teotihuacán is a compact city, which at its height was populated by over 200,000 people who shared in the prestige of a capital which influenced and integrated many cities and towns within and beyond the central plateau. Our present understanding of this city's profound and widespread significance is largely due to the excellent work of the Teotihuacán Mapping Project, which has provided startling discoveries and intriguing hypotheses for further testing. The project's director, René Millon, has demonstrated that by understanding the urban character of Teotihuacán we learn a great deal about other cities and city-states in Middle America.[9]

Prior to the rise of Teotihuacán, the primary pattern of social integration was the scattered ceremonial centers, predominantly in the Olmec lowlands. Teotihuacán became the greatest city of its time through the development of a complex network of ritual, craft, marketplace, and agricultural institutions that were directed by elites who effectively organized the world of Teotihuacán's dominance. While we will not dwell on the strictly ecological potentials and processes of Teotihuacán, it is important to repeat René Millon's general remark: "This process took place in a setting of strategic importance, in a valley rich in obsidian and potentially rich in cultivable land, and in a basin with a lake system whose resources and potential for communication were unparalleled in this part of the world."[10]

When Teotihuacán reached its greatest effluorescence, around A.D. 500, it was a cosmopolitan city, a community of the Mesoamerican world which drew all manner of peoples to visit, worship, trade, and work in the shrines, marketplaces, palaces, and workshops. The pilgrimage routes to the great holy places, which had been traveled and expanded since around 100 B.C., were filled with pilgrims from nearby as well as distant cities and towns who sought blessings, messages, revelations, and inspiration from the patron deities and temple communities of Teotihuacán. These pilgrims also came to Teotihuacán to visit the markets where abundance, adventure, and a fair deal were possibilities. The great marketplace located at the center of the city hummed with the transactions of competing and bartering merchants from local and from far away communities, fields, workshops, and storehouses. Craftsmen and painters, musicians and dancers, royalty and visiting ambassadors, ball players and warriors, thieves and con men worked and celebrated, played and schemed, argued and compromised, worshiped and sought ways to accumulate

surplus goods, influence, and power. Teotihuacán became the microcosm of its own geographical region and the epitome of urban culture
for many regions of Mesoamerica. As we will see, religion was an
organizing system for life in Teotihuacán.

Teotihuacán as *Imago Mundi*

Teotihuacán was laid out as an image of the cosmos. It was not
only a container of religious symbols, it was a religious symbol itself.
It was oriented and constructed to imitate the celestial archetypes and
cosmological patterns perceived and constructed by its sacerdotal and
royal elites. While we do not have written or pictorial documents to
tell us exactly how the Teotihuacános perceived the cosmos, we have
enough evidence in the shape and order of the city to see reflections
of that cosmos and its design.

The city's thousands of residential, ritual, and craft buildings followed a grid pattern that was organized by two main avenues, the
Street of the Dead and the East-West Avenue, which crossed at right
angles in the center of the city dividing the urban space into four
great quarters. This axial design, reflected in the city's original shrine,
conformed to a series of precise observations of celestial bodies and
natural features. As the city grew, enormous effort went into the
construction of monumental architecture which conformed to the in-

FIG. 6. Pyramid of the Sun at Teotihuacán. This majestic ceremonial structure
was located along the Street of the Dead in the imperial capital, which flourished between A.D. 200 and A.D. 750. Courtesy of Lawrence G. Desmond.

fluences associated with particular astronomical meanings. For instance, the Street of the Dead, along which were located most of the important ritual and residential buildings, cut a line along the axis of the entire valley between the two highest peaks of the mountain range, Cerro Gordo and Patlachique.[11] At the northern end of this unique ceremonial avenue sat the Pyramid of the Moon, which appears to have been shaped to replicate the mountain behind it. The initial impression was that a Mesoamerican form of geomancy, sensitive to both cave and mountain space, was used to orient the city.

The Street of the Dead is oriented 15°25' east of north, an orientation very similar to many other north-south alignments on the central plateau. Along this highway, the largest ceremonial structure, the Pyramid of the Sun, was constructed to create an important right angle to the skewed northern alignment. The great stairway of the pyramid faces a westerly point on the horizon where the sun sets directly in front of it on the day of its first passage through the zenith. What exact auspicious moment in Teotihuacán's schedule of activities this day signified will never be clear, but it is obvious that there was a noble attempt to achieve a harmony between the great pyramid and celestial dynamics. This is demonstrated further by the fact that the Pleiades, a very important star cluster in Mesoamerican religion, made its first yearly appearance above the horizon before the sun rose on the day it passed through the zenith. It also appears that these two great stellar events heralded the onset of the rainy season and a new year of agricultural, managerial, and religious activity. Archaeoastronomers have shown that the East-West Avenue, which passed through the Ciudadela and the Great Compound, the administrative and market centers of the city, roughly marked the western horizon point where the Pleiades set during the heyday of Teotihuacán's development. Conclusions based on these observations must be tentative, but it seems likely that the ceremonial city was planned to reflect precise and significant geographical, geological, and astronomical patterns which guided the general schedule of activities during the year. Teotihuacán's prestige as the model of urban spatial order may be reflected in the fact that all contemporary and later ceremonial cities within 100 kilometers show a strikingly similar axial orientation, which is called Teotihuacán north.

The central core of Teotihuacán consisted of finely worked temples, palaces, platforms, market areas, and administrative buildings. Covering an area of about 3 square kilometers, this central zone was organized by two immense compounds, the Ciudadela and the huge market area called the Great Compound. These two structures functioned, according to René Millon, as "the bureaucratic, religious and commercial center of the ancient city." A significant fact, to which we will return later, was that the most imposing structure in this zone was the Pyramid of Quetzalcoatl.

Beyond this core area were numerous residential barrios of about 3000 square meters, each ordered by streets parallel to the main avenue. The barrios replicated, in a fashion, the pattern of the ceremonial core. Each barrio was organized around a ceremonial precinct consisting of a plaza that contained a temple, a ritual platform, and an open space. The barrios contained more than two thousand apartment compounds, and each compound had a central courtyard which held a local temple and a ritual platform. Sixty to one hundred people lived in each apartment compound. Thus, the smallest living units replicated the pattern of organizing the community around a ceremonial area. René Millon stated that common economic and ritual activities were probably carried out by residents of each compound. Some of the finer palaces were decorated with marvelous and fantastic murals of deities, mythical animals, and priestly processions.

Beyond this zone, the city consisted of a "suburban" area which, although less well planned, duplicated the temple plaza complex of the inner city neighborhoods. It is obvious from the morphology of the city that religious structures, great and small, played a crucial role in the layout and concept of space.

Teotihuacán's Golden Day

The evidence uncovered by generations of archaeologists and historians working in Teotihuacán suggests that there were three major components within the "intertwined circumstances" which created and sustained Teotihuacán through its history. First, although the evidence for large-scale agriculture is limited, it is obvious that a complex agricultural system was developed which supported the massive population.[12] Moreover, the existence of the high marketplace, with signs of steadily increasing numbers of obsidian and craft workshops and the Teotihuacán artifacts discovered in nearby and distant cities, testifies to the significant role that crafts and economic exchange played in Teotihuacán's history. Third, the presence of monumental architecture, with its sophisticated orientation and abundant religious symbols, clearly indicates that religion was a major force throughout Teotihuacán's history. These three components—agricultural expansion, craft development and trade, and religious organization—were united to create a great capital of an empire. In the following section, the character of this imperial capital is discussed by focusing on its centripetal and centrifugal tendencies, as well as the pattern of sanctification which accompanied the expansion of the empire.

One of the great challenges to students of Mesoamerican society and religion is the task of historical reconstruction. The present view of Teotihuacán's phases is the result of long-term collaborative efforts by scholars from various disciplines. Rather than discuss Teotihuacán history in terms of the development of each phase, we will outline two broad stages of the city's influence and dominance: (*a*) the formative period between 200 B.C. and A.D. 400, and (*b*) the Middle Classic fluorescence from A.D. 400 to 700.[13]

The processes and institutions that sustained Teotihuacán throughout its history were taking shape during the second century B.C., and by the end of the second century A.D. a fully urban way of life had developed along the major thoroughfares of the city. Early in this formative period, by 150 B.C., two large villages with populations of about five thousand each were settled on different sides of the Street of the Dead on the northern side of the city. Village life revolved around obsidian workshops, agricultural fields, and pyramid temple complex, all of which stimulated a growing trading and pil-grimage system. Millon believes that the union of marketplace and shrine enabled Teotihuacán to function as the center of an increasingly attractive and complex trading system and sacred center. The cave shrine was probably covered by a small sun pyramid before the Christian era began, although it was still used.

The first two hundred years of the Christian era witnessed an urban revolution at the site. A boom in the obsidian industries involved Teotihuacán in the importation of obsidian from distant mines and stimulated craft specialization. By A.D. 150, thirty thousand people occupied a 20 square kilometer area dotted by at least twenty-three temple complexes including another level of the Sun Pyramid. The first Moon Pyramid was built at this time and periodically enlarged. The major axes of the site were laid out and the four-quartered settlement became the capital city for the region. The centripetal tendencies so important in the development of capitals were in full swing by A.D. 100. Large quantities of mined obsidian were shipped into the city, and large numbers of traders and pilgrims came to Teotihuacán to trade, work, and worship. The construction activity and celebrations of Teotihuacán became the great events of the valley. René Millon notes that "the attraction of the pyramid was a testament to a faith that transcended Teotihuacán itself and also would have involved others from the Teotihuacán valley and beyond in its construction."[14] Between A.D. 150 and 200, Teotihuacán's population increased to more than forty-five thousand and the city covered an area of 22.5 square kilometers. The Street of the Dead was reoriented and extended. The Pyramid of the Sun, with the cave shrine below still in use, was completed, and the Moon Pyramid enlarged. But the most important development was the construction of the large and unusual "Ciudadela" at the point where the two major avenues crossed. This magnificent and spacious compound consisted of a rectangular walled structure which supported twelve small pyramids surrounding a central temple pyramid decorated with 365 alternating heads of Quetzalcoatl and Tlaloc. Pedro Armillas has made the suggestion, supported by some evidence, that this was the residential compound and special shrine area of the rulers. If this was true, then the Ciudadela was the religious and political center of the city. We will discuss further the implication that the Feathered Serpent's image and Tlaloc's image were identified prominently with the elites of Teotihuacán during its powerful rise.

By A.D. 200, Teotihuacán was showing its plumes, displaying itself in a rigorous and extravagant gesture of spatial control. The splendid ornamentation of the Street of the Dead, with its visually overwhelming ceremonial structures and striking murals and palaces, was an elaborate statement of balance revealing a self-conscious attempt by the elites to impress the viewer with an immense, theatrical concept of religious space and action. The political and intellectual power revealed to pilgrim, citizen, merchant, and foreign ambassador no doubt convinced them that this city was the center of the Mesoamerican world.

As noted, the city surrounded two large precincts straddling the Street of the Dead at the center of the settlement. Through the use

FIG. 7. Temple of Quetzalcoatl located within the great courtyard of the Ciudadela in Teotihuacán. This pyramid marked the center of the city. Note the alternating heads of Quetzalcoatl and Tlaloc on the friezes. Courtesy of Lawrence G. Desmond.

of aerial photography, the Mapping Project discovered a huge marketplace situated across from the Ciudadela. Millon writes, "The latter two gigantic precincts together appear to have formed the symbolic as well as the geographical, political, religious center of the city. Nothing approaching them in scale of conception is known from anywhere else in the Prehispanic New World."[15] The implication of this spatial order is that the builders of Teotihuacán were immensely self-conscious about their special status in the Mesoamerican world. They were building the center of an empire and by the end of the second century A.D., the city had impressed itself on the wider social world of Mesoamerica. For instance, the importation of great obsidian industries and the exportation of worked figures known as "eccentrics" into the Mayan region, as far south as Altun Ha in British Honduras, developed during this period.

Between A.D. 200 and 450 (the Tlaminilolpa phase), Teotihuacán experienced a population explosion, an enormous increase in ceremonial and residential buildings, and a further extension of its imperial power. The most significant internal development was the construction of apartment compounds that probably housed large corporate groups who shared kinship and labor ties. These apartments were an entirely new type of domestic living space which, strangely, were never built again in later urban centers. Also during this time, the Pyramid of the Moon was completed and the Temple of the Plumed Shells and the Quetzalpapalotl Palace were carefully constructed and decorated. In addition, an extraordinary mural, today called "Mythological Animals," was painted. One of the prominent images was a feathered serpent battling another mythical figure. This mural may be a depiction of a creation myth, which would indicate that Quetzalcoatl's role as a creator deity was celebrated in Teotihuacán.[16]

The Great Compound was completed at the other end of the ceremonial complex. Around A.D. 400 the Temple of Quetzalcoatl was partially covered, and the Quetzalcoatl images were not destroyed, but preserved underground. Meanwhile, industry and trade experienced a boom. Nearly four hundred obsidian workshops were opened, including blade, tool, knife, and point industries. These workshops were clustered near the Moon Pyramid, the Ciudadela, and the Great Compound, suggesting the tie among crafts, trade, and the religious elites. There appears to have been an especially important tie between obsidian industries and the priesthood of the Moon Pyramid.

Teotihuacán's Expansion

Teotihuacán was a visually impressive, carefully organized ceremonial center dominating the Valley of Mexico, but it also became the center of a commercial, artistic, and religious empire which influenced nearly all regions of Mesoamerica during the Middle Classic period, A.D. 400 to 700. During this time Teotihuacán exercised enormous influence in the Mayan, Oaxacan, Vera Cruz, and northern regions. Recent analysis of art and architecture found in these areas revealed that the Middle Classic period was characterized by intense cross-cultural communication of trade products, ceremonial objects, artistic styles, and religious iconography and ideas. While a number of large and developing cities exchanged these cultural elements, Teotihuacán consolidated the exchanges, even after its apparent dominance began to weaken during the last century of the Middle Classic period.

Esther Pasztory has demonstrated that Teotihuacán's widespread influences were both material and symbolic. Distant cities such as Kaminaljuyu, Tikal, Áke, Dzibilchaltun, Monte Alban, Matacapan, Tajin, Xochicalco, and Cholula either utilized mundane and ceremonial objects made in the capital or produced artifacts that imitated the Teotihuacán style in hybrid forms. Teotihuacán's art style, which emphasized rectilinear designs, has been found on Mayan stelae, Oaxacan sculpture, murals, frescos, and pottery. More important, entire buildings and general architectural designs found in distant cities reflect the direct influence from the great city on the plateau. In a few cases it appears that whole ceremonial centers were spatially constructed to replicate the grid plan and four-quartered shape of Teotihuacán.

Teotihuacán's influence was ideological as well as symbolic. Pasztory noted that Teotihuacán's involvement in the Mayan regions stimulated more complex forms of social stratification including the imposition of Teotihuacán dynasties, or at least their symbols and patrons, onto local governments. Most significant was that the Teotihuacán elites developed a new standard of religious concepts and expressions. Pasztory has outlined the new organization of the religious iconography and of the pantheon that diffused from Teotihuacán into distant regions. The new religious system consisted of at least six major cultic forms: fertility, warfare, ball games, dynastic rulers, burial, and titular patrons. In short, a Classic religious tradition was developed in Teotihuacán, which was imposed upon and adapted by many other city-states. Significantly, this system continued to influence religious and political order during the Post-Classic period.

While Teotihuacán contributed to the consolidation of the trading system and religious conceptions of the Classic world, no significant political integration of peoples was achieved. Little evidence of territorial control has been found to suggest that the same institutions of marketplace and shrine that created the city became the major instruments of interaction and dominance in other regions. Yet it is clear that the city attracted foreign populations. One of the most important pieces of evidence for the capital status of Teotihuacán has been the discovery of a Oaxacan barrio within the city. Generations of peoples from the Zapotec culture around Monte Alban, two hundred miles to the southeast, lived in Teotihuacán and carried on many of their local customs. Archaeologists have found funerary urns, domestic utilitarian wares, and fine pottery which reflect the Oaxacan culture.

Teotihuacán's golden day began to dim during the last part of the sixth century when the trading relationships and religious prestige of the capital were disrupted by a number of competing cities developing new routes and ideas. Called by scholars the peripheral cities of the coastal lowlands, these settlements developed routes that skirted the areas of Teotihuacán's dominance. Within the central area of Mexico, however, Teotihuacán continued to grow and prosper, although its centrifugal power was weakened by the vigorous expansion of smaller but strategic capitals like Xochicalco, Cholollan, and Tula.

Between A.D. 600 and 750, Teotihuacán's power became more sharply focused on local regions within the central plateau. Although there was not a serious decline during this period, the city finally suffered a strategic burning of its ceremonial area around A.D. 750, and the capital became a mere fragment of its former structure. But we should not think that the end of the city's dominance meant the end of Teotihuacán's influence. Long after the society of Teotihuacán collapsed, its iconography, institutions, symbols, and prestige as the center of the world continued to reverberate as the living substance of later cities.

Secularization and Sanctification

In general, discussions of the secularization of cities in Meso-america are guided by old and in some ways specious models of social evolution which view, and sometimes celebrate, the ascent of man from theocratic, closed, and rigid world views toward secular, rational, innovative, and open systems of inquiry and problem solving. The nineteenth-century model of ancient society's development from savagery, to barbarism, to civilization has been restated in the twentieth century; Formative, Classic, and Post-Classic stages replace the offending categories of the earlier version, but the view remains that urban history is the history of theocracy and religion giving way to the secular and the military. While there is no doubt that the expansion of Teotihuacán was accompanied by the institutionalization of powerful social groups like traders, craftsmen, and warriors, there is doubt that these groups were insignificant prior to the rise of institutionalized military and economic elites. After viewing the evidence we also doubt that religious symbols became less significant through time. Rather, as our little history of the city shows, the sacred and secular forces existed together at every stage of the urban process. As the capital city developed, both secular groups and sacred symbols were expanded and joined together to validate all developments within and beyond the core of the ceremonial precincts. Groups that developed independently of the celebrations within the shrine community were validated through the sanctification of their goals and methods. When new types of social exchange or social aggression developed, the sacred, which provided the general context of meaning, was expanded and applied in new ways to the new situation and was itself revitalized in the process.

This pattern of the expansion of all dimensions of urban society and their sanctification has been referred to by Robert McC. Adams in his discussion of the impact of gross surpluses on urban evolution. He notes that as cities evolve, through the stimulation of various surpluses and their regulating institutions, there will be an expansion of monumental architecture, the use of luxuries by the elites, and a proliferation of religious symbols. New classes and groups of specialists will be formed to concentrate and to reallocate surplus accumulations.[17] It appears that in Mesoamerican society, and especially in Teotihuacán, three groups that benefited from the growth and handling of surpluses were the merchants, craftsmen, and warriors. While these groups have a strictly secular nature, their presence does not demonstrate that a secularization of the city has taken place. As these social groups asserted themselves during the expansion of Teotihuacán, the application of sacred symbols also expanded. The record shows that all major processes in Mesoamerican cities—economic, political, military, or artistic—were accompanied by the intimate association with supernatural and cosmo-magical attitudes, although all purposes and activities were not restricted to shrine and ceremony. Certainly, the Olmecs and early Teotihuacános carried out secular activities in the organization of their states, but it appears that transport, construction, warfare, and trading were legitimated by supernatural associations. A brief view of several dimensions of Teotihuacán's development will demonstrate the concomitant expansion of sacred and secular elements.

It is important to remember the limitations facing us when we discuss evolutions from sacred to secular, from theocratic to military, or the internal revolutions that take place within a city and repeat themselves in various capitals. Without written evidence, as in the case of Teotihuacán, we must make distinctions on the basis of circumstantial evidence. Yet, if we have sound indications of circumstances, we are not lost. As J. C. Beaglehole notes, "Circumstances are also facts. Circumstances indeed may become the essential facts."[18] The notion of circumstances refers to "facts or events accompanying one another," the conditions "standing around" something or someone. In a remarkable sense the mute evidence we have presented reveals some of the circumstances of Teotihuacán in the form of structures that accompanied one another and organized the living activity of the city. René Millon displays a special acumen by his insistence that various intertwined processes form the main circumstances of this center. What the Teotihuacán Mapping Project clearly demonstrates is that, from the beginning to the end of the great capital, economic forces and institutions, religious worship and faith combined to consolidate the city's power, authority, and sphere of influence. The project demonstrates that the immense expansion of ceremonial buildings and obsidian craft workshops is accompanied by the growth of many other types of workshops and industries including ceramics, figurines, shell, lapidary, basalt, and ground stone. These craft items are part of the crucial network of exchange by which Teotihuacán received raw materials and other crafted items from the lowlands. The Teotihuacán center for such exchanges is probably the Group Compound located, as we have noted, directly across from the Ciudadela and the Temple of Quetzalcoatl. This seems to be a significant circumstance which shows that religion and economics, the sacred and the secular, rather than evolving sequentially, grew up together on the site and were the most important intertwined processes of all. The implication is also that the feathered serpent symbol, at least for a time, was vital to the growth of both processes. As Millon says: "Shrine and marketplace, ritual and economic exchange probably nourished and supported one another, supporting and supported by the Teotihuacán state."[19]

Another significant circumstance that throws critical light on the ascendance of secular values concerns the defensive and military nature of the city itself. It is usually argued that the rise of military elites and constructions is a sign of the ascendance of secular groups and ideologies. Teotihuacán's morphology undermines this view as well. While Teotihuacán has no specifically defensive fortification surrounding it, the Mapping Project notes that the complex groups of walls weaving around and throughout the city probably constitute a defensive barrier. The many walled precincts within the city suggest a conscious attempt to impede access to the inner part of the city. Moreover, the natural barriers of the southern *chinampas*, the Barranca Malinalco, and the masses of organ cactus, plus the layout of the apartment compounds suggest that Teotihuacán is a fortress for its own time and place. This plan appears to have existed throughout the city's history, meaning that a military cult developed to new intensity during the Middle Classic period; again, however, religious symbolism and patronage were of primary importance in the city's activities and ideology.

A third argument made to illustrate the secularization of Teotihuacán is that no great religious structures were built in the city during its final centuries. However, the Mapping Project revealed that the elites ordered the construction of new palaces, the painting of new murals, and a vigorous renewal of the ceremonial structures in the city. The Ciudadela, the scene of calendrical rituals, was renovated during the final century of Teotihuacán's power. Allied cities also continued to use Teotihuacán's religious iconography even during the waning years of the empire. Internally, the Mapping Project discovered that during the city's last centuries there was an enormous proliferation in the creation and use of ritual objects called *candeleros*, small two-chambered ceramic objects. It seems that the use of these ritual objects reflects a change in ritual activity and not a reduction in religious faith, practice, or authority. While new religious movements may have been developing and perhaps even threatening some of the traditional religious beliefs, some kind of ritual was on the rise rather than on the decline.

The sum of this short discussion of the circumstances and tendencies reflected in the evidence is that sanctity does not wane in the last part of the Classic period, but that in fact it expands. When new groups appear to pursue what S. N. Eisenstadt called "autonomous political goals," their activities are associated with and sanctified by new religious meanings and forces. While it is true that the boundaries and content of Teotihuacán's religious system changed, sanctity continued to pervade and influence new concepts of social order, space, and time. This pattern will be borne out in the other Tollans we will visit.

Plumes of the Feathered Serpent

We have shown that Teotihuacán was not only a container of significant religious objects and symbols but was also a religious symbol itself, paralleling and interacting with the dynamic motions and forces of the heavens and the special terrestrial features of its landscape. The sacred capital mediated and managed the complex social processes of a pulsating empire. Within this general cosmo-magical and social setting, one building glares out at us with such intensity that we are drawn to its shape, symbols, and carvings. The Temple of Quetzalcoatl, located near the center of the Ciudadela, is important because it is a key to understanding how Teotihuacán's elites conceived of their own authority.

When we remember that the Ciudadela and Great Compound formed the geographical, political, and religious center of the city and that the rulers most likely lived in the Ciudadela, we can infer that the Temple of Quetzalcoatl participated in a special way in the general integration of the city's many parts and influences. This spatial arrangement suggests that this structure was the *axis mundi*, par excellence, of the city. Mircea Eliade has shown how "centers" operate in the symbolic systems of traditional cities. He wrote concerning the "symbolism of the center" that

> the architectonic symbolism of the center may be formulated as follows:
> 1. The sacred mountain—where heaven and earth meet—is situated at the center of the world.
> 2. Every temple or palace—and by extension every sacred city or royal residence—is a sacred mountain, thus becoming a center.
> 3. Being an axis mundi, the sacred city or temple is regarded as the meeting point of heaven, earth, hell.[20]

The relevant application of this scheme in Teotihuacán would mean that the Temple of Quetzalcoatl, located at the center of the royal residences at the axis of the city, was appreciated as the quintessential meeting place of cosmic levels and forces, the point of ontological transition between the supernatural world and the world of men. The Temple of Quetzalcoatl probably functioned not only as the opening toward the supernatural world of the vertical, but also as the pivot of the horizontal sociopolitical cosmos. This shrine functioned as an instrument for the dissemination of religious beliefs and political decisions into all parts of the city and empire, thereby justifying the policies, goals, and programs of the elite. Quetzalcoatl was intimately related to this expansion of power and authority.

A review of Teotihuacán's major ceremonial buildings would suggest, however, that the true cosmic mountains were the Pyramid of the Sun and the Pyramid of the Moon. Towering above the entire city, they were no doubt regarded as the great points of communication between the populace and the divine society of the gods. But these pyramids were also the sacred centers for the pilgrim and citizen of Teotihuacán. They were visible from long distances, situated in open spaces to catch the eye and attention of the approaching worshiper, merchant, worker, ambassador, or warrior. The Pyramid of the Moon was situated at the end of the Street of the Dead in order to focus the worshiper's eyes from a distance and so that the pyramid grew in size, color, and magnificent detail as the worshiper approached. These shrines were the great holy places for the people of Mesoamerica.

FIG. 8. Quetzalcoatl, the Feathered Serpent, on the Temple of Quetzalcoatl in Teotihuacán. Note the carved seashells. Courtesy of Lawrence G. Desmond.

They were the theaters where the orderly and ecstatic solar and agricultural festivals galvanized attitude, schedule, faith, respect, and religious awe.

The Temple of Quetzalcoatl, on the other hand, was the center of a different part of the world. The Ciudadela was an enclosed area, a miniature *imago mundi* which replicated the elite's view of time and space. It was a ceremonial center ordered by the cosmic mountain of the rulers whose secret deliberations among themselves and with the gods was a matter of higher prestige and courtly status. The twelve platforms that surrounded it were the stages for elaborate calendrical ceremonies urging the motion of the seasons toward fulfillment. In the middle was Quetzalcoatl's and Tlaloc's platform with 365 carved heads of the deities marking the days of the year. Sacred space and sacred time were meshed together in this elite center of the world. Recent archaeological work has suggested that the temple was bounded by two large palaces, perhaps the dwellings of Teotihuacán's two dynasties, who presided over the balance of cosmos and society.[21] The dynasties' supernatural patrons can be seen when we turn to the iconography of the temple itself.

It is clear that more than just cosmic levels and social authority were integrated in this structure because it also reflects a sophisticated degree of cooperation between Teotihuacán architects, artists, and engineers. The Pyramid displays a balance of line and curve, rectilinear forms, and three-dimensional sculpture which was unique in Mesoamerica at that time. H. B. Nicholson writes of this special structure: "With almost dramatic suddenness one of the greatest tours de force of monumental stone sculpture in world history appears as a massive decorative frieze in all four sides of the six stages of the pyramidal substructure known as the Temple of the Feathered Serpent."[22] The frieze consists of alternating giant stone heads of Quetzalcoatl and possibly an early version of Tlaloc. Quetzalcoatl's head deserves special mention because in it we see the divine grin of this great deity, an expression that is continuous in its sculptured image in many Mesoamerican cities. Quetzalcoatl appears as a monumental jutting figure with open jaws displaying white curved teeth beneath obsidian eyes. The head emerges from a bouquet of feathers which join it to a thickly stylized serpent body undulating horizontally along the temple over and under various shell and aquatic figures.

These images plus the clusters of images found throughout the city are expressions of a deep commitment to agricultural regeneration. Teotihuacán's elites shared, among many other concerns, what can be called an agricultural mentality. This mentality springs from the insight that agriculture is not just a profane skill but that it deals with the powers and life forces which dwell in the seeds, furrows, rain, and sunshine. Human society and the agricultural process are viewed as set within and dependent upon the dramatic and tense cosmic cycles that insure the vital process of plant fertilization, ripening, harvest, decay, death, and rebirth. The forces in the plants and the rains are viewed as sacred forces that reveal themselves in dramatic and critical moments which are never to be taken for granted. The agricultural year is accompanied by elaborate rituals that dramatize the scenario of plant development. The onset of the rainy season, planting, and harvest are viewed as tense, critical, and tentative moments, especially in regions of uneven rainfall and water resources. Anxiety and creativity are bound together in symbol, ritual, and labor management. It appears that just such a dramatic attitude dominated Teotihuacán's schedules and ideas. The city's iconography clearly shows that the major concern of Teotihuacán's priests and artists was the continuation of the great cosmic cycles dramatized in the patterns of the sun, moon, and planets and the delicate balance of the rainy and dry seasons. Sophisticated energy went into portraying this pattern and its tensions in art compositions and iconography. Agricultural deities and symbols appear in all the cults of Teotihuacán and its neighbors; Esther Pasztory has shown that the agricultural fertility cult became the state cult of the great city.

This agricultural emphasis suggests at least two things in regard to the Ciudadela. First, that the Temple of Quetzalcoatl was the shrine where these processes, as a unity, were celebrated by the sacerdotal elite. Second, the two deities on the temple must be seen as more than just fertility figures. They are clearly associated with the rulers and must have had something like a patron relationship with the rulers and the city. They sanctified authority. It would appear then that both Quetzalcoatl and Tlaloc, in these early versions, are not only great fertility symbols but also cosmo-magical symbols of supreme authority. They empowered the rulers to carry out their sacred functions of insuring cosmic order, social balance, and agricultural abundance. When we realize that by Toltec times, the feathered serpent symbol was not only a fertility symbol but also a kingship symbol, it is possible that this dual meaning developed in Teotihuacán where marketplace and royal palaces converged.

There is another source for this interpretation. The mural of the sowing priests in the Tepantitla Palace shows a priestly procession involved in a fertility ritual. Elaborately costumed priests with feathered serpent headdresses walk along with streams of water or pulque flowing from their hands to the ground. The water contains green oval dots representing precious stones or seeds. Drops of blood or water drip off stylized sacrificial knives within their headdresses. Giant speech scrolls full of water symbols rise up from their heads. This scene shows a clear tie not only between Quetzalcoatl and fertility but also between Quetzalcoatl, the priesthood, and fertility. Is it possible that these are "Quetzalcoatl priests," the precursors of the Toltec and Aztec priests who held that title? This possibility is strengthened when we see an undulating Quetzalcoatl with Tlaloc-like images superimposed over his body enclosing the scene. A forceful stream of water flows from Quetzalcoatl's mouth. This celestial figure appears as a supernatural model for the priests and either guides or imitates the ritual process. Here, Quetzalcoatl could represent the sky, which yields the life-giving rain and dispenses the authority to the priesthood. If this is true, then Quetzalcoatl is more than just a symbol of water and fertility: he is also the patron of the priesthood which carried out vital ritual actions.[23]

Teotihuacán Tollan: The Vision of Place

Its monumental magnificence, precise spatial order, exuberant craft and market systems, and sacred prestige helped make this city the center of an expanding, pulsating empire. Although its position of absolute dominance over many other cities appears to have lasted for less than two hundred years, its status as the center for the Mesoamerican world cannot be limited to the time when its art styles were imitated. For Teotihuacán was the first Tollan, the first great place in central Mexico where a fully integrated, harmonious, rich, and well-fed society operated under the authority of supernatural forces and cosmo-magical formulas. This abundance and order, symbolized in the careful layout of the city and its widespread rectilinear iconography, gave birth to the concept of Tollan, a capital city which organized the world into an effective space. Also, it was the first center where this process was associated in a direct way with Quetzalcoatl.

XOCHICALCO: THE PERIPHERAL CAPITAL

Xochicalco means "Place of the House of Flowers." Archaeologists have discovered that it was a garden containing clusters of artistic compositions which demonstrate the city's complex relationships with many societies of the Late Classic period. In many respects, Xochicalco was the peripheral capital of central Mesoamerica. It was a city of transition and eclectic creativity located on the edge of two major cultural areas. It maintained its own integrity, in part, through its most prominent symbol, the feathered serpent.

As outlined in the previous section, the Classic period was characterized by the oscillation between the intense centralization of Teotihuacán's empire and the decentralization of authority and cultural unity into a number of competing centers. During the ebb of Teotihuacán's influence and following its dramatic collapse, Xochicalco, along with Cholollan and Tula, became a regional capital of great importance. Its strategic location, its role as a corridor for the movement and redistribution of goods and ideas into and from the highlands, its prominent image of Quetzalcoatl, and its role as an heir of some of Teotihuacán's line of influence, all these suggest that Xochicalco was a Tollan of the periphery. In the short discussion that follows, we will make a brief tour of the site, taking special note of its eclectic iconography, its morphology, its connections with distant cities, and its attractive central shrine. Although Xochicalco is hardly mentioned in the primary sources and we have nothing approaching the Mapping Project here, a series of excavating seasons have uncovered the remnants of a truly impressive ceremonial center. Still, much remains to be learned about this puzzling sacred city.

Xochicalco was a peripheral capital in terms of space and time. It flourished between the disintegration of Teotihuacán and the full development of Tula's kingdom in the tenth and eleventh centuries. For a brief time it was also one of the most powerful settlements located between the Valley of Mexico and the southern Mesoamerican regions where the Classic Mayan centers were in full swing.

Xochicalco suprises the modern visitor. This exquisite hilltop ceremonial center traditionally receives scant attention from historians and is occasionally neglected in reconstructions of Mesoamerican history. Given the limited nature of the evidence, this is partially understandable. Yet it must be noted that Xochicalco is not an isolated ceremonial precinct on the edge of Mesoamerica, but a vibrating capital of a high-density settlement consisting of more than twenty-five thousand inhabitants during its heyday. The ceremonial center is located on seven hundred acres of land in the arid climate of southern Morelos, built on several steep, terraced hills surrounded by walls and moats. The main part of the site is called the Acropolis. The majority of the population lived and farmed in the valley surrounding the ceremonial precincts while the elite residences filled terraces around the Acropolis. Xochicalco was the center of a sizable political region, which covered an area akin to the modern state of Morelos. According to W. T. Sanders, Xochicalco ruled an autonomous state within Teotihuacán's sphere of influence which grew in size and power around A.D. 700.[24]

As Jaime Litvak's archaeological research suggests, Xochicalco became a regional capital with important extraregional relationships extending into distant parts of Mesoamerica. From its early development in the Pre-Classic period, when it had contact with Oaxaca, eastern Morelos, and local settlements, through its florescence in the Classic period, when it had contact with Teotihuacán, central Vera Cruz, Guerrero, and the southern, central, and northern Mayan regions, to its waning in the Post-Classic period, when it had contact with Tula and other centers in the Valley of Mexico, Xochicalco's external relations were largely influenced by the shifts in the extensive trade networks of Mexico. The hilltop city was in a favored position to participate in some of the major patterns of exchange between the Valley of Mexico and far away regions. This encouraged the flow into Xochicalco of the valued crafts and goods of many city-states as well as the integration of the dominant symbolic forms of the period.

An examination of the morphology and iconography of Xochicalco reveals that a mediation of foreign artistic influences took place here. Various combinations of iconographic styles display a new level of integration of lowland and highland traditions. Contact and utilization of foreign designs by Xochicalcan artisans is evident as Mayan, Teotihuacáno, Zapotec, Toltec, and Nahuan forms are woven together on stelae and temples. Such a reception and reexpression of different forms indicates the cosmopolitan and transitional nature of the city.

Specifically, some of the glyphs in Xochicalco are identical to glyphs found in Teotihuacán, Mayan, and Oaxacan centers. This suggests an intimate exchange not only of artistic styles, but also of the symbolic meanings that animated these centers. Stone sculpture and ceramics at Xochicalco show influence and synthesis from the distant regions of Vera Cruz and Teotihuacán. The relationship with the Vera Cruz region may have had special significance for the elites, since Vera Cruz iconography appears on ceremonial objects used primarily by Xochicalco's rulers in ritual contexts. Further, the ball court at Xochicalco not only shows strong similarity to those at Tula in the north, but also to those at the Mayan centers of Copan and Cobá. Jorge Hardoy has noted the strong similarity between the entire plan at Xochicalco and the Mayan centers of Piedras Negras and Yaxchilan, where important constructions were elevated on hillsides and terraces, while spatial sequences were carefully planned to introduce the visitor to the principal plazas. This evidence of interaction with Mayan centers indicates that the Mayan symbolic system penetrated the highlands during the Late Classic period partly through the mediation of Xochicalco. As proof of this, some centers to the north display combinations of Xochicalcan and Mayan motifs. Also, Xochicalcan platforms are similar to those found in Tula, Piedras Negras, Copan, and Uaxactun, suggesting a widespread interaction between Xochicalcan and Mayan architects. There are also striking similarities between the stelae representations of cosmic cycles at Xochicalco and those found in Palenque. This complex series of relationships has been described by H. B. Nicholson in his comments on sculptural styles in Mesoamerica:

> The sculptural style of Xochicalco presents certain problems. It is clearly linked to Teotihuacán, on the one hand, and to Monte Alban, on the other. It is also obviously connected with the Nuine tradition of northern Oaxaca–southern Puebla. It is a sophisticated, successfully integrating partial blend of these earlier stylistic traditions, while at the same time exhibiting a distinctively individual personality of its own. The style is less angular and heavy than Teotihuacán, emphasizing curvilineality, to a much greater extent. It is neater, less overcrowded with detail, and executed with more technical skill than is generally true of Monte Alban. . . . In spite of its obviously composite origins, the style exhibits a strong inner cohesion and integration, and its influence was to linger on after the abandonment of the type site.[25]

It appears that Xochicalco's elites borrowed and reworked, according to their own special religious and political views, the time-honored traditions of the Middle Classic period.

The architectural forms of Xochicalco reveal a culture with deep iconographic sensibility. Not only can we see the use of various artistic styles throughout the center, but also the entire ceremonial precinct is itself an image of artistic imagination and manipulation. The natural hill was flattened, rounded, shaved, redesigned, and decorated to make it more illustrative of the contemporary conceptions of powerful space and effective authority. Given the traditions of pyramids in Teotihuacán and in Cholollan, indeed throughout Middle America, one can consider the entire site as a cultural pyramid overlying and reforming a natural one. This is an important point. Many interpretations of Xochicalco's hilltop location emphasize its military significance. It seems quite possible that it had such a military value. But it is equally likely that the rulers and citizens of the center considered it a replica of a sacred mountain, the great *axis mundi* where communication between humans and supernatural forces was optimal. Throughout pre-Hispanic Mexico, as Doris Heyden demonstrates with a wealth of examples, mountains are prominent sacred spaces. Mountains are perceived as the abodes of gods, the sources of springs, the places for the most important rituals. They are points of geomantic orientation, the location of pilgrimage shrines, and the places where religious ecstasy is encouraged. Significantly at Xochicalco, as at Teotihuacán, the ceremonial precinct is built over caves which went into the heart of the hill. These caves are turned into chambers with decorations and ventilation shafts, and are probably used for special initiation rituals and ceremonies. The entire center is an elaborate expression of sacred geography. Let us make a brief visit to the site in order to appreciate Xochicalco's religious character.

Like pyramids of the Mexican tradition, Xochicalco consists of a series of terraces. Above the system of walls and moats, the first terrace sits proudly, 25 meters below the main plaza. Known to us as the La Malinche group, this lower level contains a rectangular pyramid located at the end of a causeway which passes a small but splendid ball court, several palaces, and courtyards on both sides of the causeway.

A steep stairway leads up to the second terrace where we are confronted with a medium-sized courtyard balanced by two small pyramid temples, centered by a square altarlike structure. Off to one side, a large pyramid draws the visitor's eyes upward toward the partially hidden upper platform. From this second level, we can clearly see the sprawling structures of the first level as well as the features of the valley stretching around the hill.

Ascending a steep pathway alongside the large pyramid, we enter a small plaza-antechamber which suspends the hike for a moment and prepares the visitor for the treasures ahead. As we step out of this antechamber into the main elongated plaza, which measures about 15,000 square feet and contains a cluster of platform balconies, palaces, and terraces, a true blossom of architectural craft rises before our eyes in the form of the Temple of Quetzalcoatl. Its size, shape, splendid tilting lines, and aggressive carvings attract our gaze toward a structure which seems at once vibrant and about to ascend beyond the top of the hill.

Archaeologists are unanimous in their agreement that this temple is the most important structure in Xochicalco and that it is the crowning glory of the highly innovative central plaza. Professor Hardoy, who considers Xochicalco "the best example of urban design in central Mexico during the centuries after Teotihuacán and before Tenochtitlan," notes the innovative use of topography by Xochicalcan architects who utilized the sides and shapes of the hilly layers to introduce changing visual sequences. "Almost all the buildings were set back from the edges of the platform bases, creating a balcony effect that offered an exceptional view of other sectors of the city and surrounding valley."[26] This spatial invention is most prominent in the main plaza of the ceremonial center. In a fashion similar to Teotihuacán, although more pronounced here, the axis of the center falls directly on the Temple of Quetzalcoatl. At the pivotal point of this peripheral city stands Quetzalcoatl's temple. Hardoy notes, "All lines of vision converge on this structure from any angle of the main plaza; its massiveness breaks up the space into various sectors, diminishing the

FIG. 9. Temple of Quetzalcoatl located at the center of the ceremonial city of Xochicalco. The entire structure was surrounded by a frieze depicting undulating, grinning feathered serpents. Courtesy of Lewis Messenger.

impression of the plaza's vast size." Reinforcing the idea that Xochicalco is a structured pyramid replicating a sacred mountain, this Temple, located at the center of the highest courtyard, is the peak of the ceremonial precinct.

The Temple of Quetzalcoatl is about 400 square meters in area and rises majestically 5 meters off the ground with an inventive change in the *talud/tablero* style. A slanting cornice (a Classic Mayan detail) executed with superb skill, glides above *talud* slabs carrying huge carvings of a feathered serpent. Circling almost the entire structure are radically undulating bodies of Quetzalcoatl with divine grins, which enclose human figures who wear elaborate headdresses and sit in typical Mayan postures. The upper gallery, now largely damaged, depicts warriors armed with darts and spears and calendar glyphs which dot the friezes. This relatively small pyramid temple is one of the most impressive religious structures in Mesoamerica.

In this building we see evidence of the integration of external cultural influences in a dynamic fashion. What appear to be figures of ranking authorities seated in the typical Mayan position are enclosed by Quetzalcoatl's curved body. This undulating style is a more pronounced version of the shape of Teotihuacán's feathered serpent, and it must be important that at both sites the substructure of the central temple pyramid carries the feathered serpent as the principal decorative motif. It is possible that in Xochicalco we have a significant identification among central shrine–royal priest–feathered serpent, a series of relations identified in Teotihuacán as well.

There appears to be no master plan in the organization of Xochicalco; indeed, its multicultural style and spatial sequences suggest a spirit of spontaneity. The presence of Quetzalcoatl as the main ornamental feature of the central shrine is a remarkable example of continuity with the other Tollans. As in the much larger Teotihuacán, the plumed serpent with its divine grin also dominates the ceremonial space at Xochicalco, where priests and rulers lived, dreamed, argued, and called down the powers of ancestors and deities. And just as Xochicalco makes some claim as a "peripheral capital" to have woven together historical periods and cultural traditions, so Quetzalcoatl's image supports and weaves together the *axis mundi* of this hilltop place, uniting not only the ceremonial precinct but also the emblems and symbols of other urban traditions. A kind of artistic and spatial mediation is implied. And if, as some scholars hold, Xochicalco is one of the birthplaces of new military traditions in Mesoamerica, Quetzalcoatl may have presided over their birth, justified their growth, and like the images on the temple above the god's body, supported the lives of the military's protagonists.

A detail on the Temple of Quetzalcoatl offers a little more substance to the proposition that Xochicalco was a peripheral capital
where significant transitions occurred. Near the gaping head of Quetzalcoatl appears a most unusual sign. A hand gripping a rope attached
to a calendrical sign appears to be pulling the date out of one position
and into another. It is, perhaps, a sign of the renewed synchronizing
of the calendar with new observations of celestial spheres, or some
other standard. The coincidence of this sign with Mayan personages
seated in official postures and other sculptured representations has
led some scholars to suggest that Xochicalco was the site of a mul-
tiregional priestly congress which resulted in calendrical adjustments.

FIG. 10. Quetzalcoatl at Xochicalco. Courtesy of Lawrence G. Desmond.

Whether or not such a congress took place seems beyond proof, but it does appear that we have a clear association between the calendar, the priesthood, and Quetzalcoatl. It is possible that Quetzalcoatl was the patron of Xochicalco's priest-kings, who perceived and redesigned the cosmological formulas that guided ceremony and politics in the region.

Xochicalco is a peripheral capital of central Mexico, where significant historical, artistic, and conceptual transitions took place. As in Teotihuacán, Quetzalcoatl integrates and sanctifies the ceremonial center with his striking presence, except here he appears to dominate the setting instead of sharing his power with Tlaloc. The tie between priest-ruler, Quetzalcoatl, and ceremonial precinct that appeared in Teotihuacán is elaborated in Xochicalco and it appears that the military activities of this city received some kind of legitimacy from the god. The power of Quetzalcoatl to integrate and inspire the major cultural and political institutions of the urban process is expanded even further in the next Tollan we will examine, the pilgrimage capital of Tollan Cholollan.

Tollan Cholollan: The Religious Capital

Tollan Cholollan was pilgrim's paradise. Located in a plain just east of the great volcanoes Iztaccíhuatl and Popocatepetl, it has been the goal of pilgrim's progress for over a thousand years. One of the oldest inhabited cities in the Americas, Cholollan's long and illustrious history was partly due to its strategic location in the center of the Puebla-Tlaxcala region. Here it became a giant market and religious center of the eastern regions—a fact which had widespread significance in Mesoamerica. Its special status was bolstered by its intimate relationship to the Toltec tradition, which was firmly transplanted here following the fall of Tula.

Cholollan underwent the "Tollanization" of central Mexican space. The Toltec pattern of political centralization and expansion, sanctified in part by cosmo-magical symbols associated with Quetzalcoatl, was transferred to this city. One source notes that "Quetzalcoatl . . . was a native of Tollan . . . his principal seat was Cholollan," suggesting that the tradition of sanctity and order that had flourished in Tollan's golden day was re-established here.[27] According to one text, the city was called Tollan Cholollan Tlachihualtepetl, and it was stated that the people were known as "the Great Toltecs" because they possessed the classical Toltec qualities of wisdom, creativity, business acumen, superior artworks, and appreciation for precious things.[28] Cholollan was not merely a replica of Tollan's cultural richness, but also a city where the model of Toltec sanctity and excellence was expanded, altered, and applied in new ways. Cholollan, more than any other city, had a special kind of centripetal power that attracted to its many shrines elites and commoners, warriors and traders, kings and their entourages, all seeking direct access to the supernatural powers, divine blessings, and peaceful interludes available there. It appears that Quetzalcoatl, while maintaining and sharpening his association with kingship, was also popular and revered by the masses of people who sought his protection and aid. While such an inclusive cult may have existed in other centers as well, this expanded dimension of the deity's power appears to have been developed along special lines in Cholollan. In order to appreciate this other Tollan and the enrichments of Quetzalcoatl's significance, let us look first at the city's impressive spatial structure and then view the important ritual actions that took place there.

Spanish Views

People have always gone to or passed through Cholollan. Long before Aztec times, the city was a holy center of pilgrimage which attracted pilgrims from many parts of Mesoamerica to its countless shrines. Today it remains a pilgrimage city into which small and large processions of the faithful carry the images of their local virgins, amid musical ensembles and fireworks, to the Christian churches constructed on pre-Columbian foundations. Eric Wolf writes of the most significant shrine:

> At Cholula the old gods now sleep, banished into the foundations of new churches. What was once the largest man-made pyramid in the world now serves as a pedestal for the sanctuary of Our Lady of the Remedies, who peers out in her stiff Spanish gown at the two luminous volcanoes towering above the valley.[29]

Other pilgrims from a different part of the globe arrived at this city in 1519 on their way to the conquest of Tenochtitlan. Bernal Díaz del Castillo, a member of Cortes's advancing troops, described the city as the center of a highly populated region with rich resources, crafts, and special pottery.

> The city is situated on a plain, in a locality where there were many neighboring towns, and it is a land fruitful in maize and other vegetables and much chili pepper. And the land is full of magueys from which they make their wine. They make very good pottery in the city of red and black and white clay with various designs, and with it supply Mexico and all the neighboring provinces.[30]

When the Spaniards entered the city, enormous crowds filled the streets and rooftops, but above all the noise and clamor rose the great pyramid. "At that time there were many Cues (pyramids) in the city where the idol stood, especially the Great Pyramid which was higher than that of Mexico, although the Mexican pyramid was very lofty and magnificent."[31] As the Spanish observations suggest, Cholollan's power stemmed from a combination of religious attraction and economic exchange. The city was renowned for its many temples as well as its great market days. Both the temple communities and the trading fairs were intraregional in character. They attracted pilgrims and traders from nearby and distant settlements who contributed to what Ronald A. Grennes-Ravitz calls an "intraregional reciprocity" of goods, crafts, ideas, symbols, and information.[32] Our short history will show that the Quetzalcoatl cult was at the center of this reciprocity and that it existed in the city prior to the Toltec migration.

Quetzalcoatl's Invitation

In spite of the fact that Cholollan is one of the most poorly excavated major sites in Mesoamerica, tunnels driven into the heart of the Great Pyramid reveal that there were at least four major rebuilding programs carried out during a thousand-year period. These rebuilding programs were not merely new facades, but entirely new structures superimposed upon previous ones. The city apparently experienced significant periods of expansion symbolized in the impressive enlargements of this shrine. Related evidence shows that Cholollan developed slowly under Teotihuacán's influence, but that when the great northern capital weakened, Cholollan began to flourish as a capital of a special nature. The city was conquered and ruled by the Olmeca Xicalanca, who organized a growing city-state which exercised its authority through a dual rulership consisting of two priest kings, called Aquiach ("Elder of the Above") and Tlalchiach ("Elder of the Ground"), who presided at the great pyramid known as Tlachihualtepetl, which means "constructed mountain."[33] One of the most fascinating and useful primary sources, the *Historia-Tolteca-Chichimeca*, tells us that in the twelfth century, another cultural group, the Tolteca-Chichimeca, migrated to Cholollan and eventually took control of the city. According to the text, fifteen years after internal rivalries split the stability of Tollan, the priest-ruler of the Tolteca-Chichimeca traveled to the Great Pyramid in Cholollan to seek guidance and divine favor in finding a new city for his people. The pyramid was believed to be the opening to celestial forces as well as the covering over the primordial waters of the underworld. Greatly impressed with the abundance in the land and the wealth of the people and their lords, Couenan, in a state of ritual ecstasy, asked the god Ipalnemouani

("Through Whom All Live") for mercy and permission to bring his people to Cholollan. Interestingly, the priest received a response from Quetzalcoatl, who generously invited the Toltec leader to bring his people because "this will be your home." Before returning to relay the divine invitation, Couenan plucked a white reed from the land as a sign of his successful visit. Back in Tollan he gathered the four leaders of the people, showed them the white reed, and announced that the lord Quetzalcoatl urged them to abandon Tollan and move to their new home. The people cried out with joy and it was announced that the precious Quetzalcoatl Nacxitli Tepeuhqui was the authority who commanded their exodus. It was Quetzalcoatl, already established as the speaker of divine wisdom in Cholollan, who invited the Toltecs to resettle there and in effect, to refound the city.

Following their long migration to Cholollan, the Tolteca-Chichimeca lived under the rule of the Olmeca Xicalanca. The Toltecs organized themselves into four *cabeceras*, each ruled by a chief who was part of a governing council under the guidance of Couenan. Each of the four communities had a principal temple in which the tribal deity was worshiped.[34] But the major ceremonial center was dedicated to Quetzalcoatl, "a captain who brought the people to the city" and later died. Following the rise to dominance of the Tolteca-Chichimeca, this ceremonial center became the most important ceremonial precinct in the land. It consisted of a large pyramid temple which loomed above a ceremonial patio where the most important ritual processions and dances took place in honor of the gods of the land. Interestingly, this patio was surrounded by the palace where the priests and lords lived, demonstrating again an intimate relationship between supreme authority and Quetzalcoatl.

What was especially significant about this shrine was that it attracted both rulers and commoners to Cholollan. For instance, Gabriel Rojas tells us that the Quetzalcoatl cult was part of the sanctification of the authority of rulers from all over central Mexico. The two high priests mentioned earlier had the responsibility of validating the rulership of "all the governors and kings of New Spain," who came to the city to "do obedience to the idol of Quetzalcoatl." These royal officials came in processions with lavish gifts and precious feathers, mantles, gold, and jewels for the god's temple. Following the presentation of these offerings, the investiture ceremony was moved to another building where the high priests pierced the earlobes, lower lips, or nasal septums of the new rulers and inserted jewels symbolizing the confirmation of their titles and the preciousness of their persons.[35] This is a valuable example of the conservative yet flexible nature of the Quetzalcoatl tradition. Also, it tells us clearly how authority was conceived in Cholollan. Political authority had a supernatural source which was dispersed through the offices of the high priesthood presiding in the ceremonial center associated with the Toltec tradition and Quetzalcoatl. Pilgrim kings came to the center in order to receive the divine justification for their exercise of power. In addition, the masses came to receive Quetzalcoatl's blessing in Cholollan. In the early morning of festival days, groups of Cholollan's citizens and pilgrims from other towns came to the ceremonial center carrying offerings of chickens, rabbits, quail, copal, perfume, fruit, and flowers. Rojas made an important observation about these pilgrimages when he wrote that the pilgrims came to "visit the temple of Quetzalcoatl because this was the great capital and was venerated like Rome in Christianity and Mecca among the Moors."[36]

This comparison of Cholollan with Mecca and Rome suggests that this city and its patron deity constituted the point of religious orientation for much of Mesoamerica. It also suggests that the elite Quetzalcoatl of Teotihuacán and Xochicalco became accessible to a wider populace in Cholollan while expanding his significance for rulers. Although such a relationship with the masses may have existed elsewhere, it appears to have matured here where Quetzalcoatl was not just a special emblem of the high priest and rulers, but also the spiritual beacon of other levels of the social structure in nearby and distant cities.

The breadth of the city's centripetal power is reflected in the fact that many towns and cities constructed shrines dedicated to their local deities within Cholollan's ceremonial area. Thus, other settlements oriented themselves within the religious capital in an attempt to participate more directly in the sacred power and social integration manifested there.

The integration stimulated by Quetzalcoatl's shrine had an unusual political dimension. In a world of pronounced sociopolitical fragmentation, expressed by warring groups who formed alliances and combinations of alliances among each other, Cholollan became a truce city. Apparently all political groups, even though they were considered enemies of the city, were welcome to make pilgrimages there for special religious ceremonies. Also, following a war there was a massive ritual pilgrimage to the city, apparently as a means of initiating a new period of peace. The text reads:

> In the year 7 Wind, Cuetlaxtecatl was conquered. And as was the custom, the chichimecas, totomiuaques, quauhtinchantlacas, texcaltecas, malpantlacas zacatecas, zauhctecas y alcolchichimecas, visited again in Cholollan the house of the oracle of Quetzalcoatl, offering quail, serpents, deer, and rabbits. [37]

The pilgrimage reunion united the kingdom after a period of warfare. Paul Kirchhoff maintains that the seven Tolteca-Chichimeca tribes used the religious prestige of Quetzalcoatl's shrine to insure a fundamental political unity within their sphere of influence.

We have seen that Cholollan was the religious capital of central Mexico which, partially through the symbol of Quetzalcoatl, integrated different parts of the social structure as well as different sociopolitical groups. Our understanding of the religious character of this integration can be enriched by referring to Victor Turner's studies on the "liminal" and "antistructure" nature of pilgrimages. Turner noted that pilgrimages can be understood as institutionalized rituals of "communitas" which coincide with fiestas, extensive marketing systems, and other inclusive social forms. He wrote that in cultures where factional strife, segmentation, and conflict abound, rituals such as pilgrimages were utilized to emphasize ideals and values that were common to many groups and transcended the narrow goals of specific factions. During these massive liminal events, a ritual topography was created in which categories of distinction and division were broken down so that new structures that were inclusive and even universal could begin to emerge. He called this condition "communitas" and said, "communitas strains toward universalism and openness."[38] Tollan Cholollan attracted rulers and commoners alike; it held provincial shrines, was a truce city, and had a synchronized fiesta market system; it periodically suspended both social and martial practices; and it accented common ideas and ideals in a culture full of conflict and change. It was, in short, a place where a unique kind of communitas was experienced, with Quetzalcoatl serving as the transcendent inspiration of this special integration.

The Paradigm Elaborated

In Cholollan evidence points convincingly toward the continuity of a socioreligious pattern of the kind speculated about when we discussed Teotihuacán, that is, the dual governing system which seems at least partially authorized by Quetzalcoatl. We have already mentioned the two rulers who were intimately related to Quetzalcoatl. Several sources tell us that there were two distinct major religious cults in Cholula, one dedicated to the water god Chiconnauhquiahuitl, whose temple was on the top of the pyramid, and one to an earth deity represented by the feathered serpent, who, according to Maria Nolasco Armas, had a sanctuary on top of the pyramid and one at the base as well.[39] Although there is no direct proof of such a significance in Teotihuacán, Armas says of this dual-deity structure in Cholollan, "Both gods guaranteed the conditions of fertility necessary for the subsistence of a settlement whose economy was based pri-

FIG. 11. A rear view of the great pyramid of Cholula (Cholollan), which contained a shrine to Quetzalcoatl. Note the Christian church on top of the partially excavated pyramid. Courtesy of Lawrence G. Desmond.

marily on agriculture, while on the other hand, the second important economic occupation in Cholula, commerce, was under the advocation of Quetzalcoatl."[40] This combination of shrine, agriculture, and marketplace reflects quite well the Teotihuacán situation we looked at previously. Interestingly, the evidence in Teotihuacán reflects Quetzalcoatl's patronage of agriculture, while the evidence here emphasizes his relation to both, but especially to the marketplace. Diego Durán states outright, "Quetzalcoatl was the god of the merchants" who was highly revered because of the things he taught the people about jewels and stonework. One chapter in Durán's work tells of the elaborate preparations by merchants and other groups for the great festival of Quetzalcoatl which took place yearly in Cholollan. Did a similar relationship between Quetzalcoatl and the marketplace exist in Teotihuacán? In Xochicalco?

In its later history, Cholollan competed with the other great Post-Classic city, the Aztec capital of Tenochtitlán. The tight combination of shrine and marketplace were crucial to its survival as a great city under the shadow of the military and tribute networks of the Aztecs. Pilgrims flocking into Cholollan with goods and trading capabilities made exchanges at the great ritual ceremonies and intraregional fairs which often fell on the same date. Victor Turner, in his fine article "The Center out There, Pilgrim's Goal,"[41] has noted the worldwide pattern in which societies often have two centers, the official, ideological, and bureaucratic center of a state, balanced by the ritual center where pilgrims go in order to receive the blessings from the gods, the renewal of their spirits, and the reorientation of their lives in space. It is possible that just such a tension existed between Cholollan and Tenochtitlán, contributing to some type of balance within the Aztec empire. Ronald Grennes-Ravitz has shown that the pilgrimage-market function of Cholollan was one of the chief factors in the establishment of an intraregional religious and trade nexus which united central Mexico. He suggested that this pattern of integration and dissemination of goods and ideas competed effectively with the tribute paradigm of the Aztec capital and may represent the oldest religioeconomic pattern of integration in Mesoamerica. In this regard he speculated that this pattern was the basis for Teotihuacán's eminence. We have shown how these periodic integrations depended on the complex institutions of the ceremonial center which in central Mesoamerica derived its organizing principles in part from the image of Tollan and the symbol of Quetzalcoatl.

From this brief look at Tollan Cholollan, we saw more about how Quetzalcoatl integrated and mediated a complexity of forces and institutions. Not only was he the deity par excellence of the religious capital which called the pilgrim from distant places, Quetzalcoatl also sent the merchant on his journey, summoned foreign peoples to establish their shrines in the city, calmed warring communities, and validated kings, providing them all with a foundation to stand on in the social upheavals and periodic revolutions of the region.

CHICHÉN ITZÁ: THE COLONIAL CAPITAL

Chichén Itzá was the colonial capital of the Toltec empire.[42] Like Xochicalco it did not have the distinction of being called "Tollan" in the primary sources, but its history, spatial order, its intimate relationship to Toltec expansion, and the Quetzalcoatl tradition certainly allow us to apply that prestigious title to it. Originally built near a sacred well, this ancient Mayan city became the center for the diffusion of highland Toltec urbanized culture into the southern lowlands. Like the other great urban centers we have studied, it had a long and exciting history, but it was with the appearance and revitalization of the Feathered Serpent cult that Chichén Itzá flourished and became a city of destiny.

Chichén Itzá is a fruitful place to study the continuity and change of Quetzalcoatl's significance for the city tradition because here we see extensive blending of Toltec with Mayan iconography and architecture and the creation of new symbolic forms.[43] For instance, the feathered serpent's plumes are spread throughout the architecture and history of the city. However, in a number of instances we see a clear association of Quetzalcoatl with human sacrifice, a conspicuous break with what we know about the Quetzalcoatl of Tula. More important, the written texts and architectural forms give evidence that Quetzalcoatl as god and god-man was the symbol of rulership.

Chichén Itzá has long been part of the Classic Mayan culture, which expressed extraordinary quality in artistic, political, and spiritual accomplishments and which flourished during the first millennium. Around A.D. 900, the majority of great lowland Mayan centers came to an abrupt and still puzzling end. Coinciding with the end, although not the direct cause of it, the Yucatan area experienced two significant invasions of foreign peoples during the tenth century, invasions that initiated a new political era called by scholars the "Mexican period." Around the year 918, a "Mexicanized" branch of a group known to us as the Putun Maya entered Yucatan from both land and sea and established themselves in the city of Chichén Itzá. These peripheral Mayan peoples introduced the Mexican rain god Tlaloc into the city. Seventy years later, in 987, a larger and more warlike wave of northern invaders took over Chichén Itzá and began a major transformation of the site. Mayan sources tell us that at the head of the Mexican warriors and another group of Mayas moved a great lord named Kukulcan, the Mayan name for Quetzalcoatl. Although the sources were seriously confused about the dates of Kukulcan's invasion, it was clear that he led a conquest both bloody and thorough and that he rebuilt and established his capital in Chichén Itzá, modeling it after Toltec Tula. This city became the capital city of an expanding city-state that controlled the agricultural, craft, market, and religious networks of the area. Within a short time after these conquests, Chichén Itzá became the center of a Toltec-Mayan kingdom which spread north to Tabasco and south into Honduras. Merchants, artists, warriors, and priests, inspired by the new sense of cultural and cosmic order associated with Kukulcan, turned the city into a capital of an expanding state. The city dominated the area at least until 1225, when the Toltec line apparently abandoned the city by the well and a resurgence of local forms took over. However, a new Toltec-Mayan city, Mayapan, was constructed nearby and again the cult of Kukulcan dominated.[44]

Consistent with their style in the central plateau, the Toltecs strove to create an impressive and well-ordered ceremonial center. Archaeological work has revealed that at Chichén Itzá a rapid and large-scale renewal of the ceremonial precinct took place. Michael Coe has noted that Toltec architectural techniques and motifs were synthesized with Puuc Mayan forms and that a hybridization of Toltec and Mayan religious and social elements took place. Local Mayan institutions were incorporated into the new Toltec city-state, which, according to Muriel Porter Weaver, was inspired by a new perspective.

> Earlier Maya ceremonial structures were built with thick walls, narrow doorways, and dark, mysterious interiors symbolizing the heart of the earth from which the priests would emerge to transmit messages to the waiting congregations. The Toltecs introduced a new concept in religion that replaced the earth gods with celestial worship of the sun, moon, and stars; consequently they constructed buildings and courts open to the heavens for more effective mass communication between the gods and men. Emphasis was placed on human sacrifice, carried out for the glory of the group and for the benefit of all, and therefore expedited under conditions of maximum spectator participation, pomp, and ceremony.[45]

To insure a continuity with Toltec cosmo-magical principles, the city was reoriented to conform to the typical orientation of 17° degrees east of north. Among the most prominent Toltec-inspired edifices were the Temple of the Warriors, the Group of the Thousand Columns, a Tzompantli, the Temple of the Chac Mools, and a gigantic ball court measuring 480 feet long and 120 feet wide.

At the center of the city, as we might expect, was constructed a marvelous pyramid dedicated to Kukulcan. Known today as El Castillo or the Temple of Kukulcan, it was designed as the *axis mundi* of the city-state. It consisted of a finely sculptured pyramid temple with steep stairways ascending on all four sides past jutting feathered serpent heads, which appear to grin with delight. The temple at the top was supported by serpent columns and within it sat a red stone jaguar throne encrusted with eyes of green and a shell-fang mouth. Standing on top of the structure one can look across the ceremonial precinct and see the similarities to the architecture in Tula.

Recently, Carlos R. Margain has used the morphology of this ceremonial area to make an interesting interpretation about sociocultural change in Post-Classic urban society. He notes that the Classic Mayan architectural style, called the acropolis complex, consisted of ceremonial precincts with small open spaces crowded with contiguous buildings. This style reflected the separation of a well-integrated theocratic elite from the masses over which it held supreme religious and political control. Contrasted with this was the Toltec-Mayan architectural style, which emphasized large ceremonial structures in open spaces, reflecting the constant interaction between the elite and the masses, to insure unity of purpose and mind. Margain's interpretation of the meaning of this change is as follows:

FIG. 12. El Castillo, or the Pyramid of Kukulcan in Chichén Itzá. Chichén Itzá was the capital of the Toltec-Maya kingdom which flourished from the tenth century to the thirteenth. Courtesy of Lawrence G. Desmond.

> The leitmotif of Maya-Toltec architecture is war and death . . . features related to war or warriors . . . shields, dart throwers . . . skulls and decapitated individuals. . . . We conclude therefore a) that Maya-Toltec society required the presence and even the participation of the mass of the population in the ceremonies and meetings celebrated in the most important temple-pyramid of Chichén Itzá; b) that this was required because one of the principal activities was war, for which were needed soldiers drawn from the common people; c) that war activities were decidedly and intimately associated with religion.[46]

If Margain has presented an accurate reflection of social change in architectural change, then it follows that the Quetzalcoatl/Kukulcan Temple was the supernatural source for the legitimation of military activity and the institutions of warfare. This would be another example of the continuity and change of Quetzalcoatl, who remains at the center of the sacred enclave but who also sanctifies new processes extending far beyond the ceremonial precinct and the original meaning of the symbol.

It is as though each capital, from Teotihuacán on, regardless of its individual social character, is riveted to the cosmic forces and conceptions of authority through this symbol of Quetzalcoatl and the structure it adorns. The elite sacred enclave in Teotihuacán, the symbolic place which spatially and socially oriented that city, appears to reflect and express a vision of how capital cities were to be structured and sanctified throughout Mesoamerica. Xochicalco, Cholollan, Tula, and Chichén Itzá, appear to repeat and elaborate the pattern of orientation expressed there. To return to Jonathan Z. Smith's comment, "Once an individual or culture has expressed its vision of its place, a whole language of symbols and social structures will follow."[47] It appears that Quetzalcoatl is the repeated word in this language of symbols and his temple is the ceremonial and social structure that follows. In the multiple circumstances of the capital cities we have examined here, we see that Quetzalcoatl is intimately associated with the symbolic centers of the world. The significance of this is that Quetzalcoatl stood not for sacred power over or against secular power, but for the cosmo-magical conception of sovereignty itself. Carrying this kind of prestige, the symbol was used and enriched to serve the various goals, institutions, and purposes of different elite groups. It provided the place upon which evolving institutions of power and authority could stand, move, and expand.

The Office of Quetzalcoatl
In Bishop Diego de Landa's *Relación de las Cosas de Yucatan*, we have a description of the Hombre-Dios Kukulcan who looks suspiciously like the Topiltzin Quetzalcoatl of Tollan. We are told that when the Itzá took over Chichén Itzá, a great lord, Kukulcan, became the city's ruler and ordered the construction of a great temple to be called Kukulcan in honor of the god. This king established a great reputation as a religious and political genius. Part of his renown came from the new religious practices he introduced which included the ceremonial worship of idols and new sacrificial rites, including heart sacrifice. According to Landa, he was identified as the Mexican Quetzalcoatl and the lords and people of Yucatan "considered him a god . . . on account of his being a just statesman and this is seen in the order he imposed on Yucatan after the death of the lords, in order to calm the dissensions which their deaths had caused in the country."[48] He achieved wide renown as a king and builder of a capital "to whom were tributary all the lords of this province and even beyond this province. From Mexico, Guatemala, Chiapas, and other provinces they sent him presents in sign of peace and friendship."[49] Here we see the pattern of centralization and expansion that was evident in the great Tollan of Topiltzin Quetzalcoatl. The ruler Kukulcan, representing the god Kukulcan, commanded respect and authority and directed commerce from his great shrine that sat at the center of the kingdom. Tribute, obedience, and loyalty were drawn into the capital which had been revitalized by a renewed pattern of cosmo-magical

thought. Sacred ritual and sacred ruler were joined together in the figure of the feathered serpent.

One of the key questions facing us is, Who was this Kukulcan who refounded the city? Who is referred to in the striking passage from the book of *Chilam Balam of Tiziman Tizimin:* "This is the time when it came to pass that Kukulcan tightened that which was loose, in the *katun* when he who shakes the rattle sits on his buttocks"?[50]

Michael Coe believes that this leader is the same Quetzalcoatl who was cast out of Tula. We remember that Mexican sources tell that following his disgrace in Tollan, Quetzalcoatl set out "until he reached Tlapallan," that is, the Yucatan area. And the Mayan sources seem to refer to a similar person entering the area about the same time. Further examination of the sources shows a number of parallels to the religious hero of Tollan. For instance, the conqueror of Chichén Itzá is referred to as a chaste man with a beard who taught new rituals including fasting and confession. As in Tollan, he was taken as a god. Beards, the custom of fasting, and the hero's religious mission reflect some of the characteristics of Topiltzin Quetzalcoatl (who was also described as having a beard). Bearded figures accompanied by a feathered serpent as their emblem appear in Chichén Itzá. Could this captain who became a god be the individual from the central plateau? Although that is a possibility, it is more likely that we are seeing references to different historical figures who fill the "charismatic office" of Quetzalcoatl.[51] It also seems more likely that by the time the Toltecs moved into the Yucatan area, Quetzalcoatl was the title for certain leaders who derived their authority from the Toltec paradigm. One of the main arguments for this position stems from the forceful appearance in Chichén Itzá of human sacrifice under the patronage of the feathered serpent. It is stated that this captain introduced new types of blood sacrifice including heart sacrifice into the area. As with the later Quetzalcoatl of Tenochtitlán, the earlier prohibitions on human sacrifice so important in the religious history of Tula, have been completely reversed. Quetzalcoatl celebrates and achieves his conquests through human sacrifice. If this is the same Topiltzin, how do we explain such a complete reversal in religious theology and ritual strategy? Is this turnabout the result of a king who was educated to the military necessities of political power and religious dominance, necessities which included human sacrifice? Although this is an interesting possibility, I find no basis for it in the material. It is more likely that the Toltecs who led the invasion of Chichén Itzá filled the royal office of Quetzalcoatl and performed the ritual and political activities necessary to win kingdoms and divine favor.

There are other reasons besides theological ones for arguing that we are witnessing the expansion and application of the Toltec tradition and not the journey of a particular king. When we look at the sources again, confused as they are, we find that in the thirteenth century another city called Mayapan was also founded by a great leader named Kukulcan. As was the custom in Tula, Cholollan, and apparently Xochicalco, a great temple was built in honor of Kukulcan. It was a replica of the Temple of Kukulcan in Chichén Itzá with four doors facing the four directions of the cosmos. This indicates that there was a second invasion by the Toltecs and that Kukulcans were the warrior-priests of conquering peoples. The elite classes of Yucatan apparently understood the legitimating function of this title since, according to Juan de Torquemada, the kings of Yucatan, called the "Cocomes," claimed descent from the Toltec lords.[52]

The Kukulcans of Chichén Itzá and Mayapan are the titles of conquerors and founders of cities who carry the prestige of the Toltec paradigm but no longer practice the religious beliefs of Topiltzin Quetzalcoatl. In the Yucatan area relentless aggression and new sacrificial rites were used to establish new Tollans.

Eternal Tollan

In this chapter we have attempted to discern how the Toltec paradigm, with Quetzalcoatl and Tollan as its organizing principles, functioned in those cities that appear to have been the regional capitals, a paradigm on which the ancient culture stood and from which the symbolic language and social structures that dominated society came. These places, in the estimation presented here and following the implications of the primary sources, justify the title of "Tollan." Given the erratic nature of the evidence, we began with René Millon's amazing study of Teotihuacán to demonstrate the revolutionary and complex nature of Mesoamerican urban society and the meaningful circumstances of shrine, marketplace, and Quetzalcoatl. We found that Teotihuacán served as a kind of malleable archetype influencing subsequent Tollans. To quote Robert Nisbet, "we need constantly to see the ideas of each age as responses to crises of events and the challenges formed by major changes in the social order."[53] It is quite possible that the social and symbolic changes brought about in that greatest of cities, imperial Teotihuacán, made it the place that in some form or other was constantly "taking place" in ancient Mexico.

We have also seen the varieties of Quetzalcoatls, the enrichments and changes of the symbol within social situations, and we have traced the ways in which the Toltec paradigm was altered by social changes and yet continued to sanction those changes.

In all of these other Tollans we are confronted with the meaningful union of the central shrine and Quetzalcoatl. From stone and/or written evidence, Quetzalcoatl builds, speaks from, or is worshipped at the *axis mundi* of each capital. In each situation, there appears to be a special tie between the elites and the feathered serpent. This implies that Quetzalcoatl was a major cosmo-magical symbol of the authority that legitimated the decisions and processes that organized these different city-states. Yet there are impressive changes in the associations, processes, and practices sanctified by this figure. In Teotihuacán, we found circumstantial evidence that Quetzalcoatl was, for a time, a dynastic patron sanctifying the agricultural life and commercial expansion of the city. In Xochicalco, Quetzalcoatl appears to have a direct relationship to the calendar and the activities of the warrior. Quetzalcoatl also appears to integrate culture and cultural synthesis. In the religious capital of Cholollan, Quetzalcoatl's cult legitimated rulers, guided merchants, and encouraged peace. Further, it appears that this god contributed to the successful competition Cholollan had with Tenochtitlan in the area of economics and religious faith. In addition, Quetzalcoatl was a deity of the masses, the great enclosing numen who integrated social structure. Finally, in Chichén Itzá, we have the reappearance of the Hombre-Dios pattern where the hero Kukulcan organized kingdoms which were centered by the shrine to the deity Kukulcan. In this Toltec colonial capital, we saw the possibility that Kukulcan referred to the "office" of conquering ruler and was not limited to a specific historical person. But the reappearance of the Hombre-Dios figure in Chichén Itzá was accompanied by the practice of human sacrifice, a reversal of what we saw in Tula.

In each capital, the sanctity emanating from the symbol of Quetzalcoatl contributed to and was used by generations of priest-kings who constructed and ruled capital cities through the authority they derived from cosmo-magical symbols. As we shall now see, it was this sacred symbol that finally undermined the imperial authority of the Aztec empire.

Four

The Return of Quetzalcoatl
and the Irony of Empire

The geography of Mexico spreads out in a pyramidal form as if there existed a secret but evident relationship between the latter and what I have called an invisible history. . . . If Mexico is a truncated pyramid the valley of Anahuac is the platform of that pyramid. And in the center of that valley stands Mexico City, the ancient Mexico—Tenochtitlán, seat of Aztec power.[1]

And it is said when he died he disappeared for four days. Then he dwelled in Mictlan, they say. And for four days also he made himself arrows. And so in eight days he appeared, the great star. And they said it was Quetzalcoatl. Then, they said, he ascended his lordly throne. And when he appeared they knew also, according to sign, whom he would shoot with his arrows, and strike and wound. If he comes on 1 Crocodile he strikes the old men, the old women, all whomsoever. If on 1 Jaguar, if on 1 Deer, if on 1 Flower, he strikes little children. And if on 1 Reed, he strikes at kings.[2]

When the Spaniards arrived in the Valley of Mexico and first saw the Aztec capital of Tenochtitlán in 1519, they were startled by its architectural wonders, social complexity, and spatial organization. Bernal Díaz del Castillo, a sergeant in Cortes's troop, has left us this memorable first impression of the Aztec capital:

During the morning we arrived at a broad Causeway and continued our march towards Iztapalapa and when we saw so many cities and villages built in the water and other great towns on dry land and that straight and level Causeway going towards Mexico, we were amazed and said that it was like the enchantments they tell of in the legend of Amadis, on account of the great towers and cues and buildings rising from the water, and all built of masonry. And some of the soldiers even asked whether the things that we saw were not a dream. Gazing on such wonderful sights, we did not know what to say . . . and the lake itself was crowded with canoes and in the Causeway there were many bridges at intervals and in front of us stood the great City of Mexico. . . . we went to the orchard and garden, which was such a wonderful thing to see and walk in, that I never tired of looking at the diversity of the trees, and noting the scent which each one had, and the paths full of roses and flowers, and the many fruit trees and native roses and the pond of fresh water . . . and all was cemented and very splendid with many kinds of stone [monuments] with pictures on them, which gave much to think about. I say again that I stood looking at it and thought that never in the world would there be discovered other lands such as these, for at that time there was no Peru, nor any thought of it. Of all these wonders that I then beheld today all is overthrown, and lost, nothing left standing.[3]

This description of Tenochtitlán is a fitting introduction to this final discussion of the ancient Mexican city and Quetzalcoatl. The last of the "other" Tollans was the crowning illustration of the complex set of processes that characterized urbanization in Mesoamerica, and it was the scene of Quetzalcoatl's most dramatic and ironic display of power and authority.

Tenochtitlán is the central piece in our discussion of the city and symbol puzzle. It was the geographic and political center of a young and pulsating empire. It was the metropolis in which the ancient traditions and innovations from a variety of cultural areas were restated, joined, and mixed. The Aztec elites had reshaped the honored Toltec traditions of cosmic order and political legitimacy, combined them with their own expanding cultural heritage, and constructed a new vision of cosmic and political destiny to guide and to justify the policies and ends of the military state of Tenochtitlán. This new vision fused the rhythms of the city and empire with the rhythms of the heavens and strove to integrate all the previous eras, cultures, and symbols within the Fifth Sun of the Aztecs. Tenochtitlán was viewed not merely as the next sacred city in a line of sacred cities but as the capital par excellence which internalized all cosmic forces and cultural traditions within its own space and time. The Aztecs claimed that their city was the center of the universe, contemporary and eternal.

The sources we have present a rich panorama of the process of the construction of this cosmological and social center, including the details concerning the city's origin and evolution, its revolutions and enigmatic fall. As we shall see, it was the place where the critical questions of sanctity, authority, political hegemony, imperial destiny, and cosmic order were reworked and tragically settled. Apparently the inhabitants of Tenochtitlán understood their city to be the quintessential example of a capital city, for they boasted:

> Who could conquer Tenochtitlán?
> Who could shake the foundation of heaven?
> With our arrows,
> With our shields
> The City exists
> Mexico-Tenochtitlán remains.[4]

But there was a fatal irony in the mythology and history of the Aztec capital. The sources tell us that while Mexico-Tenochtitlán "remained," its kings and priests and nobles awaited the return of a royal ancestor whose coming might "shake the foundation of heaven" and who would conquer the city. It was to Tenochtitlán, the "altar" of Mexico (to develop Octavio Paz's metaphor) that Quetzalcoatl was to return one day and reestablish the kingdom he had abandoned centuries before. In fact, the Aztec account of the conquest states that when Hernán Cortes arrived in Tenochtitlán, he was welcomed as an illustrious predecessor by the last Aztec *tlatoani*, Moctezuma Xocoyotzin, who "thought that this was Topiltzin Quetzalcoatl who had arrived." The irony of the situation begins to show when we see that the return of Quetzalcoatl uncovered an atmosphere of cosmic instability and cultural inferiority that had apparently plagued the Aztec capital since its foundation. While the Aztecs had claimed divine right to the Toltec legitimacy and had spatially ordered their capital according to the cosmo-magical formulas of ancient capitals, they suffered the anxiety that their authority was illegitimate and that their city would be subject to a lethal blow from the gods. Both their claim to legitimacy and their anxiety about destruction were partly identified with Quetzalcoatl and Tollan.

For students of Mesoamerican religions the unusual mythologem concerning Quetzalcoatl's flight from Tollan and return to Tenochtitlán presents a major problem of interpretation. The problem is aggravated by the fact that most of the sources that relate this story were constructed or reconstructed at the time of the conquest of Mexico, or shortly thereafter. Though there is ample proof that the belief in a returning king antedated the appearance of Europeans, it is clear that the arrival of "strangers in the east" in 1519, followed by the Spanish penetration and attacks on Tenochtitlán, revived in the Aztec mind the riddle of this story; it became for the Aztecs part of the initial and sustained interpretative framework of the events of the conquest. Quetzalcoatl's significance in Aztec society may be understood by focusing on the way in which Moctezuma Xocoyotzin applied this mythologem to the social crisis associated with and caused by the confrontation between Spaniards and Aztecs.[5] This will enable us to see the deep contours of influence which the paradigms of the Toltec tradition had on the society that told, sang, and relived it in educational, ceremonial, and, in the case of Cortes's *entrada*, political events. By concentrating on the Aztec capital and on Quetzalcoatl's contribution to its dramatic collapse, we will see that the ideal image of Toltec creativity with Quetzalcoatl at its core had a surprising double-edged influence on the Aztecs. On the one hand, it served as a primordium, a vital source for the legitimation of Aztec authority and power. It guided, inspired, and stabilized the Aztec city. On the other hand, there was a buried irony in this primordium which surfaced with a vengeance when the element of Quetzalcoatl's return was applied by Moctezuma during the conquest. It was in this application that Quetzalcoatl "struck at kings" and subverted the sovereignty he had supported. Following the brief reunion of ancestral king and capital city, the boast of Tenochtitlán turned into the lament

> The Aztecs are deserting the city
> The City is in flames and all is darkness,
> destruction.[6]

This chapter, including a concise reconstruction of Tenochtitlán's history and an interpretation of the spatial order of the capital, focuses on the social drama of the confrontation between Cortes and Moctezuma. We will see that the fall of Tenochtitlán, alternately called a conquest or a rebellion,[7] is enhanced by an abdication of sovereignty expressed in a series of political and symbolic gestures inspired by the mythologem of Quetzalcoatl's return. Our argument is that the story of Quetzalcoatl's return operates, during the critical events of 1519, as an ironic critique of the official and normative perception of order and destiny of the Aztec capital. This critique is offered by the Aztec king against himself. The Aztecs, striving to align themselves with the tradition of legitimate power in Mexico symbolized by the Toltecs and to capture its precious influence, are themselves captured by forces within the tradition that subverted their claim to authority.

That Quetzalcoatl did not actually return in 1519, or that he is still expected to return to Mexico, does not weaken the argument about abdication. Quetzalcoatl's image was incarnated, for too long a time, in the figure of Cortes, and this return of an a priori structure weakened Aztec authority fatally. Although the *Florentine Codex* tells that Topiltzin Quetzalcoatl sailed across the sea and was expected to return in some future time, it is clear that Quetzalcoatl never really left Mexico—he was present in the invisible history of Tenochtitlán. He was lurking in the shadows on the day when Díaz del Castillo saw "the great towers, cues and buildings rising from the water" and was active in the process lamented in the sentence, "Of all these wonders that I then beheld today all is overthrown . . . nothing left standing."

THE LAKE CULTURE AND CHICHIMEC INTRUSIONS

Seldom has a capital city fit the category of "center of the world" more completely than Tenochtitlán. While the high plateau of Mexico was roughly the center of Mesoamerica, the Valley of Mexico was the heart of the plateau, the lakes formed the center of the valley, and Tenochtitlán was built near the middle of the lakes. As chapter 3 demonstrated, the central highlands had been the dominant cultural region from Teotihuacán times on. Even though Middle American civilization had periodically fragmented, its reintegration was controlled by cities located at the top of the geographical pyramid. Between 1300 and 1521, all roads of central Mesoamerica led into the lake region of the valley from which the magnificent capital arose.

Friedrich Katz has given us an insightful discussion of the social and economic significance of this central region and its interconnected network of lakes which covered a large area of the central valley. He states that in a sense it was the lakes which gave birth to Aztec power. The combination of the exceptional fertility of the soil along the shores and the irrigation systems, which were developed to insure a steady water supply, allowed the inhabitants of the lake area to produce two harvests each year.

> Perhaps even more favorable for agriculture than the soils on the lake shores, however paradoxical it may sound, was the lake itself. The inhabitants of the Valley of Mexico practiced a system of cultivation called the Chinampa system. The Chinampas were erected on lakes like artificial islands. In the shallow waters of the lakes, rafts were made of branches, roots and brushwood which were then covered with soil from the lake bottom. This soil was unusually rich and resulted in a uniquely productive agriculture. In this way a far greater population could be maintained than in other regions of Mesoamerica. [8]

This unusual degree of fertility, along with the lake's capacity to enhance a complex system of transportation and communication, stimulated a shift of the center of culture into the Valley of Mexico during the early Post-Classic period. These potentials and stimuli became the basis for the establishment of the Lake Culture—the system of city-states located on or near the lakes which were sustained by the complex processes of economic, cultural, political, and symbolic exchange—as well as the basis for coercion and cooperation among the various centers. Long before the Aztecs entered the valley, the most fertile and cultivated regions were under the control of competing city-states, or *tlatocayotls,* in constant warfare with one another. These city-states consisted of small capital cities surrounded by dependent villages and towns which worked the agricultural lands and paid tribute and performed services for the elite classes in the capital. The most prestigious settlements combined a direct link to Toltec tradition with successful military conquests. When a new wave of Chichimec tribes entered the region in the thirteenth century, they encountered a long-standing Lake Culture dominated by the social form of the city; this urban situation was the "prior structure" that challenged, intimidated, and transformed Aztec life.

The urban character of the Lake Culture is extremely important for understanding Aztec history and myth. We have long had the impression that the Aztecs somehow magically transformed themselves from wandering hordes to civilization's keepers by establishing their city in the lake. Their own mythology, as we shall see, attempts to convince us of this. The Aztecs' rise to the position of the most powerful center in ancient Mexico was meteoric and amazing, but the rags to riches scenario obscures important social facts. The Aztecs were not a barbarian horde, but a peripheral group with long-standing ties to urban cultures, including the Toltec kingdom. This prepared them to adapt systematically to the cultural layers of civilization and to rise through them in order to achieve their dominance in the lake. They were not successful simply because they terrorized their neighbors or constructed their empire on the ruins of others, nor were they a collection of mad geniuses emerging from generations of incest.[9] Rather, they adapted to the urban style that had dominated Mesoamerica for over a millennium by undergoing an internal transformation including the intensification of social stratification, the development of an ambitious military elite, and the acquisition of cultural sanctity identified with the Toltecs and Quetzalcoatl.

Known to us collectively as the Chichimecas, "Sons of the Dog," the peoples who followed the roads into the Valley of Mexico from the north consisted of different groups, most of which became acculturated to the Lake Culture. While they cannot be reduced to a common denominator, it appears that they included tribes of hunters and gatherers as well as horticulturalists. Pedro Armillas believes that many groups were northern farmers displaced by ecological changes on the frontiers, whose horticultural traditions prepared them to utilize the lake's potential. While it is not known precisely where the builders of Tenochtitlán originated, it seems clear that they had some peripheral contact with the Toltec empire and its traditions. The ancestors of the Mexica had lived on the outskirts of the great Tollan and had probably served as mercenaries, farmers, and hunters within Tollan's sphere of influence. They were somewhat familiar with the prestige of the Toltec tradition, although they carried among themselves no royal status or blood as it was conceived of in central Mexico. This was a deficiency they would soon eliminate through shrewd social and symbolic constructions.

The early history of the Aztecs in the lake area was rough and sometimes miserable. The intense rivalry, raiding, and warfare between communities plus the distinct differences in social organization and world view intimidated the Aztecs and forced them to adapt to and serve the dominant communities. According to the sources, the Aztecs had catastrophic social experiences as early as A.D. 1299 when they moved into the region of Chapultepec. This area was prized by many of the local communities because it was the source of fresh water springs. Fearing Aztec aggression, the local warriors drove the intruders out and executed their captured leaders. Following this expulsion, the Aztecs spent what Katz calls "the gloomiest and most wretched period in Aztec history, a period in which they leaned constantly on the brink of famine." They survived by combining their hunting and gathering practices with mercenary activity for various city-states. While living in a place called Tizapan, renowned for its unrivaled number of snakes, the Aztecs developed a reputation as ferocious warriors and as having an unusual cuisine. They became great snake hunters and were famous for concocting delicacies made from snakes.[10]

During this early period, the Aztecs displayed special religious and political practices which alienated them from other people. Consider their relationship to Culhuacán, which was one of the local seats of Toltec heritage: Aztec mercenaries were instrumental in helping Culhuacán conquer several other city-states including a fierce rival, Xochimilco. Following a victorious battle, the Culhuacan king requested evidence of their exploits and the Aztecs responded by cutting off the ears of all the dead enemies. When the great collection of bloody ears was delivered to the throne, the king banished the Aztecs in disgust. On another occasion, according to legend, the Aztecs asked that the daughter of Culhuacan's king be married to one of their young leaders. Instead, they sacrificed her to the gods. The Aztecs then held a great religious festival and invited the king, who had no knowledge of the use to which his daughter had been put. In the middle of the festivities, an Aztec priest paraded through the palace wearing the daughter's skin, to the complete horror of the father. Enraged, the king had the Aztecs driven out. Whatever the historical truth, the Aztecs distinguished themselves as possessing a radically different life style and religious system.

THE SACRED LINEAGE

A later alliance led to the most fortunate social development in the Aztecs' history. The infamous tribe became allied to the most powerful city-state in the lake, Azcapotzalco, which not only rested its authority on Toltec Tollan but had an even more ancient tie to Teotihuacán. Azcapotzalco was in the process of developing a small empire within the Valley of Mexico and the Aztecs were allotted a barren island near the center of the lake in return for their expert military service. Under this arrangement the Aztecs founded their city around 1345. During the next nine decades their society underwent radical social and symbolic changes which prepared the way for an empire. Among the most important changes was the establishment of a dynastic lineage appropriate to the urbanized setting of the Lake Culture. This lineage was ultimately sanctified by its tie to the Toltecs and the memory of Topiltzin Quetzalcoatl. The Aztecs, through shrewd maneuvering, gained access to a sacred genealogy which insured their legitimacy as rulers of a growing city. It was this combined social and symbolic action, the creation of the office of kingship and its Toltec identity, which allowed the Aztecs to make a critical adaptation to the social structure of the Lake Culture. Let us look briefly at this important development.

As our short historical narrative suggests, the Aztec social order was different from the social order of the Lake Culture. The Aztecs apparently had a loosely organized social structure governed by a priestly group dedicated to Huitzilopochtli and a council of *calpulli* chiefs. We shall not go into an analysis of the controversial *calpulli* ("big house")[11] structure here, except to say that while the fundamental social ties were based on kinship, the wealth, lands, and social prestige were usually distributed unequally among members according to lines of privileged access to an original ancestor. Thus, some form of social stratification existed even though there were no fully formed classes. But the Aztecs faced a highly complex social order with clear-cut class distinctions, which included supreme rulers with immense authority and power, nobles with great privileges, merchants, warriors, specialized workers, and institutions that had evolving complexities. In order to become full-fledged members of the Lake Culture, the Aztecs had to adapt to the style of city life.

Robert McC. Adams best analyzed the significance of social stratification and the institutionalization of political authority within the ancient Mexican City. In his comparative study of Mesopotamia and Mesoamerica, he notes that the problem facing the Aztecs was crucial to their identity as an urban people. He states that "the available evidence supports the conclusion that the transformation at the core

of the Urban Revolution lay in the realm of social organization . . .
primarily a change in social institutions that precipitated changes in
technology, subsistence and other aspects.[12] The point is that the basic
development in the urban process is in the area of social structure,
or to put it differently, the change which must take place for a group
to become urbanized is a change from a society based on kinship and
ascriptive relationships to one which is hierarchically organized along
symbolic, political, and territorial lines. This does not mean that corporate kin groups like the early Aztec *calpulli* disappear—they continue to play vital roles in the city—but as Adams states, they "become
encapsulated in a stratified pattern of social organization that was
rigidly divided along class lines."[13] A later view of the Aztec social
structure reveals that by the sixteenth century, the Aztecs had clearly
managed such a development and encapsulation. At the apex of the
fully urbanized Tenochtitlán was a polygynous royal household which
drew its sanctity and legitimacy from a divinely descended lineage.
Tlatoanis, or kings, literally "chief speakers," married daughters of the
leading rulers of the empire and produced an expanding nobility
which was "sharply differentiated from the rest of the population in
wealth, education, diet, dress and other prerogatives."[14] It would
follow that if we can locate the origins or early examples of the formation of an aristocracy based on a divinely prestigious genealogy,
we would discover one of the crucial social and symbolic events that
transformed the Aztecs into urban peoples.

Professor Adams places the beginning of this process for the Aztecs at the revolutionary war which the Aztecs led against their former
rulers of Azcapotzalco in 1425. He and others have rightly seen that
the distribution of conquered lands to the new military elite created
an independent economic base of immense proportions and potential.
Subsequent Aztec history involves the expansion of these spoils of
war to include nearby and distant city-states. It appears that the rules
of succession to the office of kingship were altered following this
momentous victory to ensure that only close relatives of the king
could succeed him to the throne. This was clearly a decisive turning
point in the institutionalization of royal authority in Tenochtitlán. But
an equally significant social event with rich symbolic meaning took
place decades before this war, and that event more authentically represents the initiation of social stratification crucial to the city.

In 1376, thirty-one years after the foundation of Tenochtitlán, the
Aztecs reconstituted the structure of their society by creating a new
position at the top. In a sense they jumped upward into the authority
structure of kingship by acquiring legitimacy and inventing a new
royal office for themselves. Their leaders would now fill an office
more in line with the authoritarian structures of the other cities in the

lake. The sources clearly tell that the Aztecs formed an alliance with the Toltec remnant of Culhuacan for the purpose of establishing the cherished connection with the ruling class that traced its origin to the Toltecs of Tollan. Diego Durán recorded the famous appeal by the Aztecs in their attempt to gain access to the sacred genealogy:

> Great Lord, we the Mexicans, your servants and vassals, shut in as we are among the reeds and rushes, alone and unprotected by any nation, directed only by our god to the place where we now are, which lies within the jurisdiction of Azcapotzalco, of your kingdom, and of Texcoco. In view of this, since you have permitted us to stay there, it would not be just that we should remain without a chief or lord, who might command and guide us, and show us how we are to live: who might free us and defend and protect us from our enemies. For this reason we come to you, knowing that among your people there are sons of our blood, related to yours, brought forth from our bodies and yours. And among those of your blood and ours we have learnt that there exists a son of Opichiztahuatzin, whose name is Acamapichtli. He is also the son of your daughter called Atotoztli. We beg that you give him to us as our lord, so that we may maintain him as is fitting, since he is of the lineage of the Mexicans and of the kings and lords of Culhuacan.[15]

The point about this speech is that we are witnessing not only an act of social acquisition but also an act of symbolic acquisition. The Aztecs have understood that in order to function fully in the Lake Culture they must acquire the social and symbolic foundation which will legitimate their social group and sanctify their leaders.[16] This development points directly to the significance of Quetzalcoatl. For though we have no reference such as "they did this in order to gain the legitimacy of Quetzalcoatl," the subsequent relationships of Aztec kings to Quetzalcoatl as manifested in rituals, coronation speeches, the carvings of sacred effigies, and especially in the crisis of kingship that faced Moctezuma II a century and a half later, show that this symbol of Quetzalcoatl worked as the sacred genealogical source for the keepers of the Aztec empire. While the defeat of Azcapotzalco and the formation of the triple alliance in 1427 solidified economically and socially the Aztec drive toward full participation in the direction of control of the Lake Culture, it was the earlier connection to the sanctified tradition of kingship and urban culture that was the foundation of their claim to urban status and authority.

A parallel scenario of acquiring the social and symbolic prestige of Toltec culture can be found in an important document, the *Codex Xólotl*, which portrays the fortunes and rise of the Chichimec tribe that built the city of Tezcoco, Tenochtitlán's greatest ally and rival. This document, like many primary sources, draws a cultural dichotomy when picturing and describing the peoples of central Mexico following the fall of Toltec Tollan. On the one hand, the codices are full of praise concerning the remnants of the Toltec kingdom who were transplanted in the central region. These groups are understood to carry the legacy of wisdom, artistic excellence, farming techniques, and the civilized language, Nahuatl. An opposite picture appears of migrating Chichimec tribes, who are hunters, inhabit caves, dress in animal skins, sometimes eat human flesh, and speak rude languages. The *Codex Xólotl* presents the story of the progressive integration of one such tribe into the cultural pattern of the transplanted Toltec world of the lake.[17]

The story begins with Xólotl's grandson Tlotzin, who is half Toltec on his mother's side. Tlotzin, a truly marginal man, is out on a hunting trip when he meets a stranger who begins to instruct him in the techniques of farming, in the art of cooking tamales, and in speaking a superior language, Nahuatl. Tlotzin enters into a long tutelage with the benefactor and begins to acquire the customs of Toltec culture. A descendant of Tlotzin, named Quinatzin, who has grown up with the benefits of his ancestor's transformation, begins to build the city of Tezcoco by constructing a system of fences that signifies a new spatial and social order for the Chichimecs. (It must be said that some Chichimecas rebel against the fence, the new language, and the farming life and return to the mountains to hunt.) Meanwhile, the descendants of this half Toltec Chichimec continue to intermarry with migrating remnant Toltec families who bring more high culture into the lake. They bring painted histories, new farming techniques, and a complex set of religious concepts from Tollan. The major event is the marriage of Quinatzin's son into a Toltec family, which results in the first fully Toltecized Chichimecas. The transformation is complete when the child is a Nahuatl speaker. The descendants of this child grow up in the Toltec educational system, adopting the correct legal, military, and cultural traits, while the town of Tezcoco develops into a great cultural center. The *Codex Xólotl* story follows the pattern of Chichimec acquisition of the Toltec heritage that we saw dramatized in the Aztec acquisition of kingship. It is important to note that the crucial act in both instances is not the acquaintance with farming or the acquisition of a new language or even the establishment of a new political office, but the possession of the blood line of Tollan through intermarriage with Toltec families. It is partly a genealogical change which prepares the Chichimecs, Sons of the Dogs, to become the heirs of Quetzalcoatl, and this is the crucial step toward entering the world of the city.

In 1426, Aztec fortunes changed radically when Tezozomoc, the greatest ruler in the Lake Culture up to that time, died after sixty-three years of commanding the Tepanecs of Azcapotzalco. His charismatic personality was apparently the lodestone of Tepanec power and support because a widespread revolution began almost immediately which led to the transfer of power to a Triple Alliance of cities. We remember that the Aztecs had been a potent instrument in the rise of Tepanec power. In a tactical turnabout, they organized an alliance with two other city-states that were eager to expand their power but that had suffered under Azcapotzalco's rule. One of these centers was Tezcoco, which had recently suffered a merciless defeat at the hands of the Aztec-Azcapotzalco alliance and whose heir apparent, Nezahualcoyotl, one of the most outstanding and brilliant personalities in ancient Mexican history, waited in exile to return and claim his throne. Together with the smaller center of Tlacopan, these two originally Chichimec centers led a four-year revolution against Azcapotzalco, destroying its grip in the valley and taking over the direction of the next era of social history. Already possessing the proper claim to legitimacy, the Aztecs now began to fill the place of the Tepanecs and the road to empire was broadening. This immensely important event resulted in the creation of a new aristocracy and new ideological tendencies in the Aztec city. A meritorious military aristocracy, which influenced and operated alongside the hereditary aristocracy, became the new pillar in Aztec society. The *tlatoanis* could now depend on two noble sources of power, the royal elite consisting of family members of the king and the warrior class. The former group was known as the Pipiltin and drew their legitimacy from Toltec culture; the latter drew their power from the great victories which established and expanded the Triple Alliance.

THE SYMBOLIC CONSTRUCTION OF REALITY

This short historical reconstruction of a people struggling to fit into the developed social world of the lakes is a far cry from the glorious mythological story of divine guidance that appears in the sacred histories of Tenochtitlán. When the Spaniards saw Tenochtitlán in the early sixteenth century, not only was it a splendid expression of symbolic urban planning, but the stories of its origin and supernatural patronage reflected a supreme confidence in the imperial destiny of a great people and a great god. Before discussing the ways in which the city was constructed as a symbol of cosmic order, it will be helpful to comment on the possible meaning of the incongruity between myth and history. We have learned that foundation myths and stories of origin provide a sanctified framework for the development of a culture.[18] Myths tell how a people understand the incarnation of divine order and intention within their world. These myths provide models for human activity and regeneration. In the Aztec case it is clear that the myth of Tenochtitlán's foundation and of the birth of Huitzilopochtli served as primordial models for ritual construction and celebration. Yet, given the historical conditions of social inferiority and cultural illegitimacy that plagued the Aztecs' beginnings, the sacred histories of Tenochtitlán reveal another intention at work among Aztec cosmographers. It seems that we have a coercive sociopolitical intention revealed in the striking incongruity between myth and history. Faced with the overwhelming evidence of their predecessors' monumental achievements, sacred genealogies, and complex social structures, the Aztecs felt immensely inferior and strove to construct a city, mythology, and destiny in order to impress and intimidate others and to legitimate themselves. Their myths and capital were symbolic constructions designed not only to provide a theater for the repetition of archetypes, but also to establish the social truth that the Aztecs had divine sanction to be where they were and to do what they did—ritually, politically, and culturally. In building Tenochtitlán as a symbol of cosmic order, they learned how to combine social and symbolic creativity to establish their place in the Lake Culture.

Tenochtitlán: Symbolic Space and Cosmic Time

The city that developed under the leaders of the Triple Alliance was truly magnificent, monumental, and dramatic. Fortunately, we have a "renaissance image" of this site in the 1520 map attributed to Cortes, which was likely drawn by his geometrician Alonso García Bravo for the purpose of plotting strategy for the upcoming siege by the Spaniards in 1521. First published in Nuremberg in 1524 as an illustration of the Latin edition of Cortes's second and third letters, it presents the city as a great circular world in the lake. It consists of neighborhoods, fortresses, ceremonial precincts, with manned canoes moving alongside a series of large causeways which lead toward the most prominent area—a great ceremonial center. The city seems to be divided into four quarters.

Internally, the city was a metropolis of noise, motion, exchange, and competition. As Edward Calnek has shown so well,[19] on a given day it was filled with lapidaries from Xochimilco, warriors from different towns, nobles, workers, war refugees, merchants, beggars, prostitutes, and sweatshop owners, all of whom participated in the activities of the city including market days, weddings, festivals, riots, trials, athletic contests, and ritual processions. In Cortes's account of the marketplace in Tlatelolco, we can almost hear the transactions:

The city has many squares where trading is done and markets are held continuously. There is also one square twice as big as that of Salamanca, with arcades all around, where more than sixty-thousand people come each day to buy and sell, and where every kind of merchandise produced in these lands is found . . . provisions as well as ornaments of gold and silver, lead, brass, copper, tin, stones, shells, bones, and feathers. They also sell lime, . . . adobe bricks . . . tiles. . . . There is a street where they sell game and birds of every species found in this land. . . . There are streets of herbalists . . . shops like apothecaries, . . . shops like barbers where they have their hair washed and shaved . . . There are also men like porters to carry loads. . . .they sell . . . honey, wax, and syrup made from maize canes . . . as many colors for painters as may be found in Spain . . . deerskins, maize both as grain and bread, chicken and fish pies . . . there is in this great square a very large building like a courthouse, where ten or twelve persons sit as judges. They preside over all that happens in the markets and sentence criminals.[20]

One of the most important documents available concerning the life in Tenochtitlán is the Codex Mendoza, which was painted in the native style with accompanying Spanish glosses in the 1540s.[21] The beautiful frontispiece is extremely helpful in understanding the religious importance of the capital. As in Cortes's map, we get the impression that the city was conceived and laid out as a symbol of the Aztec cosmos. In fact, the city's startling ceremonial center was the place where the Aztec vision of cosmic order and dynamics was expressed most clearly in stone, wood, color, sound, and drama. This was the religious center of the Aztec world and from the ceremonial theater, Aztec symbolic language, social character, and political authority flowed outward to influence more than four hundred towns and cities in central Mesoamerica. At the center of the precinct stood the Templo Mayor, which became the quintessential example of Aztec symbolization of cosmic order and political aggression. It is clear from an analysis of the painted and archaeological texts associated with the city's layout and ceremonial buildings that the Aztecs saw their city and empire as the center of the universe, contemporary and eternal. In the section that follows, I will focus on the evidence concerning Tenochtitlán, especially the Great Temple, to show how the Aztec city was a symbol of cosmic order reflecting a magnificently ordered universe held firmly at the capital and shrine of Huitzilopochtli. We will see that the city's spatial order was directed by three cosmological principles: (a) the symbolism of the center, (b) cardinal axiality, and (c) repetition in architecture of a creation myth.

THE FOUNDATION OF HEAVEN

As an Aztec poem reveals, Tenochtitlán was considered a majestic place:

> Proud of itself
> Is the city of Mexico-Tenochtitlán
> Here no one fears to die in war
> This is our glory
>
> This is Your Command
> Oh Giver of Life
> Have this in mind, Oh princes
> Who would conquer Tenochtitlán?
> Who could shake the foundation of heaven?[22]

The city was eulogized as a proud, fearless, and glorious place, an invincible center linking the world of men with the universal god, the Giver of Life. Conceived of as the "foundation of heaven" Tenochtitlán was the sacred center of cosmological space. This has the special significance of thirteen celestial levels and nine levels of the underworld. Vertical space was a great column of layers, each containing deities, forces, and colors. Tenochtitlán, as the foundation of heaven, was the point of union between celestial powers and the underworld. It joined parts of the cosmos together. In Aztec thought it had to be unshakable, for if it were disturbed or conquered, the cosmos would collapse.

Tenochtitlán's prestige as the center of horizontal space is reflected in the comment by Diego Durán's informants that the capital was the "root, the navel, and the heart of this whole worldly machine."[23] The Aztecs conceived of horizontal space as a cross or four-petaled flower with a jade bead in the middle. The surface of the earth was surrounded by a disk of sea water which extended to the four corners and rose to the heavens like a wall. At each of the four corners was a sacred tree with a sacred bird perched on top. Each quadrant of celestial space was supported by one of the principal gods who held up the heavens. This cosmic order was made when four creator deities dispersed the primordial waters, carved four roads to the center of the earth and lifted the sky. Tenochtitlán was situated in the center of this four-quartered universe and received the full benefit of the qualities, forces, and deities of cosmic space. It was the navel of the cosmos.

How Tenochtitlán gained this special position was told in the Aztec foundation myth, a version of which is embroidered on the flag of modern Mexico. According to their sacred history, the Aztecs emerged from Chicomoztoc, the "Seven Caves," which was on an island surrounded by a lagoon. Their patron deity, Huitzilopochtli, appeared to their shaman priest, commanding him to lead the people south to a place where the god would appear in the form of a great eagle perched on a blooming *nopal* growing from a rocky island in the middle of the lake. The Aztecs traveled south and beheld the omen, realizing that this was to be the place of their future city, which according to the divine promise would become "the queen and lady of all the others of the earth, and where we will receive all other kings and lords and to which they will come as to one supreme among all the others."[24] The Aztecs rejoiced at the sight of their new land and enthusiastically built the first shrine to the patron god Huitzilopochtli.

Another version of the foundation story reveals the fuller character of Tenochtitlán as the center of vertical space. Following the sighting of the eagle, one of the Chichimec priests dove into the lake and disappeared. Thinking him drowned, his companions returned to their camp. Soon, he returned to report that beneath the lake he talked with the old god of the earth, Tlaloc, and had received permission for the Aztecs to settle there. The city's existence was thereby sanctified by the forces of both the earth and the sky.

From these stories of the city's origin we can see that Tenochtitlán was conceived not merely as the new settlement, but as the royal city of the world to which the various royal authorities would come "as to one supreme among all the others." This special prestige and spatial conception is reflected in the frontispiece of the *Codex Mendoza*, which pictures the four-quartered city surrounding the eagle, *nopal,* stone, and a similar image above a giant Aztec shield with seven eagle-down feathers and seven arrows attached to it. This is the ideogram for "Place of Authority" and the painted image can be read "The Aztecs have arrived in Tenochtitlán, the Place of Authority." The persistence of Tenochtitlán's status as the center for royal authority in central Mesoamerica is demonstrated by the fact that when Cortes wrote his second letter in 1520 to the emperor of Spain, he reported that "all the lords of the land, who are vassals of the said Montezuma, have houses in the city and reside therein for a certain time of year."

During the two hundred years of Tenochtitlán's existence, an elaborate ceremonial center was constructed around the original shrine. This sacred precinct grew to be about 440 meters on each of its four sides. It contained more than seventy structures including schools for nobles, temple-pyramids, priests' dormitories, seven skull racks, a gladiatorial stone, two ball courts, a dance court, and administrative structures, all surrounded by a ten-foot high serpent wall. One of the most unusual examples of Tenochtitlán's status as the *axis mundi* of the empire can be seen in the special temple built by Moctezuma II for the purpose of housing all the images of deities from towns and cities throughout the Aztec Empire. All supernatural powers were integrated into the empire's center in order to control them.

NAUHCAMPA

The Aztecs divided their city into four quarters, referred to as *nauhcampa* or four directions of the winds. In fact, the Templo Mayor was located at the meeting point of the four major avenues that divided the city into four zones. This four-quartered plan was dictated by Huitzilopochtli, who ordered his *teomama* ("god-bearer") to divide the people into four major neighborhoods, "placing at the center the house that was built for my rest."[25] It is clear from archaeological evidence, the *Codex Mendoza*, and Cortes's map that the city was divided by four major highways which crossed at the base of the Templo Mayor and which drove straight out of the ceremonial precinct connecting the city with the mainland. These avenues, carefully aligned to conform to major celestial events, determined the directions of the city's many streets and canals.

This spatial order, as we have noted, imitated the Aztec concept of the four-quartered universe. What is equally important is that within this urban microcosm were smaller microcosms. Each of the city's four quarters, as Edward Calnek has shown, was a replica of the larger design in that each quadrant had its own central temple complex housing the deities of the group who inhabited that section. A marketplace and administrative center were part of each quarter's central precinct. Each quarter had its own sacred pivot reproducing the pattern that dominated the city as a whole. Further, within each quarter, the many barrios had their own local ceremonial precinct, repeating again the symbolism of the center.

It is becoming increasingly clear that the Aztec conception and practice of cardinal orientation, with the Templo Mayor as the great pivot, influenced virtually all aspects of the Aztec world. One example is the manner in which the immense tribute system was organized. Johanna Broda has shown that the Aztecs organized their entire tribute system into five great imperial regions, which corresponded to the five major sections of the horizontal cosmos: north, west, south, east, and center.[26] The influence of the cosmological pattern apparently extended into the palace of Moctezuma, which in the *Codex Mendoza* is divided into five principal rooms, with Moctezuma's throne room at the center and at the highest level. The *Codex Mendoza* image also suggests that the apex of Aztec government consisted of Moctezuma as the supreme ruler with four counselors assisting in his royal judgments. The Aztec perception of the universe as a four-cornered world surrounding the center influenced not only the spatial structure of their city, but also the tribute system, the image of the royal palace, and the balance of government.

The Templo Mayor as Imago Mundi

The most imposing and powerful structure in Tenochtitlán is the Templo Mayor. Its importance as the sacred center is reflected in the fact that it was enlarged frontally eleven times during the two hundred years of its existence. At the important moments of Aztec political expansion within and beyond the Valley of Mexico, the temple was expanded to symbolize, celebrate, and sanctify the manipulation of peoples, goods, and meanings. Recent excavations of the shrine's base and surrounding area have uncovered a stunning example of the architectural attempt to translate into a ceremonial structure the great cosmogonic acts that legitimated and inspired the central conceptions of Aztec life and authority.

In February 1978, electrical workers excavating a pit beneath the street behind the National Cathedral uncovered a massive oval stone more than 10 feet in diameter with a mint-condition image of an Aztec goddess carved on it. The image consisted of a decapitated and dismembered female goddess whose blood streams were depicted as precious fluid. Her striated head cloth, stomach, arms, and legs were encircled by serpents. A skull served as her belt buckle. She had earth monster faces on her knees, elbows, and ankles. Her sandals reveal

FIG. 13. Model of the Templo Mayor of Tenochtitlán with the circular temple of Quetzalcoatl in the foreground. The Templo Mayor contained twin temples to Huitzilopochtli and Tlaloc. Courtesy of Lawrence G. Desmond.

a royal figure and the iconography shows that this was the Aztec goddess Coyolxauhqui. As a result of this incredible discovery, Proyecto Templo Mayor was initiated to excavate the foundation of the entire structure. The Templo Mayor was the location of the great shrines to Huitzilopochtli and Tlaloc.

The myth of Huitzilopochtli, the patron god of the Aztecs who not only guided them to their new home but who was also the ferocious inspiration of their military expansion and the personification of their spirit, helps us understand the meaning of this image of Coyolxauhqui and the relationship it has to the Aztec vision of place.

On Coatepec ("Serpent Mountain"), the mother of the gods, Coatlicue ("Lady of the Serpent Skirt"), was sweeping out the temple. A ball of feathers "descended upon her" and she placed it in her bosom. Later she discovered it had disappeared and immediately she realized that she was pregnant. When the Huitznahua (the Southern Four Hundred, her children) heard of this development, they were outraged. Led by their sister, Coyolxauhqui, who was furious "as if bursting her heart," they decided to attack and kill their mother. Coyolxauhqui, "greatly excited and aroused the siblings to prepare for war." They "dressed themselves in war array with paper crowns, nettles, painted pipe streamers and bells" and marched in military order to attack their mother. Coatlicue was frightened for her life but a voice spoke to her from her womb, "Have no fear, already I know what I must do." The army, in full fury, rushed the mountain top and just at the moment of attack, the god Huitzilopochtli sprang from his mother's womb fully grown, dressed himself as a warrior and engaged his brothers and sisters in combat. He grabbed a serpent of fire, charged his sister in a rage, and decapitated her in one swipe: "Her body went falling below and it went crashing to pieces in various places, her arms, her legs, her body kept falling."[27] Huitzilopochtli then turned to the others, attacking them, and took "them into his destiny."

As the precise studies of Johanna Broda have shown, this myth "comprised several layers of symbolism, ranging from a purely historical explanation to one in terms of cosmovision and possible astronomical content." At one level, Huitzilopochtli's birth and victorious battle against the four hundred children represent the character of the solar region of the Aztecs in that the daily sunrise was viewed as a celestial war against the moon (Coyolxauhqui) and the stars (*centzon huitznahua*). Another version of the myth, found in the historical chronicles of Diego Durán and Alvarado Tezozomoc, tells the story with strong historical allusion and portrays two Aztec factions in ferocious battle. The leader of one group, Huitzilopochtli, defeats the warriors of a woman leader, Coyolxauh, and tears open their breasts and eats their hearts. Both versions tell of the origin of human sacrifice at the sacred place, Coatepec, during the rise of the Aztec nation and at the foundation of Tenochtitlán.[28]

It is important here to focus on the meaning of Coatepec in the drama. The Templo Mayor, called Coatepec by the Aztecs, consisted of a huge pyramid base supporting two temples, one to Huitzilopochtli and one to Tlaloc. Two grand stairways led up to the shrines. The Coyolxauhqui stone was found directly at the base of the stairway leading up to Huitzilopochtli's temple. On both sides of the stairway's base were two large grinning serpent heads. The image is clear. The Templo Mayor is the image of Coatepec or Serpent Mountain where the divine battle took place. Just as Huitzilopochtli triumphed at the top of the mountain, while his sister was dismembered and fell to pieces below, so Huitzilopochtli's temple and icon sat triumphantly at the top of Templo Mayor while the carving of the dismembered goddess lay far below. This drama of sacrificial dismemberment was vividly repeated in some of the offerings found around the Coyolxauhqui stone in which the decapitated skulls of young women were placed. The suggestion is that there was a ritual reenactment of the myth at the dedication of the stone sometime in the latter part of the fifteenth century. The Templo Mayor and its parts and related actions located at the heart of the city and empire represent the dramatic cosmic victory of Huitzilopochtli and the Aztecs over celestial and terrestrial enemies.[29]

AGE OF THE CENTER

While the Aztecs were under great pressure to conform to the style of life in the Lake Culture, they also displayed a capacity for innovation. Their innovative efforts focused on the structuring of what we have referred to as the cosmomagical basis of their city. We have seen the cosmomagical pattern of the city's spatial order. But perhaps the greatest example of Aztec inventiveness can be found in the new version of temporal dynamics which undergirded and flowed through the city and empire. The Aztec cosmogony by no means excluded spatial considerations—the two dimensions are usually interwoven—but it does appear that the Aztecs' sense of place was markedly influenced by their sense of time's pattern. Tenochtitlán was a "time-factored city," a city whose character and influence can be understood in relation to the grandiose story of its destiny and mission, encoded in the great calendar stone, more accurately called the Piedra del Sol.

In this regard, Alfonso Caso has written an important introductory book called *El Pueblo del Sol*.[30] The title is important because the Aztecs did not just have a sun god whom they worshiped, but they identified themselves deeply with the sun, more specifically with the fifth sun or era of cosmic history. This cosmic history was told in the *Leyenda de los Soles,* and the pattern of cosmological time reflected there defined and guided the imperial policies and purposes of the political state. That is, the Aztecs came to identify their own cosmic era, the fifth sun, with their national destiny.

The identification of cosmic motion with social history suggests that our understanding of cosmo-magical thought must be expanded. Previous discussion of city and symbol tended to emphasize spatial principles and ignore the impact of an intimate parallel between cosmic time and human time and the character and life of the city. In the case of Mesoamerica, it is necessary to give attention to the temporal aspects of archetypal thought and action and to realize that the Aztecs possessed not just what Berthelot and Wheatley called "astro-biological thought" but something more like "astro-historical thought." This kind of thought presupposed an intimate parallelism between the rhythms of the heavens and the politically and historically determined rhythms of life on earth. Mircea Eliade has pointed to the peculiar importance of historical consciousness in Mesoamerica, especially in relation to solar cults:

> If you consider that, on the other side of the Atlantic, the solar religion was developed only in Peru and Mexico, only, that is, among the two civilized peoples of America, the only two who attained any level of real political organization, then you cannot help discerning a certain connection between the predominance of sun religions and what I may call "historic" destinies. It could be said that where "history is on the march" thanks to kings, heroes, or empires, the sun is supreme.[31]

This connection was vital for the Aztecs who identified the end of the cosmos with the end of their supremacy. In the fact of this identification, the Aztecs construed a new intention in the passage of cosmic time.

The Aztec conception of cosmic destiny appears in over twenty variants of the *Leyenda de los Soles* which were collected in central Mexico after the conquest. Wayne Elzey, a historian of religions, has shown how this widespread story of the repeated creations and destructions of the cosmos functioned as a dynamically structured paradigm for the organization of Aztec life. Rituals, the calendar, sculpture, and Aztec beliefs were permeated with the principles of temporal succession embedded in the myth, which were dynamically carved in the Piedra del Sol. Here and in other versions, it is told that the cosmos has passed through four ages and that the Aztec world constitutes the fifth. Each of these cosmic ages was destroyed in a universal cataclysm from which that age received its name. The first age, *nahui ocelotl* ("4 Jaguar"), was destroyed when jaguars devoured all living beings. The second age, *nahui ehecatl* ("4 Wind"), ended when destructive winds blew the people away. The third age, *nahui quiyahuitl* ("4 Rain of Fire"), ended when fire from the sky burned everyone to death. The people of the fourth age, *nahui atl* ("4 Water"), were drowned in a great deluge. The Aztecs live in the fifth age, called *nahui ollin* ("4 Motion"), and would be destroyed by great earthquakes. This story of cosmic time communicates the conviction that universal change is abrupt, total, destructive, and inevitable. It would appear that the Aztecs felt themselves doomed to repeat the preordained pattern of total destruction of previous ages. But Elzey has advanced our understanding of Aztec thought by perceiving that there were "two cosmogonies" in the myth of the suns and that they were graphically reproduced on the calendar stone. The first cosmogony, perhaps the one inherited by the Aztecs, presented time as an endless series of cosmic destructions, the repetition of the archetype of cosmic collapse. Each age was identified with its destructive force and led to another age in which the most important event was its destruction. But there was a second cosmogony which presented a different view of destiny. The fifth sun has a unique internal structure which transformed the notion of the fifth sun as the fifth in a sequence of suns to the fifth sun as the age of the center. In the age of the center, the energies and characteristics of each of the previous ages was internalized within the fifth age. The design of the encapsulation of previous cosmic times was on the Piedra del Sol, where four previous ages surrounded the present age as well as making up part of its structure. Elzey writes:

> All this points to the uniqueness and ingenuity of the Mexican system of world ages. The Fifth Sun is the synthesis and "center" of the four "earlier" ages. Each of the first four Suns forms one part of or aspect of the contemporary Sun. The present age, in its internal structure, is constituted by the ordered and continuous recapitulation of the other Suns, one after the other, and the sequence of the past ages becomes the model or paradigm for the organization of contemporary time and space.[32]

In other words, the Aztec age of the center was not only located in the center of the mythical design carved on the Piedra del Sol, but it was the age in which all of history, space, color, and reality was centered, encapsulated, and made alive in a regenerative way. This transformation of destiny's pattern meant that the fifth sun was the final, ultimate sun. It was no longer subject to the great law of continuous change through destructive catastrophe. In Elzey's view, for the Aztecs, a sixth sun was inconceivable. Instead the "Sun 'Four Motion,' is both the final age of the world (in linear terms) and the continuous repetition of the ages (in cyclical terms)."[33] The Aztec city was conceived as the center of universal space and time.

THE ELABORATE USES OF QUETZALCOATL

It is clear that Aztec Tenochtitlán was the site of a new design of cosmic order and national destiny. The elites took traditions which went back at least to the Toltec kingdom and used them to sanctify their own empire's development while they also manipulated segments of the cosmological and historical tradition in order to place themselves and their deity Huitzilopochtli at the center of universal space and time. In this new setting, Quetzalcoatl was conceived of as one of the supernatural and cultural patrons who legitimated important segments of Mexica society. These segments included the populace, the priesthood, kingship, and, in one case, the city itself. Quetzalcoatl was not *the* patron of Tenochtitlán, for there is much evidence that Huitzilopochtli was Tenochtitlán's patron and that Aztec kings had intimate ties to Tezcatlipoca. But there is important, if puzzling, evidence that even within the normative order of patronage associated with these deities, Quetzalcoatl continued to be a major source of inspiration and sanctification of institutions and people. This persistence derives from Quetzalcoatl's status as a creator. As a god and god-man, Quetzalcoatl created parts of the cosmos and culture. The symbol's power to legitimize stems from this creative capacity.

One version of the foundation of Tollan Tenochtitlán includes the important reference to Quetzalcoatl's association with the first shrine to Huitzilopochtli. The text states that after the omen of Huitzilopochtli appeared, the Aztecs hurried to build "a small shrine in honor of Huitzilopochtli [made of] grass and rushes of Quetzalcoatl, next to the cactus of the eagle and the spring."[34] This rare joining of Quetzalcoatl and Huitzilopochtli reflects the tie of the new city's patron god to the patron god of the archetypal city. While this alignment is not overtly expressed elsewhere, its appearance here fits with other things we know about Toltec influence.

In another text we see Quetzalcoatl's role as patron expressed in references to his paternal creativity of the citizens of the city. Following a long-winded speech by a ruler, recorded in the *Florentine Codex*, a dignitary speaking for the citizens responds, "the sons, the noble sons, precious green stones, descendants of Topiltzin Quetzalcoatl . . . those under his spell will receive thy words . . . for they are his noble descendants."[35] This paternal creativity was extended to individuals, as demonstrated in a handful of passages which tell how

FIG. 14. Quetzalcoatl in his wind god aspect as depicted in the Codex Magliabecchiano. Note the conch shell buckle, wind god mask, and four-quarter design of the shield.

rulers, noblemen, merchants, and midwives ritually address a new-born baby. They say, "verily Topiltzin Quetzalcoatl has cast thee, perforated thee." And in an extended speech addressing a new mother after delivery: "Here the truth is verily now, here in the humble mound of dirt in the humble reed enclosure, the master, our lord the creator, the master Quetzalcoatl, flaketh off a precious necklace, placeth a precious feather, here on your neck, on your bosom . . . he placeth a precious necklace, the incomparable, wonderful, the precious, the priceless, the rare."[36] It is as if the Aztec children are equivalent in some way to the Toltec creations eulogized so energetically in the portrait of Tollan.

The most outstanding example of Quetzalcoatl's influence in Aztec institutions was in the area of the priesthoods, which had immense influence in Aztec society. While the influence of the priesthood has often been understated, it is actually difficult to overstate the manner in which priestly ideas and authority permeated so many activities in the capital. Within Tenochtitlán and throughout the empire, the priesthood was hierarchically organized with the highest echelons ministering in the capital. Though the many towns and cities had autonomous sacerdotal organizations, Tenochtitlán's priestly order exercised some cultic control over the other towns. Largely from the upper classes, the priests, both male and female, were either full-time or rotational in their participation. All priestly activity originated in the priestly schools called *calmecacs*, which were usually associated with certain major temples. In these institutions the priests practiced an austere and pious discipline, which included education in the sacred traditions, ritual worship, and penitential bloodletting from different parts of the body. Elaborate rules of dress, diet, and use of ritual paraphernalia were mastered along with highly complex calendrical systems of meaning.

One thing is clear—Quetzalcoatl was the archetype for the highest priestly orders. In Tenochtitlán, there were two supreme Quetzalcoatl priests, one in charge of rituals at Tlaloc's temple and the other in charge of rituals at the shrine of Huitzilopochtli. The occupant of the Quetzalcoatl office was "respected like a lord." It is told that the Quetzalcoatl priests were "set apart and chosen to be a keeper of the god. The chief and great judges and all the nobles chose him and gave him the name Quetzalcoatl." Sahagún writes of these figures, "among these priests the best were chosen to become the supreme pontiffs, who were called *quequetzalcoa*, which means successors of quetzalcoatl."[37] They were considered "divine of heart."

These high priests, described as "having an equal level with Mutezuma,"[38] and their immediate subordinates had control over the transmission of sacred knowledge and the large-scale construction of ceremonial precincts. The priests were in charge of the complex, esoteric religious wisdom which they enlarged upon and taught to all the leaders of their communities. The mythical systems, symbols, rhetoric, dogma, and moral and cosmological teachings were in their care. The priests were in charge of perceiving, conceiving, and explaining cosmological convictions and supernatural events and forces for the entire society. But their authority extended beyond the realm of sacred education. The continual construction, reconstruction, and repair of the ceremonial buildings was under their direction. This meant they had influence over crafts, industries, architects, and sculptors. Also, the common and esoteric ritual paraphernalia including statues, idols, knives, and vessels were made and distributed under their direction. Within the ceremonial precincts and in all parts of the empire, they choreographed and directed the complex and intertwined ritual system that served to insure Aztec stability, expansion, and cosmic motion. It is also important to note that the Quetzalcoatl priest played an influential role in all major political decisions including wars, alliances, marriages, and dynastic ceremonies.

The alignment of the Aztec priesthood to Quetzalcoatl is also reflected by the fact that the deity, sometimes referred to as Topiltzin Quetzalcoatl, was Lord of the Calmecacs. When a lord or nobleman wished to dedicate his child to *calmecac* education and the vocation of the priesthood, the child was taken to the priests' house where prayers were offered up to "the lord Topiltzin Quetzalcoatl . . . who will require of your jewel, your quetzal feather" to have "awe in his heart, compassion and bravery."[39] It also appears that Quetzalcoatl had some special importance for Tenochtitlán's nobles and may have been considered the patron of the noble class. This possibility is enhanced when we are told in book 4 of the *Florentine Codex* that the day 1 Reed, which was Quetzalcoatl's birth date, was feared by the nobles of the city who made special offerings to Topiltzin Quetzalcoatl's image in the *calmecacs* of Tenochtitlán. It is possible that Quetzalcoatl had become the god of the upper class of the capital.

There are also some tantalizing references to Quetzalcoatl's role as the patron of the ruling lineage of Tenochtitlán. The evidence is not consistent and it is sometimes retrospective, but it cannot be ignored. Consider the report given to Bernal Díaz del Castillo that Moctezuma considered the Spaniards to be of "his own lineage" and that their coming was "foretold by his ancestors." Further, we have Motolinía commenting that "Quetzalcoatl was the antecedent of Moctezuma and all other lords of Mexico."[40] More important is the coronation speech given by the king of Tezcoco, Nezahaulpilli, on the occasion of King Tizoc's ascension to the throne. The new king is told that the throne was created by *zenactl y nacxitl quetzalcoatl* ("1 Reed, the fourfold Quetzalcoatl") in whose name Huitzilopochtli and Acamapichtli exercised authority. The throne, he is told, does not belong to him but to the ancestors and it will eventually be returned to them.[41]

Recently Eloise Quiñones Keber has seen the connection between the ritual activities of kings at dynastic ceremonies and the ritual traditions created by Topiltzin Quetzalcoatl in Tula. She writes, after close analysis of the sources: "the types of self-sacrifice and penance associated with Topiltzin Quetzalcoatl in the text were performed by rulers as part of dynastic ceremonies."[42] One example is quite obvious and deserves mention here. Moctezuma II is told by Nezahualpilli that his ritual bath, bleedings, and offerings to the gods should begin at the first appearance of the morning star in the sky. This can be understood as the manifestation of Quetzalcoatl's influence in the heavens marking the onset of ritual attention by the king who is his representative.

Quetzalcoatl's significance as a patron of kings is suggested more directly in an amusing scene which takes place on the occasion of the unveiling of the king's statue in the gardens of Chapultepec. The *tlatoani's* entourage is admiring the wonderful visage of their lord when the *tlatoani* states that it is written that when Topiltzin Quetzalcoatl departed, he had his image carved in wood and stone. The custom of carving the images of kings goes back to the Toltec sovereign who is the image of the archetypal king. This custom was a form of insuring legitimacy of the throne.

QUETZALCOATL AS SUBVERSIVE GENEALOGY

We have argued that the myths, stories, and images of Quetzalcoatl in Tollan, taught and symbolized in various institutions of the Aztec Empire, functioned as a sacred model for the exercise of power and authority. To understand this argument more fully, and to provide a means of approaching Quetzalcoatl's ironic history, we employ Victor Turner's notions about root paradigms. We propose to show that the Quetzalcoatl tradition operated not only as a sanction for aristocratic privilege, but also as a subversive genealogy.

In his writings on the dramatic influence of symbols in social action, Turner contends that "social action of various kinds acquires form through the metaphors and paradigms in their actors' heads." These paradigms are explicitly taught or absorbed through everyday experience in society. Of major influence are the culture's root paradigms, which operate at both conscious and unconscious levels and contain the "irreducible life stances" toward the crucial questions of life, death, authority, and the continuity of the species. These complex models for action emerge most forcefully in life crisis and are employed to deal with threats to deep social and symbolic issues. Turner writes:

> These root paradigms are not systems of univocal concepts, logically arrayed; they are not, so to speak, precision tools of thought. Nor are they stereotyped guidelines for ethical, esthetic, or conventional action. Indeed, they go beyond the cognitive and even the moral to the existential implicitness, and metaphor, for in the stress of vital action, firm definitional outlines become blurred by the encounter of emotionally charged wills. . . . One cannot then escape the presence of their consequences.[43]

The Quetzalcoatl tradition provided a cultural root paradigm for Aztec elites in the sanctification and expansion of their city and religion. While Huitzilopochtli's story provided the stereotyped guidelines for conventional action, Quetzalcoatl's power stemmed from his metaphorical character as the sovereign who manifested the maximal expression of the sacred. But as Judith Shklar has noted, we must focus on the whole sequence of deeds in a sacred genealogy to be able to perceive the full consequences of their paradigmatic presence.[44] In the case of Quetzalcoatl's end in Tollan, this presents us with a startling conflict, especially the episodes of Topiltzin Quetzalcoatl's loss of authority, the breaking of his kingly honor, and the fall of his kingdom. Since Quetzalcoatl was indeed a deep model of action for Aztec kings and priests, then this side of the paradigm must also have influenced the character, self-understanding, and destiny of those elites. The Quetzalcoatl tradition provides a model which is an example of the weakness inherent in Toltec sovereignty and which also functions as a model for the abdication of kingship.

THE KING WHO FAILED

The majority of sources that contain a version of the Topiltzin Quetzalcoatl of Tollan tale refer to the fall of Tula and the flight of Quetzalcoatl. Although only three contain elaborate accounts of these enigmatic events, they do so with such detail and general consistency and in such early sources that we may safely say that these events were widely known and most likely taught in the *calmecacs* of Tenochtitlán and the Aztec Empire. Following the period of abundance, stability, and expansion, Tollan comes to a miserable end in the following sequence: (*a*) an antagonist appears—a sorcerer usually identified with Tezcatlipoca—who organizes a small movement against Quetzalcoatl (*b*) partially around the issue of human sacrifice, and (*c*) through a series of tricks and magical deceptions, (*d*) he gets the priest-king roaring drunk, whereupon (*e*) Quetzalcoatl has some kind of sexual encounter with his sister, a high priestess, and (*f*) wakes from the debauch heartbroken; having realized that his authority has been betrayed, Quetzalcoatl decides to leave Tollan with some followers, resulting in (*g*) the immediate fall of the city or its waning over a period of years. One important aspect is the transforming power of Tezcatlipoca, the enemy magician. Quetzalcoatl appears thoroughly whipped and leaves in disgrace and great sorrow. The *Juan Cano Relación*, one of the earliest and most reliable primary sources, tells us that after Quetzalcoatl ruled in Tollan, which was the "head of a dominion like Mexico was when the Spaniards came,"[45] a religious controversy broke out concerning the appropriate victims for sacrifice. Quetzalcoatl had designated quail, butterflies, snakes, and large grasshoppers for sacrifice but the gods Huitzilopochtli and Tezcatlipoca demanded human victims and forced Topiltzin to leave Tollan with a number of his followers. This confrontation is described elaborately in the *Anales de Cuauhtitlán*. A large portion of it is included here.

> And it is told and related that many times during the life of Quetzalcoatl certain sorcerers attempted to shame him into making human offerings, into sacrificing humans. But he would not consent. He would not comply, because he greatly loved his subjects who were Toltecs. The offerings he made were always snakes, birds, and butterflies. And it is related, they say, that he thereby angered the sorcerers, so that they took to mocking and taunting him. And the sorcerers asserted and willed that Quetzalcoatl be vexed and put to flight.
>
> Then they tell how Quetzalcoatl departed: it was when he refused the sorcerers' decree that he make human offerings, that he sacrifice humans. Thereupon the sorcerers deliberated among themselves, they whose names were Tezcatlipoca, Ihuimecatl, and Toltecatl. "He must leave his city, for we shall live here," they said. And they said, "Let us make pulque. We will have him drink it, to corrupt him, so that he will no longer perform his sacraments."
>
> And then Tezcatlipoca said, "I, I say we must give him his body to see!" . . . Tezcatlipoca went first, carrying a two-sided mirror the size of an outstretched hand, concealed in a wrapping.[46]

Following some clever maneuvering on Tezcatlipoca's part, he manages to get past the palace guard and ministers. He shows Quetzalcoatl his body: "the eyelids were greatly swollen, the eye sockets deeply sunk, the face much distended all over and bilious." Shocked by his own image, Quetzalcoatl decides to stay hidden from his people. An artist is sent to him by the magicians in order to make the king a mask of turquoise, serpent's teeth, and beautiful plumage. Looking in the mirror, Quetzalcoatl felt renewed admiration and abandoned his refuge. The sorcerers gathered and made a witch's stew and "in only four days they prepared, then decanted, the pulque." Returning to Tollan with the pulque and stew, they offer the pulque to Quetzalcoatl, who refuses. Then,

> "Taste it with the tip of your finger. It's strong, it's newly made." Quetzalcoatl tasted it with the tip of his finger and finding it good, said, "I would drink more, grandfather. Three more draughts!" They answered him, "Four more shall you drink." Then they gave him even his fifth saying, "This is your sacrament."
>
> They made themselves utterly drunk. . . . And Quetzalcoatl said joyously, "bring me my elder sister Quetzalpetlatl, that we may be drunk together". . . . His pages repaired to the place

where she fasted, to Mount Nonohualca, saying, "Quetzalpetlatl, penitent lady, my daughter! We have come to fetch you.
The priest Quetzalcoatl awaits you. Go and be with him." She
said, "very well, grandfather page. Let us go." And arriving
she seated herself next to Quetzalcoatl, whereupon she was
given the pulque, four draughts and one more, the fifth, as her
portion. Thus Ihuimecatl and Toltecatl made both of them
drunk. Then to Quetzalcoatl's sister they presented a song,
singing

> "Where now is your home,
> My sister, my Quetzalpetlatl?
> Oh it's here, where you tipple!
> Ayn ya, ynya yn, ye an!"

Having made themselves drunk, no more did they say, "We
are fasting." And then they went down to the river no more.
No more did they puncture themselves with thorns. Nothing
more did they do at the break of day. And at dawn they were
filled with remorse, their spirits were heavy. Thereupon Quetzalcoatl said, "Unfortunate me!" Then he raised the lament
he'd composed for his going away. And he sang:

> "No more.
> The days will be counted no more in my house and it
> shall be empty."

Then his pages weeping sing,

> "No more we delight in him,
> Him our noble one,
> Him Quetzalcoatl
> No more thy precious crown!
> The bleeding thorns are broken.
> We mourn for him,
> We weep alas."[47]

Then a funeral urn is carved at Quetzalcoatl's request. He is placed
in it and lies there for four days. Feeling discomfort, he rises and
departs with his followers.

Another version tells this episode with emphasis on the collapse
of the kingdom. Following the description of the great kingdom of
Tollan, three sorcerers make their way into the ailing Quetzalcoatl's
quarters and urge him to drink a strange potion. He drinks it, is
cured, and is urged to drink again.

And then he drank once again, then he made himself drunk.
Then he wept, he was stricken with sorrow. Quetzalcoatl was
overwhelmed. His heart was broken. He could put it from his
mind no longer, but lived in anguish; he lived with his remorse.

Immediately following these events, Tollan begins to suffer a number of attacks by strange visitors and sorcerers who kill masses of the people and upset the entire social order. When the narrative returns to Quetzalcoatl, he is preparing to leave the crumbling city.

> Behold also how the Toltecs were cursed: It is said that the food turned bitter, utterly bitter and bitter to the core: it could no longer be placed on the lips. The Toltecs indeed had been tricked.
>
> . . . .
>
> And many another evil was done to the Toltecs that Tollan might be destroyed. And because it was so, Quetzalcoatl suffered. He grieved. Then he remembered that he was to go, that he was to leave his city of Tollan. Then he made his preparations.[48]

This is a very different Topiltzin Quetzalcoatl and Tollan, to say the least. One almost suspects he is reading about the fall of Tenochtitlán to the Spaniards! It could be said that Quetzalcoatl's opposite, the other side of the paradigm, has appeared here. We see an insecure, vain, weak, stupid, incestuous king who cannot deal with his own reflection and gives away Tollan to a powerful, more astute Tezcatlipoca. This is not the founder, but someone utterly confounded by the riddle of his own reflection and identity, and unfounded by his drunkenness and sexuality. Now the "pattern" for priest and king is complex—if not ironic—in its contradictions and comic-tragic contours. If we take seriously Turner's contention that cultural models influence social action and remember that Quetzalcoatl was the archetype for sovereign authority in the Aztec city, then it appears there is a critical weakness in the undergirding of the pivot of the four quarters. The message that comes from this side of the paradigm is that sovereigns in Mexico may become confused about their own identities and participate in the renunciation of their authority and the security of their city!

The instability of order appears at two levels. At the level of the ruler we see that while Quetzalcoatl reigns over a period of political integration, human creativity, and cosmic harmony, the destiny of the political state is total collapse initiated by the betrayal of ritual vows, confusion of identity, the disgrace of kingship, and trickery by an enemy. Tollan falls because Quetzalcoatl loses not only his piety but also his sense of authority. At the cosmological level there is the shift from orderly motion of the cosmos to its chaotic and pathetic disintegration. Could it be that this paradigm functioned as a subversive genealogy in Tenochtitlán?

CENTER AND PERIPHERY

Until now we have seen abundant evidence that the Aztec city was structured by a series of meanings and activities associated with what has been called the symbolism of the center. But it is becoming clearer that the usual way historians of religions conceive of the category of the center does not constitute a thorough interpretive approach for understanding Tenochtitlán's history and meaning. A people's capital city, which is their exemplary center,[49] inevitably reflects the intertwining of symbol and society, ontology and history. In this regard it is vitally important, in the Aztec case at least, to be aware not just of the integrating powers of the capital and its great shrine but also to acknowledge and interpret the impulses of expansion of a sacred center and the results. We have seen that this process of the expansion of Aztec sacred space paralleled the development of Tenochtitlán from the spot of the *nopal* to the shrine of Huitzilopochtli and spread to the four quarters of the city and eventually the organization of tribute payments for the empire. But it is also necessary to understand the historical, social, and symbolic tension that developed between the centripetal character of the capital and the centrifugal tendencies of the political state. For instance, Edward Shils has shown that great centers are ruled by elites whose authority has

> an expansive tendency . . . a tendency to expand the order it represents towards the saturation of territorial space. . . . Rulers, simply out of their possession of authority and the impulses which it generates wish to be obeyed and they wish to obtain assent to the order they symbolically embody.[50]

Yet these impulses of expansion will inevitably lead to involvement in peripheral and competing traditions of value, meaning, and authority. This sometimes results in tentative arrangements of power and authority between the center and the periphery. Though peripheral systems and their symbols may be weaker within a hierarchy of an empire, they nevertheless have the potential to threaten the major center with disbelief, reversal, and rebellion. It is within this kind of situation that W. B. Yeats's famous line has direct relevance: "Things fall apart; the center cannot hold." As suggested in previous chapters, ancient Mexican kingdoms were arranged around what Stanley Tambiah calls "pulsating galactic polities," that is, kingdoms in which the capital cities were in constant tension and antagonism with the surrounding allied and enemy settlements. The exemplary centers were frequently challenged by other centers, deflated by ecological crisis, and disrupted by social rebellion. This resulted in the continual relocation of capital cities within the central plateau as well as an unstable understanding of authority.[51] This is an important point because it suggests that centers not only dominate and control peripheries, but that peripheries influence and sometimes transform centers, even a center so dominant as Tenochtitlán.

With these patterns of influence in mind, let us focus briefly on the character of Tenochtitlán's hegemony in its final decades. Then we will revisit the Templo Mayor, utilizing the evidence from its recent excavation to show how the peripheries of Aztec Mexico influenced the capital. We will see that threats from the Aztec past as well as from the competing traditions of their contemporary world transformed the city and the Templo Mayor, which sanctified it.

Tenochtitlán: Domination and Crisis

It is truly astounding that by the time of Moctezuma Xocoyotzin's coronation in 1502, just three quarters of a century after the Aztecs led the Triple Alliance in a total defeat of Azcapotzalco, Tenochtitlán had become, in Friedrich Katz's words, "a world city in the true sense." The line of Tlatoque, along with their growing military aristocracy, organized a series of institutions which worked to intensify the centripetal power of Tenochtitlán. A complex irrigation and dike system, originally constructed by the city-state of Tezcoco's amazing King Nezahualcoyotl, had been brought under Tenochtitlán's control and extended to insure the effective control of the hydraulic power of the lake. This development marked an internal reversal of status among the powers of the Triple Alliance where early in its domination of the Lake Culture, Tezcoco had been the more mature and powerful center. But the power of the *chinampas* to produce surplus food for Tenochtitlán (Tezcoco was in the salt lake and did not have as direct an access to these surpluses) led to a population explosion and these increased numbers along with the growing military influence of Tenochtitlán guaranteed the growth of its power beyond that of Tezcoco.

Equally important in Tenochtitlán's rise to dominance in the lake was its tie to the sister city of Tlatelolco. This center had established its hegemony over the exchange system of the plateau and had challenged Tenochtitlán for the dominant position in the lake complex. Tlatelolco tended to drain the prizes, booty, and rewards received by the soldiers of Tenochtitlán's growing army during their expanding war campaigns into its own coffers. Eventually, however, this war effort was turned against Tlatelolco, which lost its independence and had an Aztec military leader forced into the office of *tlatoani*. It became a part of the ever expanding Tenochtitlán.

The Aztecs successfully integrated other city-states in the Valley of Mexico through the vigorous military campaigns of its elite warriors, insuring the steady expansion of tribute payments to the capital.

This expansion by conquest included a number of city-states beyond the central valley and by 1500 Tenochtitlán led the Triple Alliance which had organized over 15 million people inhabiting at least 38 provinces.

But the hegemony of Tenochtitlán was delicate and involved several devastating setbacks. In 1450, a crippling famine jolted the flourishing alliance. Intense economic, political, and theological reforms were undertaken to interpret and transform the situation. Large-scale hydraulic works were planned and executed to secure a sound water supply. The Aztec priesthood accomplished a reevaluation of the ritual responsibilities of the state religion in order to influence the celestial powers to bring abundance to the kingdom.[52] Conquests of enemy settlements increased and stricter political alliances were drawn to insure that the tribute system would serve the needs of elites.

This restructuring was further shaken by at least three threatening developments during the last decades of Aztec rule. Aztec conquests of potentially lucrative tributary settlements diminished. The influx of tribute goods ceased to expand and the internal use of luxury items was restricted. Then, major Aztec military campaigns against the independent kingdoms of Tlaxcala and Michoacan ended in defeat. The great rewards for expensive military action failed to develop and the Aztecs were paying out more than they were taking in. Finally came an even more crushing blow. In the third year of Moctezuma's reign a disastrous famine hit the central plateau. Not only was the general population starving but the structure and security of the elite order of the government was seriously threatened. Accustomed to living in a state of high luxury, the royal elite and the meritorious elite faced the humiliating necessity of changing their life-styles. The famine was a tremendous blow to the entire society, which had been deeply involved for decades in preventing such a shortage of food and goods. Now at the supposed apex of Aztec history the entire population was looking starvation and disaster in the face—for the upper class a radical reversal of their access to quality goods seemed necessary. In this situation, a crisis of confidence developed in parts of the population and more oppressive measures were employed against tributary communities.

As an antidote to this crisis, the office of *tlatoani* and the person of Moctezuma were elevated to a new, more inaccessible rung on the royal ladder, the rung of full divinity. Previously, the temporary successor to the king-god Quetzalcoatl of Tollan, Moctezuma now becomes a king-god in his own right. The accounts of Díaz del Castillo and Cortes both contain descriptions of the protocol around Moctezuma in which people are not allowed to gaze on him or eat with the divine ruler. Cortes, in particular, writes:

His personal service was equally magnificent. . . . Everyday he changed his garments four times, always putting on new clothes which were never worn more than once. The nobles always entered his palace barefoot, and those who were bidden to present themselves before him did so with bowed head and eyes fixed on the ground, their whole bearing expressing reverence; nor would they when speaking to him lift their eyes to his face, all of which was done to show their profound humility and respect. When Moctezuma went abroad, which was seldom, all who were with him or whom he met in the street turned away their faces and avoided looking at him, some of them prostrating themselves on the ground until he had passed. One of the nobles always preceded him bearing three long thin rods for the purpose, as I think, of intimating the royal presence.[53]

Moctezuma was known as Cemanahuac Tlatoani ("Ruler of the World")! But this elevation of the supreme ruler should come to us as no surprise. It is part of a decision made decades earlier when the Aztecs, in constructing their urban society and seeking to base it on a sacred genealogy, established access to a figure who was clearly a god-king. "Quetzalcoatl was looked upon as a god. He was worshiped and prayed to in former times in Tollan, and there his temple stood."[54] The Aztecs had set the stage for such a development in the social structure of their sacred city when they rooted their royal line through Acamapichtli to Toltec symbols. The royal elite was carrying out the logic of that genealogical decision: descending from a god-king, their *tlatoani* was also a god-king! Indeed, the political significance of such a decision by their ancestors was soon to be revealed in Tenochtitlán.

TEMPLO MAYOR: CENTER AND PERIPHERY

Recent discoveries at the Templo Mayor excavations reveal that the shrine's history and symbolism reflected the struggles that went on between the center and the periphery in the Aztec Empire. For instance, the Templo Mayor was the symbolic center for the extensive tribute network of the Aztec Empire. Not only was the Great Temple the material expression of Aztec religious thought, it was also the symbolic instrument for the collection and redistribution of wealth and goods from all over the empire. As the Aztec conquests proceeded to incorporate scores of these city-states into their empire, tribute payments to Tenochtitlán became enormous. The city's prestige and wealth depended to a large degree on these enormous amounts of tribute payments, which flowed into the capital and insured economic superiority for the royal house, the nobles, and the common citizens. Significantly, more than 90 incredible offerings of symbolic tribute have been uncovered at strategic points around the base of the pyramid at every stage of its construction. These offerings contain sea shells, finely carved masks, statues of deities, sacrificed humans and animals, knives, and jewelry. Over 80 percent of these objects are from distant and frontier provinces under Aztec domination. Their presence in the heart of the city displays the attempt to integrate valued and symbolic objects from the periphery of Aztec control into the foundation of the central shrine as a means of sanctifying the conquests and the expansion of Aztec sacred social order. For instance, a number of offerings contain both large and small shells, sometimes oriented toward the south, which were brought from the distant sea coasts. It seems clear that they represent the powers of fertility associated with the great bodies of water. These powers are also represented in the crocodiles and swordfish buried at the temple. Another meaning of these burials relates to the fact that the Aztec called the terrestrial world *Cemanahuac Tenocha Tlalpan*, which means the "land surrounded by water is Tenocha territory." In this light, the offerings of the shells and aquatic animals demonstrate the Aztec desire to incorporate the powers from the edges of their world into the sacred shrine. The fertility symbols from the periphery were buried at the center.

This integration of peripheral places is elaborated in one of the most stunning discoveries to date, the offering of more than two hundred finely carved masks in one burial in front of Tlaloc's shrine. These masks have noble, frightening, awe-inspiring faces carved in many different settlements under Aztec domination. They display different artistic styles, emphasize different facial features, and were apparently offered as a special tribute to the Great Temple for some auspicious ceremonial event during the latter part of the fifteenth century. They are not only offerings but also signs of subjugation. Valuable objects, perhaps symbolic faces of different allies or frontier communities, were buried at the world's axis. There is one stunning temporal aspect to this collection because the most remarkable mask is a small, mint-condition Olmec jade mask that was probably carved a full 2000 years before the first of the temple's eleven facades was constructed. In this precious Olmec treasure we see the Aztec concern to integrate the symbols of an ancient civilization into its shrine.

TWIN TEMPLES
We remember that when the Chichimec tribes, from whom the Aztecs emerged as conquerors, came into the central plateau during the thirteenth century, they encountered a world that had long been dominated by complex state societies. It is important to understand that while the Aztecs did evolve from an insignificant political group

into an imperial people in less than two hundred years, the institutions they inherited had been in existence for over 1500 years. Complex state societies with great capital cities dominating lesser cities and communities had been the order of life in central Mesoamerica since the beginning of the first millennium after Christ.

The magnificent cities of Teotihuacán, Tollan, and Cholollan, with their great pyramids, imposing stone sculpture, complex social structures, long-distance trade systems, religious iconography, and sacred genealogies for kings, intimidated and inspired the Aztecs to measure up to and integrate the Classic heritage. For instance, the truly monumental four-quartered city of Teotihuacán ("House of the Gods") was revered as the place where the present cosmogonic era was created. Aztec kings went periodically to the ancient city to perform sacrifices and reestablish ties to the divine ancestors and sanctity which dwelt there. The Toltec civilization of the Great Tollan and the cult of Quetzalcoatl was viewed as the golden age of artistic excellence, agricultural abundance, ritual renewal, and the place where giants had perceived the divine plan for human society. As Esther Pasztory has shown, these cities "cast a giant shadow over the Aztecs who could not help feeling small and inferior by contrast."[55] Plagued by a sense of illegitimacy and cultural inferiority, the Aztecs made shrewd and strenuous efforts to encapsulate the sanctified traditions of the past into their shrine. This is reflected in the fact that the Templo Mayor was a twin temple, a form invented by the Aztecs and their contemporaries. The Templo Mayor supported a great shrine to Tlaloc, and one to Huitzilopochtli. On the obvious level, Tlaloc's presence represents the great forces of water and moisture which were absolutely critical for agricultural conditions of the lake and surrounding lands. Elaborate ceremonies were held, involving the sacrifice of children to Tlaloc, in order to bring the seasonal rains to the land. But Tlaloc's prominence at the shrine displays other Aztec concerns as well. Tlaloc was the ancient god of the land who had sustained the great capitals of pre-Aztec Mexico. He represented a prior structure of reality in a cultural and supernatural sense. He had given permission to the Aztecs to settle in the lake, and therefore, he was the indigenous deity who adopted the newcomers. As a means of legitimating their shrine and city, the Aztecs were forced to integrate the great supernatural and cultural authority of the past into the Templo Mayor. Also, Tlaloc was the god of the peasant masses. He appeared in the shrines of local peasant communities and insured the fertility of their fields and the continuity of their work each year and over generations. His position at the Templo Mayor also represents the integration of peasant religion into the Aztec state shrine.

The practice of integrating the images of the great cultural past is also reflected in the recent discovery of an elaborately painted Chac Mool in front of one of the earliest Templo Mayor constructions on Tlaloc's temple. This backward reclining figure who was a messenger to the gods holds a bowl on his lap which was used to hold the hearts of sacrificial victims. But Chac Mools were definitely not Aztec but rather Toltec figures which had appeared in prominent ceremonial centers of some Toltec and Mayan cities. The statue's surprising appearance at the Templo Mayor demonstrates again the Aztec insecurity and concern to bring a legitimating predecessor into their mighty present.

TEMPLO MAYOR, PERIPHERIES, AND HUMAN SACRIFICE

The Templo Mayor was the scene of elaborate human sacrifices, which increased to incredible numbers during the last eighty years of Aztec rule. Human sacrifice was based upon a unique religious attitude. It was believed that human blood and especially the human heart contained the vital energy for the sun's continued motion through the heavens and the subsequent renewal of time, crops, human life, and the divine forces of the cosmos. In these sacrifices, human hearts were offered to the sun and the blood was spread on the Templo Mayor's walls in order to coat the temple with sacred energy. The Aztec rulers were in charge of this process and had the responsibility of obtaining human victims through war. Also, the Tlatoani and his counselors initiated heart sacrifice at many of the great festivals. As we have seen, the paradigm for this process was the myth of Huitzilopochtli's birth. But this myth alone does not account for the quantity of human sacrifice and the expansion of the Templo Mayor's role in this development.

Johanna Broda's recent analysis of ideology and the Aztec state provides valuable insights into the interrelationship of the Templo Mayor, the increment in human sacrifice, and the powers of the peripheral city-states.[56] As we have seen, within the Valley of Mexico the Aztec warrior and priestly nobility managed a high degree of centralization of agricultural schedules, technological developments, labor management, and ritual processes. But in all directions beyond the valley there was little continued success in peacefully controlling the internal organization of conquered or enemy city-states. The Aztec capital, while expanding its territory and tribute controls, was repeatedly shocked by rebellions that demanded complex and organized military and economic reprisals. This antagonism between the core area and the surrounding city-states created immense stresses within all the institutions of Tenochtitlán, contributing to the astonishing increases in human sacrifice carried out at the Templo Mayor between 1440 and 1521. Not only did the political order appear weak, but the divine right to conquer and subdue all peoples and enemies seemed unfulfilled. The anxiety the Aztecs already felt about their universal order—after all cosmic life was an unending war—was intensified to the point of cosmic paranoia. In this situation, the ritual strategy of feeding the gods became the major religio-political instrument for subduing the enemy, controlling the periphery, and rejuvenating cosmic energy.

The Templo Mayor's role in this explosive process can be seen in at least two important events. During the reign of Moctezuma Ilhuicamina, 1440–53, the shrine received its first large reconstruction. As a means of insuring quality of workmanship and allegiance to the new temple, workers from a number of city-states under Aztec control were ordered to do the job. One independent community, Chalco, refused to participate and was declared in rebellion against the Aztecs. A ferocious war was launched and eventually the Chalcans were defeated. Their captured warriors were brought to the Templo Mayor and, along with other prisoners of war, sacrificed at its rededication. This pattern of celebrating the expansion of the Great Temple with warfare and the sacrifice of enemy warriors was followed by subsequent Aztec kings. In 1487, Ahuitzotl celebrated the renovation of the Templo Mayor by ordering great quantities of tribute brought into Tenochtitlán. Newly acquired city-states were ordered to send tribute in the form of sacrificial victims who were slain at the inauguration.

Curiously, at these ceremonies of massive human sacrifice, the kings and lords from allied and enemy city-states were invited to the ceremonial center to witness the spectacular festival. The ritual extravaganza was carried out with maximum theatrical tension, paraphernalia, and terror in order to amaze and intimidate the visiting dignitaries who returned to their kingdoms trembling with fear and convinced that cooperation and not rebellion was the best response to Aztec imperialism.

On another occasion, the Aztec king, this time Moctezuma Xocoyotzin (1502–20), ordered the construction of a new temple to house the images of all the gods worshiped in the imperial domain. Before the dedication of the shrine, he ordered a war against a rebellious coastal city-state, Teuctepec. From this campaign, 2300 warriors were brought to Tenochtitlán, where the king initiated the sacrifices held at Templo Mayor.

All this shows that the tension between the center and the periphery, and the political threats and cosmic insecurities the Aztec elites felt as a result, contributed in a major way to the increase of human sacrifice at the Templo Mayor. In the long run, this increment served to strengthen *and* weaken the authority of Tenochtitlán. While many city-states were securely integrated into the Aztec sphere, others were alienated and leaned in the direction of other kingdoms and the capacity for rebellion increased. So, when the Spaniards came, Indian allies were not hard to find and in fact played a tremendous role in the conquest of Tenochtitlán. The Templo Mayor now appears to have been a much more complex *imago mundi* than we realized. It was an image of the political struggles between the center and the periphery of the Aztec Empire.

OMENS OF THE END

The sources show that there was another significant dimension of the crisis in early sixteenth-century Tenochtitlán. The indigenous accounts of the conquest tell that omens of great portent appeared in the Valley of Mexico a full decade before Cortes arrived. It is obvious from the primary sources that these signs were never understood as merely natural occurrences. Like famine and military defeat, they were viewed partly as cosmological communications reflecting the destiny of the fifth sun. Chapter 1 of book 12 of the *Florentine Codex*, a book entitled the "Conquest of Mexico," begins with the sentence, "Here are told the signs which appeared and were seen when the Spaniards had not yet come here to this land, when they were not yet known to the natives here." It is important that this text is emphatic about the fact that the omens appear in relation to but before the presence of Spaniards in Mexico. In fact, in the three different accounts of these omens, this priority of the celestial signs over Spanish influence is emphasized. The Indian informants were demonstrating that from their perspective, supernatural forces communicated that the end of their world was approaching long before the Spaniards appeared to threaten their world.

In the *Historia de Tlaxcala*, we read, "Ten years before the Spaniards came to this land, the people saw a strange wonder and took it to be an evil sign and portent."[57] Then below on the same page we find the passage concerning an omen, "This portent burned for a year, beginning in the year which the natives called 12 House—that is, 1517, in our Spanish reckoning." Now the proximity is tighter, coinciding with the year of the first major Spanish reconnaissance mission into Aztec territory. The omen was received with great terror as if it contained some message from the heavens about the future. "This great marvel caused so much dread and wonder that they spoke of it constantly, trying to imagine what such a strange novelty could signify." Apparently the omens continued, for we later hear, "Other signs appeared here in the province of Tlaxcala, a little before the arrival of the Spaniards."

FIG. 15. Quetzalcoatl as depicted in Sahagún's *Florentine Codex* showing the transformation of the symbols, shapes, and character of the figure.

If we follow Sahagún's account, which tends to be more coherent and closer to the indigenous sense of this cosmic crisis, we see that the omens appear as messages of destruction, reversal, the end of an empire. The first omen was "a fiery signal, like a flaming ear of corn or the blaze of daybreak; it seemed to bleed fire, drop by drop, like a wound in the sky . . . it was wide at the peak and narrow at the base, and it shone in the very heart of the heavens."[58]

The Aztecs witness a rip in the very heart of their universe, a rip which bleeds fire, threatening the death of the cosmos which encloses and is centered by their city and especially the Great Temple. The second omen is a more direct catastrophe:

> The temple of Huitzilopochtli burst into flames. It is thought that no one set it afire, that it burned down of its own accord. The name of its divine site was Tlacateccan (House of Authority). . . . The flames, the tongues of fire shoot out, the bursts of fire shoot up into the sky. The flames swiftly destroyed all the wood-work of the temple . . . and the temple burned to the ground.[59]

The *axis mundi* of the Aztec ceremonial center is mysteriously ignited and destroyed. The identification of temple and city is strong in Mesoamerican thought, as demonstrated in picture books like the *Codex Mendoza*, where the image of a temple tipped and burning or smoking is a sign that the city has been conquered. In this frightening event, the home of the Aztec founding deity, the victorious warrior who slew the lights of darkness, is burned and toppled reflecting the image just discussed: a burning, falling temple means a city has been conquered.

This message that the city will be conquered is sustained in the next ominous event when "the Temple of Xiuhtechutli . . . was damaged by a lightning-bolt . . . [and] the people said, 'the temple was struck a blow by the sun.' "[60] Xiuhtechutli was the "old god" of the Aztecs, the most ancient and venerated diety of all. Could this mean that the very foundation of the city was to be broken?

The fourth omen appeared when "fire streamed through the sky while the sun was still shining. . . . it flashed out from where the sun sets and raced straight to where the sun rises. . . . there was a great outcry and confusion, as if they were shaking a thousand little bells." This comet traveling across the sky in the reverse direction of the sun's path suggests the reversal of cosmic order.

The fifth omen appeared in the lake which sustained and surrounded the city. "The wind lashed the lake until it boiled . . . with rage, as if it were shattering itself in its frenzy. It . . . rose high in the air and dashed against the walls of the houses. The flooded houses collapsed into the water." Here the waters of sustenance have become the waters of chaos which break in upon the structures of the city and begin to engulf it.

The sixth omen was a "weeping woman . . . [who] passed by in the middle of the night, wailing and crying out in a loud voice: 'My children, we must flee far away from this city.' " This haunting prophetess of Tenochtitlán's doom appears in an elaborate form elsewhere in the *Florentine Codex*. In a narrative section listing the kings of Tenochtitlán and the details of their reigns, the following event is told about Moctezuma. A noble woman died and was buried, but she came back to life after four days. After bursting from her grave, she went to converse with Moctezuma about what she had seen. "She . . . said to him 'For this reason have I returned to life: I have come to tell thee that thou art come to the end. With thee the reign of Mexico ceaseth: for in thy time the city of Mexico will end. They who come, lo, these have come to subjugate the land: these will occupy Mexico.' "[61] The ghostly messenger tells Moctezuma directly, the city is about to be destroyed.

The seventh omen was "a strange creature . . . a bird the color of ashes . . . which wore a strange mirror in the crown of its head . . . Moctecuhzoma saw. ..people moving across a distant plain, spread out in ranks and coming forward in great haste." As with Quetzalcoatl in Tollan, it is a mirror which reflects a great crisis in the land.

The eighth omen was "a deformed man with two heads but only one body who appeared in the streets of the city"—a sign, perhaps, of the deformity of Aztec life soon to appear.

The splendid synchronization of the city and cosmos, symbolized in the image of 4 Motion, was about to be shattered. When the stable order of parallel worlds began to wobble and collapse, of course, it bled fire, drop by drop, on the earthly pivot of the empire, Tenochtitlán. This is a radical reversal of the vision of cosmic destiny carved on the Piedra del Sol.

The interplay of omens and political events is displayed in the account of the fall of the city. The informants have gone on to tell of Moctezuma's suffering, the battles between the two armies, and are telling of the siege of Tenochtitlán. Then comes a passage full of piercing fate. We read that, just before the surrender of the city,

> at nightfall it began to rain, but it was more like a heavy dew than a rain. Suddenly the omen appeared, blazing like a great bonfire in the sky. It wheeled in enormous spirals like a whirlwind and gave off a shower of sparks and red-hot coals, some great and some little. It also made loud noises, rumbling and

hissing like a metal tube placed over a fire. It circled the wall nearest the lakeshore and then hovered for a while above Coyonacazco. From there it moved out into the middle of the lake, where it suddenly disappeared. No one cried out when this omen came into view: *the people knew what it meant and they watched in silence* [italics added].[62]

Here we have a stunning example of the cosmo-magical consciousness which interpreted and sustained the ancient Mexican sense of order. Thirty years after the conquest, in a society ruled by Spaniards, Aztec survivors poignantly reaffirm the cosmological conviction lodged in their hearts that the collapse of their own society was influenced not solely by Spanish armies and intentions but also by the pattern of the heavens.

THE RETURN OF QUETZALCOATL: A MYTHIC DRAMA

It was in this political and religious atmosphere that the symbol of Quetzalcoatl made its final pre-Columbian appearance and through which we must make a final attempt to perceive its significance. When one reviews the narratives and fragments concerning the return of Quetzalcoatl to Tenochtitlán, it is clear that this last Tollan was the stage for an amazing "mythic drama." We are utilizing the notion of mythic drama for two reasons. First, because the story of Cortes's confrontation with Moctezuma appears in the sources like a stage drama. The scene has been set by the expectations of a returning king, the main actors are in their places in the capital, and onto the stage, in a great *entrada*, comes the Spaniard, whose enigmatic visage and actions create great tension, emotion, and a crisis of identity for the Aztec hero. Speeches are delivered, soliloquies whispered, and the plot moves through a crisis to a resolution. Second, the return narratives portray a dramatic process of transformation in which the myth of the destiny of kingship influenced the main action of the play in a major way. In this usage of "mythic drama," we benefit from the vivid development of a similar category, "social drama," in the writings of Victor Turner. In a different context, Turner utilized the category of social drama to decipher Ndembu episodes of tension irruption within a social order and the changing social relations which result. In a wider application of the category, Turner shows that when

a major public dramatic process gets under way, people, whether consciously, preconsciously, or unconsciously, take on roles which carry with them, if not precisely recorded scripts, deeply engraved tendencies to act and speak in supra-personal or 'representative' ways appropriate to the role taken, and to prepare the way for a certain climax that approximates the nature of the climax given in a certain central myth of the death or victory of a hero or heroes.[63]

A similar process of mythic influence can be discerned in the confrontation of Cortes with Moctezuma. There are, however, two important differences between social drama and mythic drama. First, the dramatic process is not merely internal to the Aztec society. The drama involves strangers whose otherness intensifies the need to find suprapersonal models of explanation. Second, it is crucial to note that while Turner has deciphered episodes of "tensional irruption," the drama of Quetzalcoatl's return is an episode of "structural disruption" telling of the break at the apex of the Aztec social structure. The social transformation usually called the conquest of Mexico was initiated by the abdication of sovereignty on the part of the king, a collapse which ironically repeats the design of Tenochtitlán's political paradigm— Tollan. It is a myth that is dramatized, not merely social relations.

There are a number of references in the primary sources to the expected return of Quetzalcoatl which help us to set the stage for the main action. These references strongly suggest that the belief in Quetzalcoatl's return was a pre-Columbian attitude and not, as some have suggested, invented by the Spaniards. They hint at the conflict which was waiting to be acted out in Tenochtitlán.

SAHAGÚN's DISPUTE

The appendix to book 1 of the *Florentine Codex* contains a section we will call Sahagún's dispute. In this postscript, the Franciscan is refuting the truth and value of Aztec beliefs. Included is a summary of the Topiltzin Quetzalcoatl story, which Sahagún labels a terrible lie. Its importance for us is that the dispute provides one of the "proofs" of the pre-Columbian nature of this mythologem. Referring to Topiltzin, he writes:

> The ancients worshiped Quetzalcoatl, who was a ruler at Tula. And you named him Topiltzin. He was a common man. . . . What he did which was like miracles, we know he did only through the command of the devil. . . . Therefore he must needs be abhorred and abominated. Our Lord God hath thrust him into the land of the dead. The ancients went on to say that Quetzalcoatl went to Tlapallan; [that] yet he will return. He is still expected . . . it is falsehood. His body died.[64]

This passage is important because it demonstrates the antagonistic attitude a Christian cleric with a great deal of knowledge about pre-Columbian thought had for the historical Quetzalcoatl. Second, it is clear that Sahagún believed the expectation of Quetzalcoatl's return to be an authentic Aztec belief and not the invention of early Christian missionaries. The ancients who expect Quetzalcoatl to return are the surviving keepers of the sacred traditions of Tenochtitlán and Tlatelolco. Also, the passage clearly identifies Quetzalcoatl with the illustrious city of Tollan.

The belief Sahagún is disputing appears elsewhere in the *Codex Telleriano-Remensis (Vaticanus A)* demonstrating that it was held by other informants besides Sahagún's, though that alone is an impressive piece of evidence. In the codex we are faced with the verbal commentary on a series of paintings depicting episodes in Quetzalcoatl's life. The narrative states that after the hero left Tollan he entered Tlapallan and was never seen again, nor was it known what became of him. Then it states that he had promised to return at some special moment in the future. The commentator adds that when the Zapotecs revolted in 1550, they were encouraged by the belief that their deity had come to redeem them. The commentator notes that Quetzalcoatl's return is still expected.

Again, we see evidence of an indigenous belief and its use, but now we see the important addition that Quetzalcoatl himself promised to return. It is not just a rumor started by others.

A third very important piece of evidence, which we have seen earlier, was the conversation that took place between Moctezuma II and his counselor Tlacaelel during the viewing of the carved image of the king at Chapultepec. Previously, we used Diego Durán's version, which made it clear that the carving of the ruler's images was a repetition of Quetzalcoatl's carved image. When we read about the same event in Alvarado Tezozomoc's account, we see a curious change in the action. It is not Moctezuma who remembers that Quetzalcoatl originated this tradition. Rather, the counselor Tlacaelel reminds the king that while it is appropriate to admire his own image, it is time to renovate Quetzalcoatl's image because it has disintegrated and the Toltec king promised to return to his throne. The second in command states:

> And in other times, the newly arrived Mexican ordered the cutting and making of an image of the god Quetzalcoatl who went to heaven, saying when he left he would return and bring our brothers—and that figure was made of wood—in time it deterioriated, so now there is no memory of it and it has to be renovated, to be the god we all wait for, who went to the sea and the sky.[65]

While this version of the speech can be interpreted in various ways, it may be seen as an embarrassing reminder to the king of the thoughtless disrepair of the original king's image. Was this a subtle cut at Moctezuma, whose kingly vanity should also have been spent on the restoration of Quetzalcoatl's image? Again, as in the *Codex Telleriano-Remensis*, Quetzalcoatl is the source of the prophecy, only now it is clearly related to kingship and kingdoms.

Still another source, the *Memorial Breve*, states succinctly that Quetzalcoatl's return was a belief held by the people and that kingship was the issue. The text notes that when the king left Tollan he promised to return and reestablish his kingdom. The writer of the text adds that all the rulers of Tenochtitlán were aware of this prophecy and kept on the alert. He also notes that the prophecy had special influence on Moctezuma, who opened his city to Cortes. In this important source, the kingdom that Quetzalcoatl is returning to claim is not just the ancient Tollan but the contemporary Mexico-Tenochtitlán.

The purpose of this short review has been to establish the probable existence of an indigenous, pre-Columbian mythologem concerning Quetzalcoatl's return to Mexico. Our impression is that the people thought the prophecy originated with Quetzalcoatl and its fulfillment was awaited by Aztec kings.

In a sense, a dramatic scenario has been outlined in which Quetzalcoatl will return to reclaim his throne. In reconstructing the drama we will follow Sahagún's text and utilize a few excerpts from other relevant accounts in order to present a fuller story. We will use direct quotations generously because a summary of some passages will not do justice to the amazing action that takes place. It is important to remember that the drama of the conquest as presented in book 12 follows immediately after the chapter telling of the omens of the end of the empire.

Primordium and Application

In 1517 a Spanish expedition led by Juan de Grijalva came into contact with coastal peoples under the dominion of Tenochtitlán. Troubled by the appearance of strange beings from the sea, a group of Moctezuma's stewards went out to spy on the strangers, thinking "that it was Quetzalcoatl Topiltzin who had come to arrive." Following a careful exchange of gifts and information, the stewards rushed to Tenochtitlán in order to warn Moctezuma of the intruders. The king was deeply concerned and ordered the messengers to "Rest. What I have seen has been in secret. . . . No one shall let it escape his lips." Careful watch is ordered along the coast and Moctezuma waits apprehensively.

The next alarm is sounded "when the year [thirteen] Rabbit was about to come to an end, was at the time of closing when [the Spaniards] came to land." This passage announces the arrival of the Cortes expedition in the ominous year 1519/Ce Acatl (1 Reed). Moctezuma is informed of the landing and his response is recorded:

Tenochtitlan.

FIG. 16. The meeting of Hernán Cortes with Moctezuma in Tenochtitlán, as depicted in the sixteenth-century *Lienzo de Tlaxcala*. Cortes was originally identified by some Aztecs as the returning Topiltzin Quetzalcoatl.

> Thus he thought—thus was it thought that this was Topiltzin Quetzalcoatl who had come to land. For it was in their hearts that he would come, that he would come to land, just to find his mat, his seat. For he had traveled there [eastward] when he departed. And [Moctezuma] sent five emissaries to go to meet him, to go to give him gifts.[66]

This passage is important because it refers to the use of an ancient myth in a contemporary situation for the purpose of interpreting and coping with an unusual presence of strangers in the landscape. The earlier encounter of the strangers on the coast was the occasion for the recall of this prophecy, but it was not Moctezuma who had that recall. Now, in the year associated with Quetzalcoatl, the thoughtful king is credited with thinking and setting the pattern of interpretation that the Toltec ancestor had returned. The king applies to a series of reconnaissance reports the archaic mythologem of Quetzalcoatl's flight and promised return to regain his throne.

As the narrative proceeds, however, we see that Moctezuma is filled with both fear and caution. His mind and spirit hover between acceptance and suspicion for a long period. When he sends elaborate treasures consisting of the jeweled costumes of major Aztec deities, including the "array of Quetzalcoatl," he instructs his messengers to honor the visitors but also to spy on them so that their true identity can be discovered.

The message sent to "our lord the god" suggests that Moctezuma is preparing to abdicate his authority as ruler. The messengers are commanded "say unto him, Thy governor Moctezuma hath sent us. Here is what he giveth thee, for [the god] hath come to reach his humble home in Mexico." This message of welcome and hinted submission is translated to Cortes as "May the god deign to hear his governor Moctezuma, who watcheth over Mexico for him, prayeth unto him." Significantly, the messengers dress Cortes in the outfit of Quetzalcoatl.

In this statement, we see that Moctezuma, who was recently elevated to a new rung of authority, has become the representative of the returning king, watching over Mexico in the interim. While it might be argued that these are exaggerated expressions of royal protocol, a further examination of the text reveals that Moctezuma is falling into a personal crisis. The text reads that while the messengers were delivering the divine clothes, "Moctezuma enjoyed no sleep, no food, not one spoke more to him. Whatsoever he did, it was as if he were in torment. Oftentimes it was as if he sighed, became weak, felt weak." This depression and feeling of powerlessness has a focus in his mind. A hint of tragedy emerges in his soliloquy: "What will now befall us? Who indeed standeth [in command]? Alas, until now, I. In great torment is my heart, as if it was washed in chili water it indeed burneth, it smarteth. Where in truth [may we go] O our lord?"[67] This blunt lament points directly to Quetzalcoatl's significance for the Aztecs. While most interpreters emphasize Quetzalcoatl's priestly influence, it is clear that Moctezuma's torment is not caused by concern for his priestly status, but by a threat to his authority as ruler. In the words of the text, who, indeed, stands in command, Moctezuma or Quetzalcoatl?

The messengers return from the coast but before Moctezuma will receive their report two captive warriors are taken to the Coacalli (Snake Temple) and sacrificed. Their blood was sprinkled onto the messengers because they had looked upon gods and were about to deliver a fateful report. Moctezuma's response to their report is extreme:

"he was . . . terror struck . . . he was filled with great dread, swooning. His soul was sickened, his heart was anguished.[68]

His chili-water heart has taken on the character of what Rudolph Otto calls a "creature feeling" of numinous dread, awe, and urgency. The more the royal mind applies the mythic theme to the quickening drama, the more anguished he becomes. He is encountering his numen, the origin of rulership, and it is an uncanny experience.

But Moctezuma has a warrior's resilience and is not convinced that Cortes is Quetzalcoatl or that his throne is doomed. He launches a magical campaign against the intruders in order to clarify their identity, cast spells upon them, kill them, or repel them from Mexico. In the meantime, confusion and emotional chaos spread through the city.

> And Moctezuma expressed distress because of the city. And indeed everyone was greatly terrified. There were terror, astonishment, expressions of distress, feelings of distress. There were consultations. There were formations of groups; there were assemblies of peoples. There was weeping. . . . fathers said: "Alas, O my beloved sons! How can what is about to come to pass have befallen you?"[69]

Now the city is gripped with dread and the citizens driven to great laments. When we remember the lament at Quetzalcoatl's departure quoted at the beginning of chapter 2, it is incongruous that this more intense lamentation, indeed near hysteria, is sweeping through the capital because of the possibility of the hero's return. Why would the return of the archetypal line cause such a panic?

Moctezuma's emotional and political crisis increases as he makes clear gestures toward an abdication of this office. He decides to escape the worldly crisis by fleeing to a magical cave where he believes he can pass into the supernatural world. Significantly, his counselors tell of four magical locations of escape which coincide with the four cardinal points of the universe. In another confused version of this episode, found in Tezozomoc's *Cronica Mexicana*, the wizards tell the king that Topiltzin Quetzalcoatl went away and died and that he need not fear. Unconvinced, Moctezuma responds: "We expect the god Quetzalcoatl because the elders of Tula are certain that Quetzalcoatl told them he would return to rule at Tula and all parts of the world."[70] The point is that Quetzalcoatl will return to rule at Tula and it will be the center of the new kingdom.

Moctezuma, taut with fear and unsuccessful in his attempt to escape into the supernatural realm, changes his royal residence. He leaves the "great palace" and moves into his "princely home"; the baffled king is making room for the true sovereign advancing toward the city.

The king continues to send spies and emissaries versed in magic to impede the Spaniards, but Cortes's troops continue toward Tenochtitlán, killing, conquering, and making alliances along the way.

CHAOS AND BAFFLEMENT

We have referred to this dramatic scenario as a "crisis situation." But the description of Moctezuma's torment or derangement, the panic of Tenochtitlán's citizens, the signs from the heavens, and the relocation of the royal residence reflect such a deep sense of disorder that the term "chaotic situation" is more apt. And as the sources present it, it seems to be fundamentally a chaos of the mind. How can we understand this complex chaos? The impact of chaotic stress on human thought has been illuminated by Susanne Langer:

> Man can adapt himself somehow to anything his imagination can cope with: but he cannot deal with chaos. Because his characteristic function and highest asset is conception, his greatest fright is to meet what he cannot construe—the "uncanny," as it is popularly called. It need not be a new object: we do meet new things, and "understand" them promptly, if tentatively, by the nearest analogy, when our minds are functioning freely; but under mental stress even perfectly familiar things may become suddenly disorganized, and give us the horrors.[71]

These lines can help us illuminate the situation in Tenochtitlán in 1519, when Moctezuma and the city are faced with conceptually chaotic situations. Indeed, it is not a new object that Moctezuma must cope with; supposedly it is a quite familiar one taught to all Aztec nobles. And it is possible to claim that the famine, the failing war effort, and the internal dissension in the aristocracy, along with the series of omens, placed Moctezuma under great stress leading to his disorientation in the face of the uncanny. But this kind of social determinism misses the point, although it is certainly part of the play. We must ask ourselves what is conceptually chaotic about Topiltzin Quetzalcoatl's return.

Clifford Geertz has suggested that the issue in dealing with chaos, "a tumult of events which lack not just interpretation but interpretability," is—at one level—the problem of bafflement![72] Geertz notes that humans tend to use beliefs to explain phenomena, "or more accurately, to convince themselves the phenomena were explainable within the accepted scheme of things." This is getting to the point of the power of the story of Quetzalcoatl's return. The city, the king, the nation had claimed descent, and therefore legitimacy, from the Toltec priest-king. The Aztec used the Tollan tale as a political myth, a myth which contained the "true" story of sovereignty and city. This myth also included the detail that the fountainhead of kingship, the founder of Tollan, would return and reestablish his kingdom. But as we have also demonstrated, the Aztecs had already reshaped their cosmology and city by placing themselves at the center of space and time. Topiltzin Quetzalcoatl had gone and now the Aztecs were lords of the world and a new pattern of destiny had been discovered. Huitzilopochtli, Tezcatlipoca, Tlaloc, and Xipe Totec demanded the attention of the Aztec realm while Quetzalcoatl, though still important in the regular expression of the sacred, became slightly crowded to the side. Thus, the appearance of strangers in the east and the return of Quetzalcoatl and the consequences promised in the myth could no longer be "conceived as being within the accepted scheme of things." In fact it was inconceivable, an attack on the accepted scheme of things. Therefore, the return of Quetzalcoatl was not understood as a renewal or regeneration of the society and cosmos but as an uncanny chaos descending on Mexico like the end of another age. This return was a reaffirmation of an older pattern of destiny, not centered in Tenochtitlán or the Fifth Sun, but in the cycles of original forces coming around again to incarnate themselves in the present moment of time. The crisis for the Aztecs is not merely political, it is fundamentally cosmological. It is this crisis of the incarnation of Quetzalcoatl's image that plagues Moctezuma whose identity becomes effaced before the approaching ancestor. Octavio Paz has written of the power of such cyclical images:

> Cyclic time is another way toward absorption, transformation, and sublimation. The date that recurs is a return of previous time, an immersion in a past which is at once that of each individual and that of the group. As the wheel of time revolves, it allows the society to recover buried, or repressed, psychic structures so as to reincorporate them in a present that is also a past. It is not only the return of the ancients and antiquity; it is the possibility that each individual possesses of recovering his living portion of the past. The purpose of psychoanalysis is to elucidate the forgotten incident, so that to a certain extent the cure is a recovery of memory. In ancient rites it is not memory that remembers the past, but the past that returns. This is what I have called in another context, the incarnation of images.[73]

And what makes this incarnation of the image, this "past that returns" so powerful is its cosmic significance. It means that not only do the priests and king have to wrench their brains to deal with a bewildering second coming, but the social order must deal with a return to beginnings, a total reorganization! The return of the date Ce Acatl and the reincorporation of the psychic and mythic structure represented by Quetzalcoatl are experienced by Moctezuma as destructive. According to tradition, Quetzalcoatl had made arrows during his disappearance and if he reappeared on 1 Reed, he would strike down kings. The conjuction of Quetzalcoatl's reappearance and the striking down of kings is portrayed in Diego Duran's account of the Spanish march to Tenochtitlán. Moctezuma sent gifts of beads and biscuits to Cortes in order to discover if it was Quetzalcoatl returning to Anahuac. The idea was that if the stranger recognized the food and ate it, then indeed it was the returning king. The Spaniards ate the food, greeted Moctezuma's messengers and sent back beads and biscuits to the Aztec monarch. They were given to Moctezuma who saw them as divine gifts from Quetzalcoatl.

> Moctezuma said they were from the gods and refused to eat them lest he show irreverence toward divine gifts. He ordered his priests to carry them to the city of Tula with great ceremony and bury them in the temple of Quetzalcoatl whose sons had now arrived. The priests took the biscuits and placed them in a richly decorated bowl, covered it with cloaks and carried it in procession to Tula. Hymns appropriate to Quetzalcoatl were sung and the biscuits were buried with great pomp at Quetzalcoatl's temple in the ancient city.[74]

This ritual return of Quetzalcoatl's food to the archetypal ceremonial capital is accompanied by an act of abdication to Quetzalcoatl at the Templo Mayor in Tenochtitlán. Taking the string of beads sent by Cortes, Moctezuma held them up as objects from heaven saying, "I receive the mercy and bounty of what the god has given me." He then ordered the beads to be buried at the feet of the god Huitzilopochtli saying that he was not worthy to use such divine objects. "And they buried it with great pomp and solemnity, accompanied by incense burners and shell trumpets and other instruments because it was a divine thing."

The incarnation of Quetzalcoatl's image in the face of Cortes persuaded Moctezuma of the imminent dislocation of the center of Mexico to Tula and the annihilation of his own image as the ruler of the empire. He was no longer worthy to be king.

Cortes continues his march into Tenochtitlán and Moctezuma continues to act out the abdication of Aztec sovereignty. The drama arrives at the point of ultimate tension when Cortes arrives in Tenochtitlán and meets Moctezuma face to face.

EXIT THE KING

It is fortunate that we have both Aztec and Spanish versions of the face-to-face encounters of Cortes and Moctezuma, including quoted excerpts from speeches by both men. While there are differ-

ences in the reports of these encounters, there are fascinating similarities. We will begin with the abdication speech of Moctezuma as
it appears in the Aztec accounts and compare the scenario and content
with Cortes's version.

After Cortes arrived in Tenochtitlán, Moctezuma "went in peace
and calm" to greet him with gifts of flowers and golden neck bands.
He addressed the captain:

> O our Lord, thou hast suffered fatigue, thou hast endured
> weariness. Thou hast come to arrive on earth. Thou hast come
> to govern thy city of Mexico; thou hast come to descend upon
> thy mat, upon thy seat, which for a moment I have watched
> for thee, which I have guarded for thee. For thy governors are
> departed—the rulers Itzcoatl, Moctezuma the Elder, Axayacatl,
> Tizoc, Auitzotl, who yet a very short time ago had come to
> stand guard for thee, who had come to govern the city of Mex-
> ico. . . . O that one of them might witness, might marvel at
> what to me now has befallen. . . . I do not merely dream that I
> see thee, that I look into thy face. . . . The rulers departed
> maintaining that thou wouldst come to visit thy city, that thou
> wouldst come to descend upon thy mat, upon thy seat. And
> now it hath been fulfilled; visit thy palace.[75]

Quetzalcoatl-Cortes is welcomed back to his city in order to reoccupy
the throne which has been guarded by Moctezuma and the other
tlatoanis who bore the Toltec mantle. Moctezuma laments that it is his
fate to face the loss of the throne and reminds himself that he is awake
and facing the true ruler. The ancient prophecy has been fulfilled and
the returning lord is invited to occupy his throne and visit the palace.
There could hardly be a clearer statement of returning the sovereignty
to the original king.

A similar speech appears twice in the second letter Hernando
Cortes wrote to King Charles during the campaigns against the Aztecs. The Cortes letter, written in 1520, is extremely important because
it contains the earliest account we have of the application of the return
mythologem. One speech is delivered, according to Cortes, at the
scene we have just witnessed, the initial meeting of the two men. The
second speech, which is an abdication speech, is delivered later in
the year. Following Cortes's account of this second speech come the
lines "All this took place in the presence of a notary public and was
duly drawn up by him in legal form, witnessed in the presence of
many Spaniards." The significance of this is that Cortes may have
been constructing his letter to the king from a document produced
on the scene of the dramatic encounter. In Cortes's account of the
first speech, Moctezuma states,

for a long time we have known from the writings of our ancestors that neither I, nor any of those who dwell in this land, are
natives of it, but foreigners who came from very distant parts;
and likewise we know that a chieftain, of whom they were all
vassals, brought our people to this region. And he returned to
his native land.[76]

In this version Moctezuma opens with reference to the sacred history
of the nation which tells of migrations and a special leader who
brought the people here and departed. The speech continues,

And we have always held that those who descended from him
would come and conquer this land and take us as their vassals.
So because of the place from which you claim to come, namely
from where the sun rises, and the things you tell us of the
great lord and king who sent you here we believe and are certain that he is our natural lord, especially as you say that he
has known of us for some time. So be assured that we shall
obey you and hold you as our lord in place of that great sovereign of whom you speak; and in this there shall be no betrayal
whatsoever. And in all the land that lies in my domain, you
may command as you will, for you shall be obeyed; and all that
we own is for you to dispose of as you choose.[77]

One suspects the clever hand of Cortes in this rendition of the
welcome speech. For instance, Moctezuma expects one of the lord's
descendants, not the lord himself. There is a distinct reference to the
change in social structure. The Aztecs, including Moctezuma, will
become vassals. The Aztec king is not receiving Cortes as the descendant of Quetzalcoatl but as a messenger of the descendant, "our
natural lord," who is Charles. King Charles is the royal descendant
in this account while in the Aztec version he is absent from the picture.
The disruption of Aztec sovereignty is clearly stated when Moctezuma
turns over the lands and command of the kingdom. Royal protocol,
offering royal power to a distinguished visitor, is mixed with an overt
gesture of turning the government over to Cortes as representative
of Quetzalcoatl's descendant. Then comes the concluding section of
Moctezuma's speech and a bizarre gesture. Asking Quetzalcoatl's
representative to disbelieve the slander of Moctezuma's enemies
against the Aztec state, he concludes, " 'I also know that they have
told you . . . that I was, and claimed to be a god.' " . . . Then he
raised his clothes and showed me his body, saying, as he grasped his
arms and trunk with his hands, 'See that I am of flesh and blood like
you and all other men, and I am mortal and substantial.' "[78] In this
symbolic "exposure" Moctezuma eliminates the mystery and majesty

of his rank and invites Cortes not only to have a look at his humanity but to take control.

If there is any doubt in our minds that this mythic drama is about the structural disruption of Aztec rulership, then we need only focus on the second abdication speech reported in Cortes' second letter to King Charles. Soon after the Spaniards are lodged in Tenochtitlán, Moctezuma is taken house prisoner. According to Cortes, this was accomplished through his constant references to King Charles's good intentions for Moctezuma and his city and by promising that it was only a temporary condition for the *tlatoani*. It is in this context that the complete abdication is offered. To appreciate the full significance of the speech, we must realize that the stage directions have been altered. Moctezuma is now facing in the opposite direction, toward his own kingdom. An assembly of "all the chiefs of the cities and lands thereabouts," was gathered by Moctezuma. Facing the elites of his empire, Moctezuma delivers a similar speech to the one he had given on Cortes's entry. Several new additions reflect his understanding of the pathetic destiny of the city. First the king recalls that the chiefs have been his vassals and his forefathers' vassals for many years and that there have always been good relations. Then comes the reference to the widespread tradition about a returning lord who

> departed, saying that he would return or would send such forces as would compel them to serve him. You well know that we have always expected him, and according to the things this captain has said of the Lord and King who sent him here, and according to the direction whence he says he comes, I am certain, and so must you be also, that this is the same lord for whom we have been waiting, especially as he says that there they know of us. . . . And I beg you—since all this is well known to you—that just as until now you have obeyed me and held me as your rightful lord, from now on you should obey the great King, for he is your rightful lord and as his representative acknowledge this is his captain. And all the tributes and services which, until now, you have rendered to me, render now to him, for I also must contribute and serve in all that he may command; and in addition to doing your duty and all that you are obliged to do, you will give me great satisfaction thereby.[79]

While it is possible that Cortes could have invented part of this speech, reference back to the earlier speech or the Aztec version or the many widespread references of the expected return will show that it is an elaboration of the theme of abdication which was initiated by Moctezuma. In this last speech to the assembly of rulers, we see the full collapse of authority in Tenochtitlán.

In this mythic drama, we have witnessed much more than the confrontation of two leaders. We see the collapse of the indigenous structure of sovereignty, fallen under the weight of a mythic force embodied in the ironic return of Quetzalcoatl. This mythic force intensified a crisis situation within the capital city of an empire, the pivot of the geographical and social pyramid that was ancient Mexico and led to the end of a long tradition of civilized history. This mythic force came upon the Aztecs from a primordial tradition which they thought could be utilized to support and legitimate their throne. But the contours of that tradition had their own shape and meaning and could not be reduced to Aztec inventions and applications. In this instance we see the impact of a prophecy that succeeded, a prophecy that was fulfilled, for too long a time, in the incarnation of an ancient visage in the face of Cortes. Ironically, the drama repeated the scenario of the end of the ideal Tollan, in which a king lost his throne to strangers who deceived him and led him to ruin. The Toltecs were correct when they claimed that Quetzalcoatl was the pattern for everything in Mexico, for he was also the pattern of the end of everything.

Exit the king.

Notes

Introduction: Mosaics and Centers

1. I am following the work of Paul Wheatley, especially the *Pivot of the Four Quarters* (Chicago: Aldine, 1971), where he interprets the emergence, in seven areas of pristine urban generation of "hierarchically structured, functionally specialized social institutions organized on a political and territorial basis" (p. xiii). Later, in Chap. 3, "The Nature of the Ceremonial Center," Wheatley summarizes the amazing emergence of cities from ceremonial centers in this fashion (pp. 225–26):

> Beginning as little more than tribal shrines, in what may be regarded as their classic phases, these centers were elaborated into complexes of public ceremonial structures, usually massive and often extensive and including assemblages of such architectural items as pyramids, platform mounds, temples, palaces, terraces, staircases, courts, and stelae. Operationally they were instruments for the creation of political, social, economic, and sacred space, at the same time as they were symbols of cosmic, social and moral order. Under the religious authority of organized priesthoods and divine monarchs, they elaborated the redistributive aspects of the economy to a position of institutionalized regional dominance, functioned as nodes in a web of administered (gift or treaty) trade, served as foci of craft specialization, and promoted the development of the exact and predictive sciences. Above all, they embodied the aspirations of brittle, pyramidal societies in which, typically, a sacerdotal elite, controlling a corps of officials and perhaps a pretorian guard, ruled over a broad understratum of peasantry.

2. Paul Wheatley, "City as Symbol," Inaugural Lecture delivered at the University College, London, November 20, 1967.

3. Robert McC. Adams, *The Evolution of Urban Society* (Chicago: Aldine, 1967). See especially chap. 4, "Parish and Polity," pp. 120–69 for a discussion of Mesoamerican patterns of rise and decline.

4. H. B. Nicholson, "Religion in Late Pre-Hispanic Central Mexico," in *Handbook of Middle American Indians,* in Guide to Ethnohistorical Sources, (Austin: University of Texas Press, 1964–77): 10:498.

5. See also Paul Wheatley, *From Court to Capital* (Chicago: University of Chicago Press, 1978) for a discussion of the rise of capital cities in ancient Japan.

6. Numa Denis Fustel de Coulanges, *The Ancient City* (New York: Doubleday Anchor Books, n.d.).

7. Mircea Eliade, "Methodological Remarks on the Study of Religious Symbolism," in *The History of Religions: Essays in Methodology*, ed. Mircea Eliade and Joseph Kitagawa (Chicago: University of Chicago Press, 1959), pp. 86–108.

8. Alfredo López Austin, *Hombre-Dios, Religión y Política en el Mundo Nahuatl* (Mexico City: Universidad Autónoma Nacional de México, 1973), p. 9.

9. Adams, *Evolution*, p. 28, and see pp. 21–34, for a concise discussion of the limits and possibilities of utilizing archaeological evidence.

10. In November 1979, the Religious Studies Department at the University of Colorado convened an international body of scholars at a conference entitled "Center and Periphery: The Templo Mayor and the Aztec Empire," to examine and interpret the abundant evidence from Proyecto Templo Mayor, which was excavating the great Aztec temple in Mexico City. Some of the results of the conference appear in my article, "Templo Mayor: The Aztec Vision of Place," *Religion* 11 (1981): 275–97. Also Johanna Broda, in her unpublished manuscript, "Aztec Ideology and Human Sacrifice" (convocation of the conference), begins a new interpretation of the history of Aztec Mexico on the basis of Proyecto Templo Mayor.

11. H. B. Nicholson, "The Late Pre-Hispanic Central Mexican (Aztec) Iconographic System," in *The Iconography of Middle American Sculpture*, ed. Ignacio Bernal (New York: Metropolitan Museum of Art, 1973), p. 72. I am aware of the debate among Mesoamericanists concerning the use of analogy and allegory in attempting to read back into the Classic and Formative stages of ancient Mexican culture from the vantage point of the Post-Classic materials. Yet I agree with Nicholson that a careful and tentative working backward from living forms to dead forms can "yield positive results of great value."

THE SOURCES: FROM STORYBOOK TO ENCYCLOPEDIA

1. Mircea Eliade, "Methodological Remarks on the Study of Religious Symbolism," in *The History of Religions: Essays in Methodology*, ed. Mircea Eliade and Joseph Kitagawa (Chicago: University of Chicago Press, 1959), p. 92.

2. Robert McC. Adams, *The Evolution of Urban Society* (Chicago: Aldine, 1967), p. 33. See Adams's excellent chapter "The Problem and the Evidence" for a concise discussion of the problems and possibilities facing us.

3. My approach to these documents has been directly influenced by the incisive essays on hermeneutics and religion by Jonathan Z. Smith, which have been collected in *Map Is Not Territory: Studies in the History of Religions* (Leiden: E. J. Brill, 1978).

4. Adams, *Evolution*, p. 2.

5. See Juaquin Garcia Icazbalceta's *Don Fray Juan de Zumárraga* (Mexico: Editorial Porrua, S.A., 1947), 2:87–162, for a spirited denial of Zumárraga's inquisitional burnings. His impressive scholarly research argues that this scene was the invention of later historians Juan de Torquemada and Fernando de Álva Ixtlixóchitl. While Zumárraga may not have been the mad burner he is sometimes represented as, Icazbalceta's strong pro-Spanish and anti-Indian biases have, no doubt, influenced his argument. Most contemporary scholars still blame Zumárraga for presiding over the destruction of manuscripts, if not actually lighting the fires at Tezcoco. But Icazbalceta's study does include

an important footnote to the manner in which picture books disappeared. The Indian owners of some picture writing destroyed their own treasures for fear of being brought before the Inquisition and burned at the stake.

6. John Glass, "A Survey of Native Middle American Pictorial Manuscripts," in *Handbook of Middle American Indians,* (Austin: University of Texas Press, 1964–76), 14:3–81. This volume is part of a four-volume group entitled "Guide to Ethnohistorical Sources," and dedicated to describing, listing, and evaluating the various groups of documentary research materials relevant to the study of Middle American Indians. It contains extremely valuable articles about the pictorial and prose archives I will be referring to throughout this chapter. The first eleven volumes in the *Handbook,* which will be utilized in other chapters, are dedicated to general topic areas such as "Physical Anthropology," "Archaeology of Northern Mesoamerica." Hereafter this series of works will be referred to simply as *Handbook* with the relevant volume noted.

7. Bernal Díaz del Castillo, *The Discovery and Conquest of Mexico* (New York: Farrar, Straus & Giroux, 1956), p. 219.

8. George Kubler, *Mexican Architecture of the Sixteenth Century* (New Haven, Conn.: Yale University Press, 1948), p. 1.

9. Angel Maria Garibay K., quoted in Arthur J. O. Anderson, "Sahagún's Nahuatl Texts as Indigenist Documents," *Estudios de Cultura Nahuatl* 2 (1960): 33.

10. See Mircea Eliade, "Paradise and Utopia: Mythical Geography and Eschatology, in *The Quest* (Chicago: University of Chicago Press, 1969) for a discussion of America as the "New World," which, it was believed, would usher in a new age for all mankind.

11. For a detailed and inspired analysis of the persistence and transformation of Pre-Columbian pictorial traditions, see Donald Robertson, *Mexican Manuscript Painting of the Early Colonial Period: The Metropolitan Schools* (New Haven, Conn.: Yale University Press, 1959).

12. Ibid., p. 2.

13. *Relaciones Geográficas,* a major group of sources concerning sixteenth-century Mexico and the Spanish Indies, consist of replies by local Spanish officials throughout Middle and South America "to a standard questionnaire developed by imperial bureaucrats in Madrid, making 50 broad queries applicable alike to European, Indian, and Maritime communities in the overseas realms." Howard Cline, in his article, "The Relaciones Geográficas of the Spanish Indies, 1577–1648," in *Handbook,* 12:183, tells us that the questionnaire "specified in detail how alcaldes mayores, corregidores, and others assigned to answer it were to do so." These documents required a *pintura* or map and the written section.

14. Kubler's "Introduction: The Mendicant Friars," in *Mexican Architecture,* provides the best general summary of the Mendicant enterprise in Mexico.

15. John Leddy Phelan, *The Millennial Kingdom of the Franciscans in the New World* (Berkeley: University of California Press, 1970).

16. Kubler, *Mexican Architecture,* p. 3.

17. Robertson, *Mexican Manuscript Painting,* p. 185–86.

18. Juan A. Vasquez, "The Religions of Mexico and of Central and South America," in *Reader's Guide to the Great Religions*, ed. Charles J. Adams (New York: Free Press, 1977).

19. I am following Friedrich Katz, *The Ancient American Civilizations* (New York: Praeger, 1972), p. 1.

20. Johanna Broda, "Algunas Notas Sobre Critica de Fuentes del Mexico Antiguo," *Revista de Indias* (Madrid, 1976).

21. Jill Leslie Furst, *Codex Vindobonensis Mexicanus I: A Commentary*, Institute for Mesoamerican Studies Publication 4, (Albany: State University of New York at Albany, 1978), p. 7.

22. Mary E. Smith, *Picture Writing from Ancient Southern Mexico* (Norman: University of Oklahoma Press, 1973).

23. See especially Charles Gibson, "A Survey of Middle American Prose Manuscripts in the Native Historical Tradition," in *Handbook*, 15:311–21, for an analysis of the nature of the prose sources generated in the postconquest situation.

24. I. J. Gelb, *A Study of Writing* (Chicago: University of Chicago Press, 1963), p. 191.

25. Charles E. Dibble, "Writing in Central Mexico," in *Handbook*, 10:324.

26. See the frontispiece of *The Codex Mendoza*, trans. James Cooper Clark, 3 vols. (London: Waterlow & Sons, 1938), for an example of this combination; the Mexican manuscript, known as the collection of Mendoza, is preserved in the Bodleian Library, Oxford.

27. H. B. Nicholson, "Phoneticism in Late Pre-Hispanic Central Mexican Writing Systems," in *Mesoamerica Writing Systems*, ed. Elizabeth Benson (Washington, D.C.: Harvard University Press, 1971), p. 3.

28. Furst, *Codex Vindobonensis*, p. 13.

29. Glass, in *Handbook*, 14:3–81.

30. H. B. Nicholson, "Middle American Ethnohistory: An Overview," *Handbook*, 14:488.

31. Toribio de Motolinía, *Motolinía's History of the Indians of New Spain*, trans. Francis Borgia Steck (Washington, D.C.: Academy of American Franciscan History, 1951), p. 75.

32. See Alexander Marshack, *The Roots of Civilization: The Cognitive Beginnings of Man's First Art, Symbol, and Notation* (New York: McGraw-Hill, 1972) for an elaborate discussion of time-factored thought in primitive culture.

33. Paul Wheatley, *The Pivot of the Four Quarters* (Chicago: Aldine, 1971), p. 384.

34. Glass, in *Handbook*, 14:28.

35. I have benefited significantly from H. B. Nicholson's detailed analysis of primary sources found in "Topiltzin Quetzalcoatl of Tollan: A Problem in Mesoamerican Ethnohistory" (Ph.D. diss., Harvard University, 1957).

36. See Robert Chadwick, "Native Pre-Aztec History of Central Mexico," in *Handbook*, 11:474–505, for an unusual interpretation concerning Mixtec-Toltec relations and exchanges of sacred historical material.

37. See Nicholson, "Topiltzin Quetzalcoatl," pp. 201–3, for the details of this version.

38. Zelia Nuttal's *Codex Nuttal* (Cambridge, 1902) is a facsimile edition of an ancient Mexican codex belonging to Lord Zouche of Harynworth.

39. Alfonso Caso, *Interpretation del Codice Selden 3135*, (Mexico, 1964), facsimile edition.

40. Nicholson, "Topiltzin Quetzalcoatl," pp. 201–6.

41. Furst, *Codex Vindobonensis*, pp. 102–9, has an elaborate description of these activities.

42. *Codex Telleriano-Remensis: Manuscrit Mexicain No. 385 à la Bibliothèque nationale*, ed. E. T. Hamy (Paris, 1899).

43. *Codex Vaticanus A: Il Manoscritto Messicano Vaticano 3738, detto II Docice Rios*, ed. Franz Ehrle (Rome, 1900).

44. *Historia Tolteca-Chichimeca*, in *Anales de Quauhtinchan* (Mexico: Antigua Libreria Robredo de Jose Porrua e Hijos, 1947).

45. Nicholson, "Topiltzin Quetzalcoatl," pp. 87–108.

46. I am following Nicholson's strategy in "Topiltzin Quetzalcoatl."

47. Eliose Quiñones Keber, "Topiltzin Quetzalcoatl in Texts and Images" (M.A. thesis, Columbia University, 1979), pp. 51–56.

48. Ibid., p. 6.

49. *Historia Tolteca-Chichimeca*, paragraph 32. Throughout this book the pre-Columbian city of Cholollan will also be referred to by its colonial rendition, Cholula.

50. Ibid. , paragraphs 81–90.

51. Ibid., paragraph 337.

52. Robert Barlow, "Anales de Cuauhtitlán and Leyenda de los Soles," *Hispanic American Historical Review* 27 (1948): 520–26.

53. Robert Bierhorst, *Four Masterworks of American Indian Literature* (New York: Farrar, Straus, & Giroux, 1974), pp. 24–26. I shall be using Bierhorst's translation of this document throughout this work because it is the best and most complete English version of the Quetzalcoatl material.

54. Ibid., p. 37.

55. Ibid., pp. 17–21.

56. "Historia de los Mexicanos por sus pinturas," in *Nueva Colección de Documentos para la Historia de Mexico*, ed. Juan Bautista Pomar (Mexico: Editorial Salvador Chávez Hayhde, 1941),pp. 209–18.

57. I am following H. B. Nicholson's decision to give the name *Juan Cano Relación* to two documents, *Relación de la genealogía y linaje de las señores que han senoreado esta tierra de la nueva España* and *Origen de los Mexicanos* (ibid).

58. *Histoyre du Mechique*, in *Teogonia e Historia de los Mexicanos: Tres Opusculos del Siglo XVI*, ed. Angel Maria Garibay K. (Mexico, 1973).

59. Alvarado Tezozomoc, *Cronica Mexicana* (Mexico: Editorial Leyenda, S.A., 1944), p. 16.

60. Ibid., p. 70.

61. Ibid., p. 490.

62. Ibid., p. 520.

63. .Nicholson, "Topiltzin Quetzalcoatl," p. 11.

64. Juan Bautista Pomar, *Relación de Tezcoco*, in *Nueva Colección de Documentos para la Historia de Mexico* (Mexico, 1941).

65. Benjamin Keen, *The Aztec Image in Western Thought* (New Brunswick, N.J.: Rutgers University Press, 1972), p. 381.

66. Diego Muñoz Camargo, *Historia de Tlaxcala* (Mexico: Chavero, 1892), I:50.

67. Ibid., II:71.

68. Hernán Cortes, *Five Letters to the Emperor*, trans. J. Bayard Morris (New York: W. W. Norton, n.d.), p. 74.

69. Nicholson, "Topiltzin Quetzalcoatl," pp. 127–28.

70. Gabriel de Rojas, "Relación de Cholula," *Revista Mexicana de Estudios Historicos* 1 (1927): 158–70.

71. A. Leo Oppenheim, *Ancient Mesopotamia: Portrait of a Dead Civilization* (Chicago: University of Chicago Press, 1964), p. 153.

72. Ibid., p. 144.

73. Broda, "Algunas Notas," p. 130.

74. Motolinía, *Motolinía's History*, pp. 137–38.

75. Ibid., p. 40.

76. Ibid.

77. Nicholson, "Topiltzin Quetzalcoatl," pp. 80–87.

78. Alfredo López Austin, "The Research Method of Fray Bernardino de Sahagún: The Questionnaires," in *Sixteenth Century Mexico*, ed. Munroe Edmonson (Albuquerque: University of New Mexico Press, 1974).

79. Phelan, *Millennial Kingdom*, p. 18.

80. Bernardino de Sahagún, *Historia General de las cosas de Nueva España*, ed. Angel Maria Garibay K. (Mexico City: Editorial Porrua, 1956), 1:27.

81. Fray Bernardino de Sahagún, *The Florentine Codex: General History of the Things of New Spain*, ed. Arthur J. O. Anderson and Charles Dibble, 12 vols. (Santa Fe: School of American Research and University of Utah, 1950–69).

82. Austin, "Research Method of Sahagún," pp. 115–20.

83. Ibid.

84. Ibid., p. 135.

85. Sahagún, *Florentine Codex*, see especially book 6.

86. Ibid., book 3.

87. Ibid., book 12.

88. Diego Durán, *Book of the Gods and Rites and the Ancient Calendar*, trans. and ed. Fernando Horcasitas and Doris Heyden (Norman: University of Oklahoma Press, 1970), p. 51.

89. Ibid., p. 35.

90. Diego Durán, *Historia de las Indias de Nueva España y Islas de Tierra Firme* (Mexico: Imprenta de J. M. Andrade y F. Escalente, 1867), 1:250.

91. Durán, *Book of the Gods and Rites*, p. 54.

92. Durán, *Historia de las Indias*, 2:5–9.

93. Fray Diego de Landa, Relación de las Cosas de Yucutan, ed. Alfred Tozzer (Cambridge: Harvard University Press, 1941).

94. Paul Westheim, *The Art of Ancient Mexico* (Garden City, N.Y.: Anchor Books, 1965), p. 89.

95. Motolinía, *Motolinía's History*, p. 105.

96. René Millon, *Urbanization at Teotihuacán, Mexico: The Teotihuacán Map* (Austin: University of Texas Press, 1973).

97. Charles Margain, "Pre-Columbian Architecture of Central Mexico," in *Handbook* 10:73.

98. Keber, "Topiltzin Quetzalcoatl."

99. Jorge R. Acosta, "El Altar 2," in *Proyecto Cholula* (Mexico: Instituto Nacional de Antropología e Historia, 1970).

100. Alfredo López Austin, *Hombre-Dios, Religion y Politica en el Mundo Nahuatl* (Mexico City: Universidad Autónoma Nacional de Mexico, 1973), p. 9.

101. Clifford Geertz, *The Interpretation of Culture* (New York: Basic Books, 1973), p. 10.

102. López Austin, *Hombre-Dios*, pp. 13–43.

103. Lewis Hanke, *Aristotle and the American Indian* (Bloomington: Indiana University Press, 1959), p. 6.

104. Alexander von Humboldt, *Vues de cordilleres et monuments des peuples indigenes de l'Amerique* (Paris: F. Schoell, 1810).

105. Daniel Brinton, *Essays of an Americanist* (New York: Johnson Reprint, 1970), p. 85.

106. See H. B. Nicholson, "Eduard Georg Seler, 1849–1922," in *Handbook*, 13:348–69.

107. Laurette Séjourné, *El Universo de Quetzalcoatl* (Mexico: Fondo de Culture Economica, 1962).

108. Miguel Léon-Portilla, *Aztec Thought and Culture* (Norman: University of Oklahoma Press, 1963).

109. Wigberto Jiménez Moreno, "Tula y los Toltecas Segun las Fuentes Historicas," *Revista Mexicana de Estudios Antropológicos* 5 (1941): 79–85.

110. Paul Kirchhoff, "Quetzalcoatl, Huemac y el Fin de Tula," *Cuadernos Americanos* 84 (1955): 163–96.

111. A summary of both positions appears in Wigberto Jiménez Moreno, "Sintesis de La Historia Precolonial del Valle de Mexico," *Revista Mexicana de Estudios Antropológicos* 14 (1954): 219–36.

112. Jacque Lafaye, *Quetzalcoatl and Guadalupe: The Formation of Mexican National Consciousness, 1531–1813* (Chicago: University of Chicago Press, 1976).

QUETZALCOATL AND THE FOUNDATION OF TOLLAN

1. *Cantares Mexicanos*, trans. Angel Maria Garibay K., in *Poesia Nahuatl* (Mexico: Universidad Nacional Autonoma de Mexico, 1968), p. 1. This powerful song was translated into English by the nineteenth-century scholar Daniel Brinton in *Ancient Nahuatl Poetry* (New York: AMS Press, 1969), p. 105. The Brinton edition contains a detailed analysis of the text which is "quite archaic and presents many difficulties." Recently, a fine rendering of the original Nahuatl into English has been offered by John Bierhorst in *Four Masterworks of American Indian Literature* (New York: Farrar, Straus & Giroux, 1974). Throughout this chapter I will be quoting extensively from the Bierhorst translation of fragments and sagas about Quetzalcoatl found in the Leyenda de los Soles, the Anales de Cuauhtitlán, the Florentine Codex, and Cantares Mexicanos. Though there was once great controversy about the pre- and post-conquest character of this song, it seems widely accepted that this text

was definitely pre-Columbian in origin. All of the translators mentioned here state that the text clearly relates to Topiltzin Quetzalcoatl of Tollan and that it is concerned with the fall of Tollan.

2. H. B. Nicholson has discussed the nomenclatural aspects of this figure, noting that Topiltzin (To-pil[li]-tzin) translates as "our prince" or "our son," while Quetzalcoatl (quetzal[li]-coatl) literally translates "quetzal feather snake" or "feathered serpent," although the latter is not literal, but acceptable. " 'Precious snake' is a reasonable supplementary interpretation, due to the precious nature of the long green tail feathers of this prized bird." But the most widespread proper name which appears to refer to this character is Naxcit(l). "The usual etymology is 'four foot' (na[hui]-[i]cxitl), which seems acceptable; it has often been interpreted (e.g., Lehmann, 1922: 293) as referring to the four cardinal points (from which the wind blows)." This name had particular play and importance in the sources relating to Guatemalan ceremonial centers where the feathered serpent cult existed. Another name which appears with this figure is Tepeuhqui, probably signifying the "mighty one." The commonest of the calendrical names for this figure is Ce Acatl, which translates "1 Reed," the supposed date of Topiltzin Quetzalcoatl's birth, death, and return to Mexico. H. B. Nicholson, "Topiltzin Quetzalcoatl of Tollan: A Problem in Mesoamerican Ethnohistory" (Ph.D. diss., Harvard University, 1957), pp. 353–56.

3. Paul Wheatley, *The Pivot of the Four Quarters* (Chicago: Aldine, 1971), p. 225.

4. Paul Wheatley, *From Court to Capital* (Chicago: University of Chicago Press, 1978), pp. 8–11.

5. Paul Wheatley, "City as Symbol," inaugural lecture delivered at University College, London, November 20, 1967.

6. Paul Wheatley, "The Suspended Pelt: Reflections on a Discarded Model of Spatial Structure," *Geographic Humanism, Analysis and Social Action*, ed. Donald R. Deskins, Jr., Michigan Geographical Publication 17 (Ann Arbor: Department of Geography, University of Michigan (Ann Arbor, Mich., 1977).

7. Paul Kirchhoff , "Mesoamerica: Sus Limites Geograficas, Composicion Etnica y Caracteres Culturales," *Acta Americana* 1 (1943): 92–107.

8. René Millon, *Urbanization at Teotihuacán, Mexico: The Teotihuacan Map* (Austin: University of Texas Press, 1973).

9. See Adams's discussion of social surplus and its role in urban development in *Evolution of Urban Society* (Chicago: Aldine, 1967), esp. pp. 38–79.

10. Ibid., p. 165.

11. Wheatley, *Pivot*, p. 319.

12. Ibid., p. 414.

13. Ibid.

14. Wheatley, "City as Symbol," p. 10.

15. See Mircea Eliade's classic discussion of the *axis mundi* in *The Myth of the Eternal Return* (New York: Pantheon Books, 1965), pp. 12–17, and Wheatley, "The Suspended Pelt."

16. Wheatley, "The Suspended Pelt," p. 6.

17. Quoted in Miguel León-Portilla, *Aztec Thought and Culture* (Norman: University of Oklahoma Press, 1963), p. 39.

18. A. Recinos, ed., *Annals of the Cakchiquels and Title of the Lords of Totonicapan* (Norman: University of Oklahoma Press, 1953), pp. 45, 47.

19. Richard Diehl, "Pre-Hispanic Relationships Between the Basin of Mexico and North and West Mexico," in *The Valley of Mexico*, ed. Eric Wolf (Albuquerque: University of New Mexico Press, 1976), p. 263.

20. Jorge Hardoy, *Pre-Columbian Cities* (New York: Walker Publishers, 1973), p. 82.

21. Nigel Davies, *The Toltecs* (Norman: University of Oklahoma Press, 1977), pp. 24–51, describes the various meanings of this term.

22. Mircea Eliade, "Cosmogonic Myth and Sacred History," in *The Quest* (Chicago: University of Chicago Press, 1969), p. 73.

23. Ibid.

24. For an elaborate discussion of aretalogy, see Moses Hadas and Morton Smith, *Heroes and Gods: Spiritual Biographies in Antiquity* (New York: Harper & Row, 1965).

25. *Historia Tolteca-Chichimeca*, see Davies, *The Toltecs*, pp. 302–12, for discussion of the various translations of this passage.

26. Fray Bernardino de Sahagún, *The Florentine Codex: General History of the Things of New Spain*, ed. Arthur J. O. Anderson and Charles Dibble, 12 vols. (Santa Fe: School of American Research and University of Utah, 1950–69), 10:168.

27. *Anales de Cuauhtitlán*, trans. Bierhorst, *Four Masterworks*.

28. Mircea Eliade, *Patterns in Comparative Religions* (New York: Meridian Books, 1967), pp. 216–39.

29. *Leyenda de los Soles*, trans. Bierhorst, *Four Masterworks*, p. 21.

30. Ibid.

31. Ibid., p. 23.

32. *Anales de Cuauhtitlán*, ibid., p. 25.

33. Sahagún, *Florentine Codex*, 10:165.

34. Ibid., p. 165.

35. Ibid.

36. Ibid., p. 166.

37. Ibid.

38. Ibid.

39. Ibid.

40. Ibid.

41. Ibid.

42. Ibid., p. 169.

43. Bierhorst, *Four Masterworks*, p. 38. The Dibble and Anderson translation reads, "These started and proceeded from Quetzalcoatl—all craft and wisdom."

44. Sahagún, *Florentine Codex*, 10:166.

45. Ibid. (quoted in Bierhorst, *Four Masterworks*, p. 38).

46. Sahagún, *Florentine Codex*, 10:167.

47. Diego Durán, *Book of the Gods and Rites and the Ancient Calendar*, trans. and ed. Fernando Horcasitas and Doris Heyden (Norman: University of Oklahoma Press, 1970), p. 64.

48. *Anales de Cuauhtitlán*, trans. Bierhorst, *Four Masterworks*, p. 26.

49. Ibid. See also León-Portilla, *Aztec Thought and Culture*, esp. pp. 29–32, for his alternate translation of the deity names and the significance of this quest.

50. Sahagún, *Florentine Codex*, 10:168.

51. Alfredo López Austin, *Hombre-Dios, Religion y Politica en el Mundo Nahuatl* (Mexico City: Universidad Autonoma Nacional de Mexico, 1973), contains an intricate and excellent discussion of Quetzalcoatl's significance for political history.

52. Sahagún, *Florentine Codex*, 3:14.

53. Ibid.

54. Ibid.

55. Mircea Eliade, "The World, the City, the House," in *Occultism, Witchcraft and Cultural Fashions* (Chicago: University of Chicago Press, 1976), p. 22.

56. Cornelius Loew, *Myth, Sacred History, and Philosophy* (New York: Harcourt, Brace & World, 1967), p. 5.

57. H. B. Nicholson, "Religion in Pre-Hispanic Central Mexico," in *Handbook* 10:397.

58. Wayne Elzey, "The Nahua Myths of the Suns," *Numen*, August 1976.

59. Ibid.

60. A. J. L. Wensinck, "The Semitic New York and the Origin of Eschatology," *Acta Orientalia* 1 (1923); Henri Frankfort, *Kingship and the Gods* (Chicago: University of Chicago Press, 1948), p. 4.

61. Sahagún, *Florentine Codex*, 2:14–15.

62. Ibid.

63. Thorkild Jacobsen, in Henri Frankfort et al., *The Intellectual Adventure of Ancient Man* (Chicago: University of Chicago Press, 1946), p. 125, and see especially pp. 125–219 for a description of the Mesopotamian cosmological conviction.

Other Tollans

1. I am influenced in my use of the term "place" by Jonathan Z. Smith's significant interpretations in the article "The Influence of Symbols upon Social Change: A Place on Which to Stand," *Worship* 44, no. 8 (October 1970): 457–74. Writing about two important religious stances, he says, "From this perspective, place (whether in an open or closed structure) ought not to be viewed as a static concept. It is through an understanding and symbolization of place that a society or individual creates itself. Without straining the point, this active sense is crystallized in the expression, 'to take place' as a synonym for 'to happen,' 'to occur,' 'to be.' It is by virtue of its view of its place that a society or an individual (that history or biography as the description of a society or individual) takes place. The insight of the poet Mallarmé may be extended as the exhaustive description of history or biography: 'Nothing shall have taken place but place' " (p. 472).

2. Mircea Eliade, *Patterns in Comparative Religions* (New York: Meridian Books, 1967), especially chap. 1.

3. Roy Rappaport, *Ecology, Meaning, Religion* (Richmond, Calif.: North Atlantic Books, 1979), p. 148.

4. Ibid.

5. Quoted in Doris Heyden, "An Interpretation of the Cave Underneath the Pyramid of the Sun in Teotihuacán, Mexico," *American Antiquity* 40 (April 1975): 139.

6. Doris Heyden, "Sacred Geography: Myths and Symbols in Ancient Mexico," mimeographed (Boulder, Colo.: Center and Periphery Conference, November 1979), p. 7.

7. Ibid., p. 8.

8. See Nigel Davies, *The Toltecs* (Norman: University of Oklahoma Press, 1977), pp. 32–47, for the evidence concerning Tollan Teotihuacán.

9. See René Millon's excellent summary of archaeological work in *Urbanization at Teotihuacán, Mexico: The Teotihuacán Map* (Austin: University of Texas Press, 1973).

10. René Millon, "Social Relations in Ancient Teotihuacán," in *Sixteenth Century Mexico*, ed. E. Wolf (Albuquerque, N.M.: University of New Mexico Press, 1974), p. 214.

11. I am following Esther Pasztory's concise discussion of Teotihuacán's setting in *The Murals of Tepantitla, Teotihuacán* (New York: Garland Publisher, 1976), p. 25.

12. Friedrich Katz, *The Ancient American Civilizations* (New York: Praeger, 1972), pp. 50–55.

13. See the excellent series of essays on the Middle Classic period in Esther Pasztory, ed. *Middle Classic Mesoamerica; A.D. 400–700* (New York: Columbia University Press, 1978).

14. Millon, *Urbanization at Teotihuacán*, p. 54.

15. Ibid., p. 55.

16. Pasztory, *Murals of Tepantitla*, pp. 110–30.

17. Robert McC. Adams, *The Evolution of Urban Society* (Chicago: Aldine, 1967), p. 46.

18. See J. C. Beaglehole, "Case of the Needless Death: Reconstructing the Scene," in *The Historian as Detective*, ed. Robin W. Winks (New York: Harper Colophon Books, 1968), pp. 279–302.

19. Millon, *Urbanization at Teotihuacán*, p. 47.

20. Eliade, *Myth of the Eternal Return*, p. 12.

21. See Millon, "Social Relations in Ancient Teotihuacán," pp. 236–39, for evidence concerning the twin rulers of the city.

22. H. B. Nicholson, "Major Sculpture in Pre-Hispanic Central Mexico," in *Handbook* 10:97.

23. I am following Pasztory, *Murals of Tepantitla*, pp. 112–21. My interpretation, however, goes beyond hers.

24. William T. Sanders, "Settlement Patterns in Central Mexico," in *Handbook* 10:3–45. Throughout this section I am utilizing the works of Jorge Hardoy, *Pre-Columbian Cities* (New York: Walker, 1973), and Eduardo Noguera, "Exploraciones en Xochicalco," *Cuadernos Americanos* 5 (1945): 37–52, and Jaime Litvak King, "Las Relaciones Externas de Xochicalco: una Evaluacion de su Significado," *Anales de Antropologia* 9 (1972).

25. Nicholson, "Major Sculpture," 10:105.

26. Hardoy, *Pre-Columbian Cities*, p. 98.

27. See Toribio de Motolinía, *Motolinía's History of the Indians of New Spain*, trans. Francis Borgia Steck (Washington, D.C.: Academy of American Franciscan History, 1951), pp. 136–38, for one source account of Quetzalcoatl's importance in Cholollan.

28. Davies, *The Toltecs*, p. 31.

29. Eric Wolf, *Sons of the Shaking Earth* (Chicago: University of Chicago Press, 1959), p. 6.

30. Bernal Díaz del Castillo, *The Discovery and Conquest of Mexico* (New York: Farrar, Straus & Giroux, 1956), p. 181.

31. Ibid.

32. Ronald A. Grennes-Ravitz, "The Extrapolation of Pre-Classic Reality from Post-Classic Models: The Concept of an Olmec Empire in Mesoamerica," *Actas del XLI Congreso Internacional de Americanistas* 1 (1975): 378–83.

33. *Historia Tolteca-Chichimeca*, in *Anales de Quauhtinchan*, (Mexico: Antigua Libreria Robredo de Jose Porrua e Hijos, 1947). See also a summary of the sources concerning Cholula in Pedro Carrasco, "The Peoples of Central Mexico," in *Handbook*, 11:459–75.

34. See the series of articles about this city in *Proyecto Cholula*, ed. Ignacio Marguina (Mexico: Instituto Nacional de Antropologia y Historia, 1970), for the best summary of evidence. Focus on Mercedes Olivera de V., "La Importancia Religiosa de Cholula," pp. 211–42.

35. Gabriel Rojas, "Relación de Cholula," *Revista Mexicana de Estudios Historicos* 1 (1927): 162.

36. Ibid.

37. *Historia Tolteca-Chichimeca*, paragraph 330.

38. Victor Turner, *Dramas, Fields, and Metaphors* (Ithaca, N.Y. : Cornell University Press, 1974), p. 185.

39. Maria Nolasco Armas, "Cuauhtlancingo, Un Pueblo de la Region de Cholula," *Proyecto Cholula*, p. 254.

40. Ibid. See also Jorge Acosta, "El Altar 2," in *Proyecto Cholula*, p. 110.

41. Victor Turner, "The Center out There, Pilgrim's Goal," *History of Religions* 12 (1972): 191–230.

42. Chichén Itzá means "at the rim of the well of the Itzá." See J. Eric S. Thompson, *The Rise and Fall of the Mayan Civilization* (Norman: University of Oklahoma Press, 1966), p. 133.

43. Alfred Tozzer, *Chichén Itzá and its Cenote of Sacrifice: A Comparative Study of Contemporaneous Maya and Toltec* (Cambridge: Harvard University Press, 1957).

44. Michael Coe, *The Maya* (New York: Praeger, 1973), pp. 117–31.

45. Muriel Porter Weaver, *The Aztecs, Mayas, and Their Predecessors* (New York: Seminar Press, 1972), p. 225.

46. Carlos Margain, "Pre-Columbian Architecture in Central Mexico," in *Handbook* 10:71–72.

47. Jonathan Z. Smith, "Influence of Symbols upon Social Change, " p. 468.

48. Diego de Landa, *Relación de las Cosas de Yucatan*, ed. Alfred Tozzer (Cambridge: Harvard University Press, 1941), p. 24.

49. Ibid.

50. *The Book of Chilam Balam of Chumayel,* ed. Ralph L. Roys (Norman: University of Oklahoma Press, 1967), quoted in Nicholson "Topiltzin Quetzalcoatl," p. 286.

51. For an important discussion of religious authority, see Joachim Wach, *Sociology of Religion* (Chicago: University of Chicago Press, 1967), pp. 331–73.

52. See H. B. Nicholson's account of primary sources from Yucatan in "Topiltzin Quetzalcoatl," pp. 269–91.

53. Robert Nisbet, *The Sociological Tradition* (New York: Basic Books, 1966), p. 9.

THE RETURN OF QUETZALCOATL AND THE IRONY OF EMPIRE

1. Octavio Paz, *The Other Mexico* (New York: Grove Press, 1972), p. 84.

2. *Anales de Cuauhtitlán,* trans. John Bierhorst, *Four Masterworks of American Indian Literature* (New York: Farrar, Straus & Giroux, 1974), p. 37.

3. Bernal Díaz del Castillo, *The Discovery and Conquest of Mexico* (New York: Farrar, Straus & Giroux), p. 191.

4. Miguel León-Portilla, *Pre-Columbian Literature of Mexico* (Norman: University of Oklahoma Press, 1969), p. 87.

5. The category of application and its relation to mythical traditions has been discussed by Adolph Jensen in *Myth and Cult among Primitive People* (Chicago: University of Chicago Press, 1963), see especially pp. 195–211. For a critical discussion of Jensen's view, see Jonathan Z. Smith, "A Pearl of Great Price and a Cargo of Yams: A Study of Situational Incongruity," *History of Religions* 16 (1976): 1–19. I take up this critique in "Quetzalcoatl's Revenge: Primordium and Application in Aztec Religion," *History of Religions* 19 (1979): 296–320.

6. Miguel León-Portilla, ed., *The Broken Spears* (Boston: Beacon Press, 1962), p. 146.

7. See Eric Wolf, *Sons of the Shaking Earth* (Chicago: University of Chicago Press, 1959), especially the chapter "The Conquest of Utopia," for an account of the complexities of the fall of the Aztec kingdom.

8. Friedrich Katz, *The Ancient American Civilizations* (New York: Praeger, 1972), p. 129.

9. R. C. Padden, *The Hummingbird and the Hawk* (New York: Harper and Row, 1967) tends toward this view.

10. See Katz, *Ancient American Civilizations,* pp. 129–37, for a concise discussion of the Aztec's early history in the Lake Culture.

11. Ibid., esp. pp. 138–47.

12. Robert McC. Adams, *The Evolution of Urban Society* (Chicago: Aldine, 1967), p. 12.

13. Ibid., p. 119.

14. Ibid.

15. Diego Durán, *Historia de las Indias de Nueva España y Islas de Tierra Firme* (Mexico: Imprenta de J. M. Andrade y F. Escalante, 1867), 1:45.

16. My interpretation appears to be supported in both Nigel Davies's *The Aztecs* (London: Macmillan, 1973), and Burr Brundage's *A Rain of Darts* (Austin: University of Texas Press, 1972). Both discuss Aztec royalty from the point of Acamapichtli's coronation.

17. Miguel León-Portilla, "El Proceso de Aculturacion de las Chichimecas de Xólotl," *Estudios de Cultura Nahuatl* 8 (1967).

18. Mircea Eliade, *The Myth of the Eternal Return* (New York: Pantheon Books, 1965), especially chap. 2.

19. Edward Calnek, "The Internal Structure of Tenochtitlan," in *The Valley of Mexico*, ed. Eric Wolf (Albuquerque: University of New Mexico Press, 1976).

20. A. R. Pagden, ed., *Hernando Cortes, 1485–1547: Letters from Mexico* (New York: Grossman Publishers, 1971), p. 103.

21. See Donald Robertson's *Mexican Manuscript Painting of the Early Colonial Period: The Metropolitan Schools* (New Haven, Conn.: Yale University Press, 1959), for detailed information about this document. See also Davíd Carrasco, "City as Symbol in Aztec Thought: The Clues from the Codex Mendoza," *History of Religions* 20 (1981): 199–223.

22. León-Portilla, *Pre-Columbian Literature*, p. 87.

23. Quoted in Wayne Elzey, "Mythology of the Ages of the World" (Ph.D. diss., University of Chicago, 1975).

24. Durán, *Historia de las Indias*, 2:343.

25. Ibid.

26. Johanna Broda, "El Tributo en Trajes Guerreros y la Estructura del Sistema Tributario Mexica,"in *Economia, Politica e Ideologia en el Mexico Prehispanico*, ed. Pedro Carrasco and Johanna Broda (Mexico City: Instituto de Antropologia y Historia, 1978).

27. Fray Bernardino de Sahagún, *The Florentine Codex: General History of the Things of New Spain*, ed. Arthur J. O. Anderson and Charles Dibble, 12 vols. (Santa Fe: School of American Research and University of Utah, 1950-69), 6:83.

28. Johanna Broda, "Aztec Ideology and Human Sacrifice" (convocation lecture delivered at the conference "Center and Periphery: The Templo Mayor and the Aztec Empire," Boulder, Colorado, 1979).

29. See Davíd Carrasco, "Templo Mayor: The Aztec Vision of Place," *Religion* 11 (1981): 275-97.

30. Alfonso Caso, *El Pueblo del Sol* (Mexico: Fondo de Cultura Economica, 1953).

31. Mircea Eliade, *Patterns in Comparative Religion* (New York: Meridian Books, 1967), p. 125.

32. Wayne Elzey, "The Nahua Myth of the Suns," *Numen*, August, 1976.

33. Ibid.

34. Sahagún, *Florentine Codex*, 6:83.

35. Ibid.

36. Ibid., p. 181.

37. See Jacques Soustelle's discussion of Aztec society and the priesthood in the important *Daily Life of the Aztecs* (Stanford, Calif.: Stanford University Press, 1962), pp. 36–94. Quequetzalcoa is the plural of Quetzalcoatl.

38. Quoted in H. B. Nicholson's splendid article, "Religion in Pre-Hispanic Central Mexico," in *Handbook* 10:395–445.

39. Sahagún, *Florentine Codex*, 6:98.

40. Toribio de Benavente O. Motolinía, *Historia de los Indios de la Nueva España* (Mexico: Editorial Porrua, 1969), p. 12.

41. Fernando Alvarado Tezozomoc, *Cronica Mexicana* (Mexico: Editorial Leyenda, S.A., 1944), p. 490.

42. Eloise Quiñones Keber, "Topiltzin Quetzalcoatl in Text and Images" (M.A. thesis, Columbia University, 1979), p. 64.

43. Victor Turner, *Dramas, Fields, and Metaphors* (Ithaca, N.Y.: Cornell University Press, 1974), p. 26.

44. Judith Shklar, "Subversive Genealogies," in *Myth, Symbol and Culture*, ed. Clifford Geertz (New York: W. W. Norton, 1972).

45. Quoted in H. B. Nicholson, "Topiltzin Quetzalcoatl of Tollan," A Problem in Mesoamerican Ethnohistory" (Ph.D. diss., Harvard University, 1957), p. 12.

46. Anales de Cuauhtitlán, trans. Bierhorst, *Four Masterworks*, pp. 28–29.

47. Ibid., pp. 33–35.

48. Sahagún, *Florentine Codex*, trans. Bierhorst, *Four Masterworks*, pp. 43, 57.

49. Stanley Tambiah, "The Galactic Polity: The Structure of Traditional Kingdoms in Southeast Asia," *New York Academy of Sciences*, vol. 293 (1974), discusses the character of exemplary centers or "center-oriented constructs," in terms of pulsating galactic polities which dominated life in Southeast Asia.

50. Edward Shils, "Center and Periphery," *Selected Essays*, (Chicago: Center for Social Organization Studies, 1970), pp. 7–8.

51. Tambiah, "The Galactic Polity." In using categories such as "center" and "periphery," I am building upon the work of Shils; Jonathan Z. Smith, "The Wobbling Pivot," *Journal of Religion* 52, no. 2 (April 1972): 134–49; Richard Hecht, "Center and Periphery: Some Aspects of the Social World of Ptolemaic and Early Roman Alexandria," mimeographed (Santa Barbara, Cal.: University of California, 1979); Alfonso Ortiz, *The Tewa World* (Chicago: University of Chicago Press, 1979). I have also benefitted from the insights of Jane Marie Swanberg, whose paper, "Center and Periphery as a Geography for Reflection: The North American Trickster Figure," mimeographed (Boulder, Colo.: University of Colorado, 1980), explores the value of these categories in a remarkable fashion.

52. See Wigberto Jiménez Moreno, "Religión o Religiónes Mesoamericanos," *Acta y Memorias, XXXVIII Congreso International de Americanistas* (1968), 3:201–6.

53. Hernando Cortes, "The Second Dispatch of Hernando Cortes to the Emperor," trans. J. Bayard Morris, *Five Letters to the Emperor* (New York: W. W. Norton, n.d.), p. 98.

54. *Anales de Cuauhtitlán*, trans. Bierhorst, *Four Masterworks*, p. 38.

55. Esther Pasztory, *Aztec Stone Sculpture* (New York: The Center for Interamerican Relations, 1977).

56. Broda, "Aztec Ideology and Human Sacrifice," pp. 20–27.

57. Quoted in León-Portilla, *The Broken Spears*, p. 7.

58. Ibid., p. 4.

59. Ibid., p. 5.

60. Ibid.

61. Sahagún, *Florentine Codex*, 8:47.

62. León-Portilla, *Broken Spears*, p. 116.

63. Turner, *Dramas, Fields and Metaphors*, p. 42.

64. Sahagún, *Florentine Codex* 1:69, Appendix.

65. Tezozomoc, *Cronica Mexicana*, p. 171.

66. Sahagún, *Florentine Codex*, 12:9.

67. Ibid., p. 17.

68. Ibid., p. 20.

69. Ibid., p. 25.

70. Tezozomoc, *Cronica Mexicana*, p. 519.

71. Susanne Langer, *Philosophy in a New Key* (Cambridge: Harvard University Press, 1960), p. 287.

72. Clifford Geertz, *Interpretation of Cultures* (New York: Basic Books, 1973), p. 101.

73. Octavio Paz, *Conjunctions and Disjunctions* (New York: Viking Press, 1974), p. 10.

74. Durán, *Historia de las Indias*, 2:510–11.

75. Sahagún, *Florentine Codex*, 12:44.

76. Pagden, ed., *Hernando Cortes*, p. 85.

77. Ibid., p. 86.

78. Ibid.

79. Ibid., p. 94.

Selected Bibliography

Adams, Robert McC. *The Evolution of Urban Society*. Chicago: Aldine, 1967.

Anales de Cuauhtitlán. In *Codice Chimalpopoca*. Mexico: Universidad National Autonoma de Mexico, Imprenta Universitaria, 1945.

Anderson, Arthur J. O. "Sahagún's Nahuatl Texts as Indigenist Documents." *Estudios de Cultura Nahuatl* 2 (1960): 31–42.

Armillas, Pedro. *Program of the History of American Indian*. Washington, D.C.: Pan American Union, 1958.

———. "La Serpiente Emplumada, Quetzalcoatl y Tlaloc." *Cuadernos Americanos* 31 (January-February 1947): 161–78.

Barlow, Robert. "Anales de Cuauhtitlán and Leyenda de los Soles." *Hispanic American Historical Review* 27 (1948): 520–26.

Beaglehold, J. C. "Case of the Needless Death: Reconstructing the Scene." In *The Historian as Detective*, edited by Robin Winks. New York: Harper Colophon Books, 1968.

Benson, Elizabeth, ed. *Mesoamerican Writing Systems*. Washington, D.C.: Trustees of Harvard University, 1971.

Berger, Peter. *The Sacred Canopy*. Garden City, N.Y.: Anchor Books, 1969.

Bierhorst, John. *Four Masterworks of American Indian Literature*. New York: Farrar, Straus & Giroux, 1974.

Bock, Kenneth E. *The Acceptance of Histories: Toward a Perspective for Social Science*. Berkeley: University of California Press, 1956.

Broda, Johanna. "El tributo en trajes guerreros y la estructura del sistema tributario Mexica." *Economia, Politica e ideología en el Mexico prehispanico*, ed. Pedro Carrasco and Johanna Broda. Mexico: Instituto Nacional de Antropología e historia, 1978.

Brinton, Daniel. *American Hero Myths*. Philadelphia: H. C. Watts, 1882.

———. *Essays of an Americanist*. New York: Johnson Reprint, 1970.

———, ed. *Ancient Nahuatl Poetry*. New York: AMS Press, 1969.

Brundage, Burr. *A Rain of Darts*. Austin: University of Texas Press, 1972.

Burland, Cottie. *The Gods of Mexico*. New York: Putnam, 1967.

———. *Montezuma, Lord of the Aztecs*. London: Weidenfield & Nicholson, 1972.

Calnek, Edward. "The Internal Structure of Tenochtitlán." In *The Valley of Mexico*, edited by Eric Wolf. Albuquerque: University of New Mexico Press, 1976.

Carrasco, Davíd. "Quetzalcoatl's Revenge: Primordium and Application in Aztec Religion." *History of Religions* 19 (May 1980): 296–319.

―――. "City as Symbol in Aztec Thought: The Clues from the Codex Mendoza." *History of Religions* 20 (February 1981): 199–220.

Carrasco, Pedro. "The Peoples of Central Mexico and Their Historical Traditions." In *Handbook of Middle American Indians,* 11:459–74. Austin: University of Texas Press, 1964–76.

Caso, Alfonso. *El Pueblo del Sol.* Mexico: Fondo de Cultura Economica, 1953.

Charnay, Desiré. *The Ancient Cities of the New World.* New York: Harper, 1882.

Childe, V. Gordon. *Man Makes Himself.* New York: New American Library, 1951.

―――. "The Urban Revolution." *Town Planning Review* 21 (1950): 3–17.

Clavijero, Francisco. *The History of Mexico.* Richmond, Va.: William Prichard, 1806.

Coe, Michael. *The Maya.* New York: Praeger, 1973.

Cornyn, John. *The Song of Quetzalcoatl.* N.p.: Antioch Press, 1931.

Cortes, Hernando. *Five Letters of Cortes to the Emperor.* Translated by J. Bayard Morris. New York: W. W. Norton, n.d.

Culbert, T. Patrick, ed. *The Classic Maya Collapse.* Albuquerque: University of New Mexico Press, 1973.

Davies, Nigel . *The Aztecs: A History.* London: Macmillan, 1973.

―――. *The Toltecs until the Fall of Tula.* Norman: University of Oklahoma Press, 1977.

Díaz del Castillo, Bernal. *The Discovery and Conquest of Mexico.* New York: Farrar, Straus & Giroux, 1956.

Deuel, Leo. *Conquistadors without Swords.* New York: Schocken Books, 1974.

Dibble, Charles E. "Writing in Central Mexico." In *Handbook of Middle American Indians,* Guide to Ethnohistorical Sources, 10:322–32. Austin: University of Texas Press, 1964–76.

Dumézil, Georges. *The Destiny of a King.* Chicago: University of Chicago Press, 1974.

Durán, Diego. *Book of the Gods and Rites and the Ancient Calendar.* Translated and edited by Fernando Horcasitas and Doris Heyden. Norman: University of Oklahoma Press, 1970.

―――. *Historia de las Indias de Nueva España y Islas de Tierra Firme.* Mexico: Imprenta de J. M. Andrade y F. Escalante, 1867.

Edmonson, Munroe, ed. *Sixteenth Century Mexico.* Albuquerque: University of New Mexico Press; School of American Research Book, 1974.

Eliade, Mircea. "Methodological Remarks on the Study of Religious Symbolism." In *The History of Religions: Essays in Methodology.* Edited by Mircea Eliade and Joseph Kitagawa. Chicago: University of Chicago Press, 1959.

―――. *The Myth of the Eternal Return.* New York: Pantheon Books, 1965.

―――. *Patterns in Comparative Religions.* New York: Meridian Books, 1967.

―――. *The Quest.* Chicago: University of Chicago Press, 1969.

Elzey, Wayne. "Mythology of the Ages of the World." Ph.D. diss., University of Chicago, 1975.

―――. "The Nahua Myth of the Suns." *Numen,* August 1976.

Encyclopaedia Britannica. 15th ed. S.v. "Encyclopaedia," by Robert L. Collison.

Florescano, Enrique. "La Serpiente emplumada, Tlaloc y Quetzalcoatl." *Cuadernos Americanos* 23 (1964): 121–66.

Frankfort, Henri. *Kingship and the Gods*. Chicago: University of Chicago Press, 1948.

Frankfort, Henri, et al. *The Intellectual Adventure of Ancient Man*. Chicago: University of Chicago Press, 1946.

Furst, Jill Leslie. *Codex Vindobonensis Mexicanus I: A Commentary*. Institute for Mesoamerican Studies Publication 4. Albany: State University of New York, 1978.

Fustel de Coulanges, Numa Denis. *The Ancient City*. New York: Doubleday Anchor Books, n.d.

Gamio, Manuel. *La Poblacion del Valle de Teotihuacán*. Mexico: Talleres Graficas de la Nacion, 1922.

Garibay K., Angel Maria. *Poesia Nahuatl*. Mexico: Universidad Nacional Autonoma de Mexico, 1968.

Geertz, Clifford. *The Interpretation of Culture*. New York: Basic Books, 1973.

———, ed. *Myth, Symbol and Culture*. New York: W. W. Norton, 1971.

Gelb, I. J. *A Study of Writing*. Chicago: University of Chicago Press, 1963.

Gibson, Charles. "A Survey of Middle American Prose Manuscripts in the Native Historical Tradition." In *Handbook of Middle American Indians: Guide to Ethnohistorical Sources*, 15:311–21. Austin: University of Texas Press, 1964–76.

Glass, John. "A Survey of Native Middle American Pictorial Manuscripts." In *Handbook of Middle American Indians: Guide to Ethnohistorical Sources*, 14:3–81. Austin: University of Texas Press, 1964–76.

Grennes-Ravitz, Ronald A. "The Extrapolation of Pre-Classic Reality from Post-Classic Models: The Concept of an Olmec Empire in Mesoamerica." *Actas del XLI Congreso Internacional de Americanistas* 1 (1975): 378–83.

Gurvitch, Georges. *The Spectrum of Social Time*. Dordrecht: D. Reidel, 1964.

Hanke, Lewis. *Aristotle and the American Indians*. Bloomington: Indiana University Press, 1959.

Hardoy, Jorge. *Pre-Columbian Cities*. New York: Walker, 1973.

Hentz, Carl. "Gods and Drinking Serpents." *History of Religions* 4 (winter 1965): 179–208.

Heyden, Doris. "An Interpretation of the Cave underneath the Pyramid of the Sun in Teotihuacán, Mexico." *American Antiquity* 40 (April 1975): 131–47.

Historia de los Mexicanos por sus Pinturas. In *Nueva Colección de Documentos para la Historia de Mexico*, edited by Juan Bautista Pomar. Mexico: Editorial Salvador Chávez Hayhde, 1941.

Historia Tolteca-Chichimeca. In *Anales de Quauhtinchan*. Mexico: Antigua Libreria Robredo de Jose Porrua e Hijos, 1947.

Humboldt, Alexander von. *Vues de cordilleres et monuments des peuples indigenes de l'Amerique*. Paris: F. Schoell, 1810.

Icazbalceta, Juaquin Garcia. *Don Fray Juan de Zumárraga*. Mexico: Editorial Porrua, S. A., 1947.

Jennings, Francis. *The Invasion of America*. Chapel Hill, N.C.: University of North Carolina Press, 1975.

Jiménez Moreno, Wigberto. "Sintesis de la Historia Precolonial del Valle de Mexico." *Revista Mexicana de Estudios Antropológicos* 14 (1954): 219–36.

————. "Tula y los Toltecas segun las Fuentes Historicas." *Revista Mexicana de Estudios Antropologicos* 5 (1941): 79–84.

Katz, Friedrich. *The Ancient American Civilizations*. New York: Praeger, 1972.

Keen, Benjamin. *The Aztec Image in Western Thought*. New Brunswick, N.J.: Rutgers University Press, 1971.

Kelly, David. "Quetzalcoatl and His Coyote Origins." *El Antiquo Mexico* 9 (1955): 397–416.

Kirchhoff, Paul. "Quetzalcoatl, Huemac y el Fin de Tula." *Cuadernos Americanos* 84 (1955): 163–96.

Krickeberg, Walter. *Las Antiguas Culturas Mexicanas*. Mexico: Fondo de Cultura Economica, 1961.

Lafaye, Jacques. *Quetzalcoatl and Guadalupe: The Formation of Mexican National Consciousness*. Chicago: University of Chicago Press, 1976.

————. "Mexico according to Quetzalcoatl: An Essay of Intra-History." *Diogenes* 78 (19//): 18–37.

Landa, Diego de. *Relacion de las Cosas de Yucatan*. Edited by Alfred Tozzer. Cambridge: Harvard University Press, 1941.

Langer, Susanne. *Philosophy in a New Key*. Cambridge: Harvard University Press, 1960.

Lehmann, Walter, ed. *Die Geschichte der Konigreiche von Colhuacan und Mexico*. Stuttgart: Verlag von W. Kolhammer, 1938.

León-Portilla, Miguel. *Aztec Thought and Culture*. Norman: University of Oklahoma Press, 1963.

————. "El Proceso de Acculturación de los Chichimecas de Xólotl." *Estudios de Cultura Nahuatl* 5 (1967): 59–86.

————. *Pre-Columbian Literature of Mexico*. Norman: University of Oklahoma Press, 1969.

————. "Quetzalcoatl, Espiritualismo de Mexico Antiquo." *Cuadernos Americanos* 105 (1959): 127–39.

————. *Time and Reality in the Thought of the Maya*. Boston: Beacon Press, 1973.

————, ed. *The Broken Spear*. Boston: Beacon Press, 1962.

Leyenda de los Soles. In *Codice Chimalpopoca*. Mexico: Universidad Nacional Autonoma de Mexica, Imprenta Universitaria, 1945.

López Austin, Alfredo. *Hombre-Dios, Religion y Politica en el Mundo Nahuatl*. Mexico: Universidad Nacional Autonoma de Mexico, 1973.

Mace, Edward Carroll. "Charles Etienne Brasseur de Bourbourg, 1814–1874." In *Handbook of Middle American Indians: Guide to Ethnohistorical Sources*, 13:298–325. Austin: University of Texas Press, 1964–76.

Margain, Carlos. "Pre-Columbian Architecture in Central Mexico," In *Handbook of Middle American Indians: Guide to Ethnohistorical Sources*, 10:45–91. Austin: University of Texas Press, 1964–76.

Marshack, Alexander. *The Roots of Civilization: The Cognitive Beginnings of Man's First Art, Symbol, and Notation*. New York: McGraw-Hill, 1972.

Mendieta, Geronimo de. *Historia Eclesiastica Indiana*. Mexico: Editorial Salvador Chávez Hayhde, 1945.

Millon, René. *Urbanization at Teotihuacán, Mexico: The Teotihuacán Map*. Austin: University of Texas Press, 1973.

Morse, Marston. "Mathematics and the Arts." *Bulletin of the Atomic Scientists* 15 (February 1959): 52–59.

Motolinía, Fray Toribio de Benavente O. *Historia de los Indios de la Nueva España*. Mexico: Editorial Porrua, 1969.

———. *Memoriales*. Mexico: Don Luis Garcia Pimentel, 1903.

Mumford, Lewis. *The City in History*. New York: Harcourt Brace & World, 1961.

Muñoz Camargo, Diego. *Historia de Tlaxcala*. Mexico: Alfredo Chavero; printed for presentation at the Columbian Exposition in Chicago, 1893.

Nicholson, H. B. "Eduard Georg Seler, 1849–1922." In *Handbook of Middle American Indians, Guide to Ethnohistorical Sources*, 13:348–69. Austin: University of Texas Press, 1964–76.

———. "Major Sculpture in Pre-Hispanic Central Mexico." In *Handbook of Middle American Indians, Guide to Ethnohistorical Sources*, 10:92–134. Austin: University of Texas Press, 1974–76.

———. "Middle American Ethnohistory: An Overview." In *Handbook of Middle American Indians: Guide to Ethnohistorical Sources*, 15:487–506. Austin: University of Texas Press, 1964–76.

———. "Phoneticism in Late Pre-Hispanic Central Mexican Writing Systems." In *Mesoamerican Writing Systems*, edited by Elizabeth Benson. Washington, D.C.: Trustees of Harvard University, 1971.

———. "Religion in Pre-Hispanic Central Mexico." In *Handbook of Middle American Indians: Guide to Ethnohistorical Sources*, 10:395–445. Austin: University of Texas Press, 1964–76.

———. "Topiltzin Quetzalcoatl of Tollan: A Problem in Mesoamerican Ethnohistory." Ph.D. diss., Harvard University, 1957.

Nicholson, Irene. *Firefly in the Night: A Study of Ancient Mexican Poetry*. London: Faber & Faber, 1959.

———. *Mexican and Central American Mythology*. London: Paul Hamlyn, 1967.

Nisbet, Robert. *The Sociological Tradition*. New York: Basic Books, 1966.

Noguera, Eduardo. "Exploraciones en Xochicalco." *Cuadernos Americanos* 5 (1945): 37–52.

Nuttal, Zelia. *Codex Nuttal*. Facsimile of an ancient Mexican Codex belonging to Lord Zouche of Harynworth, Cambridge, England, 1902.

O'Gorman, Edmundo. *The Invention of America*. Westport, Conn.: Greenwood Press, 1961.

Olivera, Mercedes de V. "La Importancia Religiosa de Cholula." In *Projecto Cholula*, edited by Ignacio Marguina. Mexico: Instituto Nacional de Antropologia y Historia, 1970. Pp. 221–43.

Oppenheim, A. Leo. *Ancient Mesopotamia: Portrait of a Dead Civilization*. Chicago: University of Chicago Press, 1964.

Orozco y Berra, Manuel. *Historia Antigua y de la Conquista de Mexico*, 4 vols. Mexico: Porrua, 1880.

Ouwehand, C. *Namazu-e and Their Themes: An Interpretive Approach to Some Aspects of Japanese Folk Religion*. Leiden: E. J. Brill, 1964.

Padden, R. C. *The Hummingbird and the Hawk*. New York: Harper & Row, 1967.

Palacios, Enrique. "Teotihuacán, los Toltecas y Tula." *Revista Mexicana de Estudios Antropologicos* 5 (1941): 113–34.

Paz, Octavio. *Claude Lévi-Strauss: An Introduction*. Ithaca, N.Y.: Cornell University Press, 1970.

——. *Conjunctions and Disjunctions*. New York: Viking Press, 1974.

——. *The Other Mexico*. New York: Grove Press, 1972.

Phelan, John L. *The Millennial Kingdom of the Franciscans in the New World*. Berkeley: University of California Press, 1970.

Phillips, Philip, and Willey, Gordon. *Method and Theory in American Archaeology*. Chicago: University of Chicago Press, 1958.

Pollock, H. D. *Round Structures in Aboriginal America*. Washington, D.C.: Carnegie Institute, 1936.

Pomar, Juan Bautista. *Relaciónes de Tezcoco y de la Nueva Espana*. Mexico: Editorial Salvador Chávez Hayhde, 1941.

Price, Barbara, and Sanders, William T. *Mesoamerica: The Evolution of a Civilization*. New York: Random House, 1968.

Radin, Paul. *Sources and Authenticity of History of the Ancient Mexicans*. University of California Publications in American Archaeology and Ethnology 17. Berkeley: University of California, 1920.

Recinos, A., ed. *Annals of the Cakchiquels and Title of the Lords of Totonicapan*. Norman: University of Oklahoma Press, 1953.

Robertson, Donald. *Mexican Manuscript Painting of the Early Colonial Period: The Metropolitan Schools*. New Haven, Conn.: Yale University Press, 1959.

Rojas, Gabriel. "Descripcion de Cholula." *Revista Mexicana de Estudios Historicos* 1 (1927): 158–69.

Roys, Ralph L., ed. *The Book of Chilam Balam of Chumayel*. Norman: University of Oklahoma Press, 1967.

Saenz, Cesar. *Quetzalcoatl*. Mexico: Instituto Nacional de Antropologia e Historia, 1962.

——. "Las Estelas de Xochicalco." *Actas y Memorias, Congreso Internacional de Americanistas*, 1964, pp. 73–85.

Sahagún, Fray Bernardino de. *The Florentine Codex: General History of the Things of New Spain*. Edited by Arthur J. O. Anderson and Charles Dibble. 12 vols. Sante Fe, N.M.: School of American Research and University of Utah, 1950–69.

Sanders, William. "Settlement Patterns in Central Mexico." In *Handbook of Middle American Indians: Guide to Ethnohistorical Sources*, 10:3–45. Austin: University of Texas Press, 1964–76.

Séjourné, Laurette. *El Universo de Quetzalcoatl*. Mexico: Fondo de Cultura Economica, 1962.

Seler, Eduard Georg. *The Tonalamatl of the Aubin Collection*. Translated by A. H. Keane. Berlin, 1901.

Shils, Edward. *Selected Essays*. Chicago: Center for Social Organization Studies, 1970.

Shklar, Judith. "Subversive Genealogies." In *Myth, Symbol and Culture*, edited by Clifford Geertz. New York: W. W. Norton, 1972.

Sjorborg, Gideon. *The Pre-Industrial City, Past and Present*. Glencoe, Ill.: Free Press, 1960.

Smith, Jonathan Z. "Birth Upside Down or Right Side Up." *History of Religions* 9 (1970): 281–403.

———. "The Influence of Symbols upon Social Change: A Place on Which to Stand." *Worship* 44 (October 1970): 457–74.

Smith, Mary E. "The Relationship between Mixtec Manuscript Painting and the Mixtec Language: A Study of Personal Names in Codices Muro and Sanchez Solis." In *Mesoamerican Writing Systems*, edited by Elizabeth Benson. Washington, D.C.: Trustees of Harvard University, 1971.

Soustelle, Jacques. *Daily Life of the Aztecs*. Stanford: Stanford University Press, 1970.

———. *Mexico*. New York: World Publishing Co., 1967.

Spinden, Herbert J. "New Light on Quetzalcoatl." *Actas y Memorias del Congreso Internacional de Americanistas* 46 (1947): 505–12.

Tezozomoc, Fernando Alvarado. *Cronica Mexicana* . Mexico: Editorial Leyenda, S.A., 1944.

Thompson, J. Eric S. *The Rise and Fall of the Mayan Civilization*. Norman: University of Oklahoma Press, 1966.

Tovar, Juan de. *Historia de los Indios Mexicanos (Codex Ramirez)*. Mexico, 1944.

Tozzer, Alfred. *Chichén Itzá and Its Cenote of Sacrifice: A Comparative Study of Contemporaneous Maya and Toltec*. Cambridge: Peabody Museum, 1957.

Turner, Victor. *Dramas, Fields, and Metaphors*. Ithaca, N.Y.: Cornell University Press, 1974.

Vaillant, George. *The Aztecs of Mexico*. New York: Doubleday, 1941.

Wach, Joachim. *The Sociology of Religion*. Chicago: University of Chicago Press, 1967.

Wauchope, Robert. *Lost Tribes and Sunken Continents*. Chicago: University of Chicago Press, 1962.

Weaver, Muriel Porter. *The Aztecs, Mayas, and Their Predecessors*. New York: Seminar Press, 1972.

Wensinck, A. J. L. "The Semitic New Year and the Origin of Eschatology." *Acta Orientalia* 1 (1923).

Westheim, Paul. *The Art of Ancient Mexico*. Garden City, N.Y.: Anchor Books, 1965.

Wheatley, Paul. "City as Symbol." Inaugural Lecture delivered at the University College, London, November 20, 1967.

———. *From Court to Capital*. Chicago: University of Chicago Press, 1978.

———. *The Pivot of the Four Quarters*. Chicago: Aldine, 1971.

———. "The Suspended Pelt: Reflections on a Discarded Model of Spatial Structure." Mimeographed. Chicago: University of Chicago, 1975.

Wolf, Eric. *Sons of the Shaking Earth*. Chicago: University of Chicago Press, 1959.

———, ed. *The Valley of Mexico*. Albuquerque, N.M.: University of New Mexico Press, 1976.

Index